COFFEE CAN INVESTING

ADVANCE PRAISE FOR *COFFEE CAN INVESTING*

'This book offers objective, fact-based and sensible advice for saving and investing that will enable readers to formulate realistic lifetime aspirations and to accumulate wealth to achieve them. Most importantly, it will teach them [how] to avoid losing a small fortune in fees and commissions and to avoid losing a large fortune through market timing attempts, bad asset allocation and overtrading. A must-read for India's emerging huge numbers of middle and upper-middle income-earners'—Avinash K. Dixit, John J.F. Sherrerd '52 University professor of economics, emeritus, Princeton University

'Sensible advice on portfolio construction and wealth management is hard to find in India. This book therefore fills a void in the Indian market. Anyone who wants to invest sensibly and retire happily should read this book'—Sanjay Bakshi, adjunct professor, Management Development Institute (Gurgaon)

PRAISE FOR *THE UNUSUAL BILLIONAIRES*

'Saurabh Mukherjea describes incisively how some great Indian companies have achieved corporate success and made a great deal of money for investors along the way'—John Kay, professor of economics, London School of Economics

'Saurabh's book highlights that the recipe for outstanding corporate results hinge on old-fashioned values'—Ashok Wadhwa, group CEO, Ambit Holdings

'An insightful—and reassuring—exposition of how steady good sense can consistently beat the unsteady Sensex'—Rama Bijapurkar, author and management consultant

'Mukherjea's book is insightful and makes for easy reading'—*Financial Express*

'Mukherjea is one of our most erudite young writers in the field of investment banking'—*Mint*

'Books that are able to describe successful businesses through a common theme or analytical framework are rare in India. This one is an addition to that small collection'—*Moneylife*

'The book does not just list the winning pack, but also traces the history of these companies'—*The Hindu BusinessLine*

COFFEE CAN INVESTING

THE LOW-RISK ROAD TO STUPENDOUS WEALTH

SAURABH MUKHERJEA

RAKSHIT RANJAN

PRANAB UNIYAL

PORTFOLIO
PENGUIN

An imprint of Penguin Random House

PORTFOLIO

USA | Canada | UK | Ireland | Australia
New Zealand | India | South Africa | China

Portfolio is part of the Penguin Random House group of companies whose addresses can be found at global.penguinrandomhouse.com

Published by Penguin Random House India Pvt. Ltd
4th Floor, Capital Tower 1, MG Road,
Gurugram 122 002, Haryana, India

Penguin Random House India

First published in Portfolio by Penguin Random House India 2018

40 39 38 37 36

ISBN 9780670090457

Typeset in Adobe Caslon Pro by Manipal Digital Systems, Manipal
Printed at Replika Press Pvt. Ltd, India

www.penguin.co.in

Contents

Foreword

Whilst I have been a finance professional for thirty-five years, it is only in the past twenty years or so that I have made a conscious effort to save and invest in a structured manner. Initially, I relied on wealth managers to advise me about my investments, but soon I realized that most of them are focused on their wealth, not mine. Therefore, around fifteen years ago, I set up my family office, which is staffed by hand-picked chartered accountants and chartered financial analysts. However, such is the paucity of sensibly priced and structured investment products in the Indian market that even my family office has to be very selective to enable me to preserve and grow my wealth.

Given this backdrop, I was more than intrigued when four years ago Ambit Capital's research team published its first Coffee Can Portfolio. Whilst I wasn't an initial convert to the idea of buying a bunch of high-quality stocks and then leaving it untouched for a decade, I soon began hearing from my friends that they were putting money into this construct. Initially, Ambit Capital offered this portfolio to private clients in an advisory arrangement, i.e. the corpus was invested by the clients in their own name but with Ambit's wealth managers helping with the stock selection. Then, after Saurabh's book, *The Unusual Billionaires*, became a runaway hit within months of its publication in August 2016, Ambit Capital started offering the Coffee Can Portfolio in a SEBI-regulated PMS construct. I was one of the first investors in this PMS scheme. Since then the Coffee Can Portfolio has given me impressive returns with low volatility and low transaction costs. I hope it does the same for you.

If the Coffee Can Portfolio is an example of homegrown innovation in the Indian stock market, then Exchange Traded Funds (ETFs)[1] are an example of an idea imported from the US which is finding rapid traction in India. As the Indian stock market matures, as it becomes better regulated, more institutionalized and more competitive, it is but natural that large-cap mutual fund managers will struggle to beat the market. Hence, for most investors, large-cap ETFs with low fees will become a cost-efficient way to participate in the growth of India's vibrant economy.

Although active management of large-cap stocks is no longer an assured way to generate market-beating returns in large-cap Indian stocks, in the small-cap space India has several talented fund managers who consistently deliver outstanding returns by investing in upcoming companies. These fund managers are able to find companies that are not only good (i.e. companies where the promoter allocates capital sensibly) but, just as importantly, are also clean (i.e. companies where the financial statements are a true and fair reflection of the underlying state of the business). Ambit Capital's Good & Clean fund focuses on investing in such companies, and three years ago I invested in this fund.

---

[1] An ETF is a basket of stocks that reflects the composition of an Index, like S&P, CNX Nifty or BSE Sensex. The trading value of ETFs is based on the net asset value of the underlying stocks that it represents. One may think of it as a mutual fund that you can buy and sell in real time at a price that changes through the day. ETFs are explained in detail in Chapter 3. (Source: moneycontrol).

These three contrasting approaches to equity investing—ETFs for large-caps; a low-cost, conservative strategy like the Coffee Can Portfolio for large and mid-caps; and careful stock selection for small-midcaps—should form the bedrock of any growth-oriented Indian portfolio. To the extent that all of us need to set aside some money for a rainy day, I strongly believe it should be done by investing in government bonds and conservatively managed liquid funds. When it comes to my 'rainy day' corpus, life has taught me that I need to focus on liquidity and complete safety of funds.

Saurabh Mukherjea, Rakshit Ranjan and Pranab Uniyal have worked in Ambit Capital for almost a decade now. I have seen them grow as finance professionals. It has been my privilege to see their wealth management philosophy evolve through intense brainstorming sessions at Ambit and then see them put their ideas to work in front of India's smartest investors. This elegantly constructed book is their attempt to share their wealth management approach with you. It uses minimal jargon and is packed with case studies that almost everyone will identify with. I hope you enjoy reading this book and make even better returns from your portfolio.

Mumbai
December 2017

Ashok Wadhwa
Group CEO, Ambit

Acknowledgements

We hit upon the idea for *Coffee Can Investing: The Low-Risk Road to Stupendous Wealth* when Saurabh was at the CNBC studio in August 2016. He was recording the second episode of a six-part programme that CNBC had come up with around Saurabh's bestselling book *The Unusual Billionaires*. Saurabh and Latha Venkatesh, the CNBC anchor, were waiting for Jalaj Dani, then at Asian Paints, to join the show. Dwelling on the contents of *The Unusual Billionaires*, Latha happened to remark that 'it has become harder to identify good mutual funds than it is to identify good stocks'. When Saurabh came back to the office and relayed the remark to us, we wondered that if well-informed market observers found it difficult to figure out how to invest in the stock market, then what hope did the average investor have. Given the existential pressures bearing down on people, can they really navigate the maze of data, regulations and distorted incentives that characterize investing in India? For giving us the germ of the idea that went on to become this book, we are thankful to Latha Venkatesh.

We believe most people do *not* invest to make a lot of money. They invest to meet goals like paying for their children's education and funding their retirement. They also invest to fulfil their dreams, which might be as modest as buying a nice TV or as grand as owning a resort in the Himalayas. Whilst we had long believed in the centrality of goals and dreams in the investment process, it wasn't until we came across Ashvin B. Chhabra's superb book, *The Aspirational Investor: Investing in the Pursuit of Wealth and Happiness*[1] (2015), that we found a structured way to link life goals with asset allocation. We owe an intellectual debt to Ashvin Chhabra and hope that he continues to write in a similar vein.

The late Robert Kirby of Capital, the Los Angeles-based American investment giant, came up with the idea of the Coffee Can Portfolio in a short note he wrote over thirty years ago.[2] As is evident from the title, the Coffee Can Portfolio is at the heart of this book. More practically, both for Ambit's clients and for ourselves, the Coffee Can Portfolio has proved to be a life-changing investing construct. We owe a huge intellectual debt to Robert and wish he was around to read this book.

Many people are able to come up with ideas that can form the kernel of a good book. However, most people (including us till a few years ago) do not have the resources to turn those ideas into a book that can reach millions of people. Were it not for the research support provided at Ambit Capital by Divesh Mehta, Sudeep Pai, Kislay Upadhyay, Karan Khanna and Prashant Mittal, we would not have been able to write *Coffee Can Investing*. We are indebted to these gentlemen for the many months of effort, including public holidays and vacations, which they invested in this book.

Much of the research about how the Indian economy is changing and how that impacts the investment landscape in the country comes from Ambit's Economics team that includes Ritika Mankar, Sumit Shekhar and Aditi Singh. We

[1] Ashvin Chhabra, *The Aspirational Investor*, Portfolio Penguin, 2015.

[2] https://thetaoofwealth.files.wordpress.com/2013/03/the-coffee-can-portfolio.pdf.

are thankful to them for turning abstract economic ideas into coherent investment takeaways.

Jestin George, our editor at Ambit Capital, spent countless hours tidying up our grammatically incorrect writing. Sharoz Hussain, Ambit's formatting guru, turned our rough sketches into charts which are more powerful than most of our text. Sudhanshu Nahta at Ambit Capital worked tirelessly to pull the chapters and the hundreds of charts into a coherent narrative. Without these gentlemen, the book would not flow as nicely as it does.

To build and manage an Indian firm that attracts and retains the best talent in the country is not easy. To then give that talent downtime for intellectual adventures such as this is unheard of in India—nobody else does it in the country. Hence, we thank Ambit's CEO and co-CEO, Ashok Wadhwa and Rahul Gupta respectively, for giving us not just a job but an opportunity to do something bigger.

Over the past seven decades, the Indian government and the institutions associated with it have rarely been seen as drivers of positive change. And yet, amidst this cynicism, over the past decade, the Securities and Exchange Board of India (SEBI) has done some outstanding work. In the face of intense lobbying from the Financial Services industry, SEBI has intervened repeatedly and decisively in favour of small investors. Whilst as industry participants we might not always benefit from SEBI's interventions, as small investors ourselves, we are grateful that it has created a space in the Indian market for the retail investor who wants to invest to meet his life goals.

Lohit Jagwani at Penguin Random House was the editor of *The Unusual Billionaires*. While guiding us through the process of publishing *Coffee Can Investing*, he demonstrated why Saurabh rates him so highly as a commissioning editor. Lohit knows how to give shape and direction to a book so that it becomes an accessible and enjoyable read for a broad range of people, instead of a learned tome which gathers dust on library shelves. We thank Lohit for supporting us in this endeavour and look forward to co-operating with him on more intellectual adventures.

Before we end, we have to thank the most important people in our lives—Sarbani Mukherjea, Roohani Sood Ranjan and Divya Uniyal respectively (for Saurabh, Rakshit and Pranab). Not only do they juggle professional and domestic commitments whilst we spend weeks on the road, they also give us precious weekend time for writing. It is in those early hours of Saturday and Sunday that we do some of our best work, secure in the knowledge that someone wiser and stronger is holding things together for us.

Pranab Uniyal would also like to thank his parents, Abhay and Kanta Uniyal, for being his guiding lights and his friends, Shailendra Tripathi and Aman Dwivedi, for being the sounding board for many of the ideas presented in the book.

Rakshit Ranjan would also like to thank his parents, Dr K.K. Ranjan and Dr Savita Ranjan, for their unwavering support and encouragement.

We hope you enjoy reading the book as much as we enjoyed writing it. You can write to us at Coffeecan@ambit.co.

List of Abbreviations

AIF	Alternate Investment Fund
AMFI	Association of Mutual Funds in India
AUM	Assets Under Management
B2B	Business to Business
B2C	Business to Consumer
Bps	Basis Points
BSE	Bombay Stock Exchange
CAGR	Compounded Annual Growth Rate
CCP	Coffee Can Portfolio
CFI	Cash Flow from Investing
CFO	Cash Flow from Operations
CWIP	Capital Work In-Progress
DCF	Discounted Cash Flow
EBIDTA	Earnings before Interest, Depreciation, Tax and Amortization
EBIT	Earnings before Interest and Tax
EMI	Equated Monthly Instalment
ETF	Exchange Traded Fund
F&O	Futures & Options
FD	Fixed Deposits
GDP	Gross Domestic Product
IMF	International Monetary Fund
InvIT	Infrastructure Investment Trust
M&A	Mergers & Acquisitions

MF	Mutual Fund
MTM	Mark to Market
NCD	Non-Convertible Debentures
NCR	National Capital Region
NDA	National Democratic Alliance
NOI	Non-Operating Income
NSE	National Stock Exchange
P/B Multiple	Price-Book Value Multiple
P/E Multiple	Price-Earnings Multiple
PAT	Profit After Tax
PBIT	Profit before Interest and Tax
PEG ratio	P/E divided by expected earnings growth of a stock
PMS	Portfolio Management Service
REIT	Real Estate Investment Trust
ROA	Return on Assets
ROCE	Return on Capital Employed
ROE	Return on Equity
SEBI	Securities & Exchange Board of India
SPV	Special Purpose Vehicle
TSR	Total Shareholder Returns
ULIP	Unit Linked Insurance Plan
YTM	Yield to Maturity

Introduction

'Risk comes from not knowing what you are doing.'

—Warren Buffett[1]

If you visit a branch of a typical private sector bank in India on a Saturday afternoon, you will notice most relationship managers (RMs) selling packaged financial products, i.e. synthetic instruments that offer exposure to more than one financial asset in a packaged form, which modifies that exposure compared to a direct holding in any one financial asset. However, if you listen closely to what the RM is saying, you will find that little of it is genuine advice; most of it is promotional literature disguised as financial advice. One of the greatest examples of mis-selling by financial intermediaries in India has been Unit Linked Insurance Plans (ULIPs).

ULIPs are 'push' products and thus require high brokerage commissions to be sold, i.e. customers do not—of their own volition—buy these products unless an RM cajoles them into doing so. The fact that the tenor runs into decades allows the manufacturer to implicitly charge the customer a hefty upfront brokerage commission (these used to be as high as 40 to 60 per cent of the first year premium) and yet promise good absolute returns.

---

1 'The Three Essential Warren Buffett Quotes To Live By', *Forbes*, 20 April 2014.

Halan, Sane and Thomas estimated that Indian investors had lost more than Rs 1.5 lakh crore (approximately US$23 billion, yes, billion!) on these products because of lapsing. This was because investors were not informed about the compulsory investment required in subsequent years.[2] This allowed insurance companies to confiscate investors' funds when they did not make payments in subsequent years. Unfortunately, such mis-selling is not just a thing of the past. It continues to characterize the financial services landscape in India.

A diligent investor seeks to avoid getting trapped in such mis-selling by reading up on his own. However, a visit to any good bookshop shows that finding a good book on investing in the Indian context is not an easy task. Though there is no shortage of great books by global gurus that can inform the Indian investor about how to build his investment portfolio, the relevance of global literature to India becomes limited because of a combination of three factors.

Firstly, there is an overwhelming dominance of physical investments like gold and real estate in most Indian households' portfolios. A recent RBI committee opined that 88 per cent of an Indian investor's wealth is in gold and real estate,[3] a dominance not seen in any other large economy of the world. Moreover, issues around illiquidity, emotional connect and unfavourable capital gains taxation make it harder for investors to move away from such existing physical investments. Secondly, the culture of stock market investments in India is only two decades old.

---

2 Monika Halan, Renuka Sane and Susan Thomas, 'Estimating losses to customers on account of mis-selling life insurance policies in India', Indira Gandhi Institute of Development Research, Mumbai, April 2013.

3 Reserve Bank of India, 'Report of the Household Finance Committee', 24 Aug 2017, https://www.rbi.org.in/Scripts/PublicationReportDetails.aspx?UrlPage=&ID=877#CH13.

With the regulatory supervision of the Indian capital markets still evolving, and given the irregular quality of financial reporting by Indian companies, it is difficult for an average investor to make an informed decision. Thirdly, unlike the stock markets in some developed countries, the Indian stock market has very few great companies that sustain leadership over long periods of time. This point is demonstrated clearly through the following analysis from Ambit Capital's research—the average probability of a sector leader remaining a sector leader five years later is only 15 per cent, implying that 85 per cent of BSE500 companies slide towards mediocrity. In fact, the average probability of a 'great' company becoming a sector laggard five years later is 25 per cent. Even the Nifty 'churns' by around 50 per cent or so every decade (as compared to around 25 per cent for developed markets and around 30 to 40 per cent in other major emerging markets). Furthermore, the tendency for large, successful companies to slide down the market-cap spectrum is not confined to the Nifty. A guide to portfolio construction and investment in India needs to take heed of these peculiarities. This book aims to be such a guide.

This book can be read in two ways. An affluent professional or entrepreneur should read it chapter by chapter, and his/her portfolio should be spread across both equities and bonds. Of particular relevance for such a reader are Chapter 1 (Mr Talwar's Uncertain Future), Chapter 7 (Pulling It All Together) and Chapter 8 (Designing Your Own Financial Plan). Alternatively, someone who seeks more specific guidance on how to build a high-quality equity portfolio should carefully read Chapter 2 (Coffee Can Investing), Chapter 5 (Small Is Beautiful), Chapter 6 (How Patience and Quality Intertwine) and Appendix 1 to see how the Coffee Can Portfolio works.

CHAPTER 1

Mr Talwar's Uncertain Future

'The best time to plant a tree was twenty years ago. The second best time is now.'

—ancient Chinese saying

An evening of celebration and reflection

Even by the standards of north India, it was an unusually hot June evening with the mercury hovering at 42 degrees Celsius. As is the norm during the evening rush hour, all roads leading away from Noida were gridlocked with bumper-to-bumper traffic. However, in flat number 901 of Aviral Housing Society, located just five minutes off the Delhi–Agra Expressway, the Talwar household was celebrating a special evening.

Yogesh Talwar beamed happily at the small gathering that had come together to celebrate his son's success in the Class XII Board exams. Ronit had scored 93 per cent and stood third in his class. It was time to celebrate as all the relatives commented on what a great future awaited Ronit. As immortalized in the classic 1967 movie *The Graduate*, relatives and family friends congratulated the young man and told him what they thought he should do with his life. Dustin Hoffman plays the graduate in this super hit movie that made him a star, earned him his first Oscar nomination and captured the spirit of that remarkable decade.

Mr Talwar felt a little uneasy about the happy predictions for his son. In the midst of the hubbub he could sense that something was not right, but he could not pinpoint the reasons for his disquiet. Once the guests were gone, he sat in the balcony with his favourite single malt and let his mind drift over his own career. As he looked out towards the sea of skyscrapers—most of them half-completed buildings abandoned by real estate developers—that is Greater Noida, Mr Talwar's mind retraced the steps of his distinguished corporate career.

He had done well academically. After completing his undergraduate degree in engineering from the highly rated Regional Engineering College in Telangana's Warangal (formerly Andhra Pradesh), he had gone on to finish his studies at a reputed business school—Management Development Institute (MDI) in Gurgaon. His MBA from MDI, coupled with a solid academic record, had helped Yogesh Talwar get a good job with a leading multinational company with an attractive salary of Rs 2 lakh per annum. He had stars in his eyes and the world was his to conquer. That was 1990, but it seemed like yesterday.

The years had flown by since then, but even in the tumult of post-1991 India, Mr Talwar had broadly done the right things. To begin with, he had married a smart girl. Kusum was a teacher at a private school in Noida. Kusum and Yogesh's children, Akanksha and Ronit, were bright, hard-working and well-behaved. Akanksha was pursuing a postgraduate degree in biotechnology in Bangalore and Ronit was awaiting his engineering entrance exam results. Mr Talwar had a settled life, and yet he felt deeply unsettled.

Over the years, especially in the last four to five years, he had started feeling like an underachiever despite working hard over his twenty-five-year corporate career. When he had started working, he told himself that he would retire at the age of forty. That forty had become forty-five and now here he was at fifty years of age. And yet, despite all the hard work, Mr Talwar felt almost as financially unsecure as he was when he graduated from business school.

He had started working in 1990, just as India was about to open its doors to liberalization. It was a good time to work with a private firm. His career had progressed better compared to some of his friends who had joined public sector companies. The yearly increments were great too. For the first few years, the young Yogesh never needed to save. He spent his income on a bike, on travel and on social outings. He was a generous man who stood by his friends. But most of the loans he gave to them never came back. He got married in 1995 at the age of twenty-eight and that didn't change his lifestyle much. It was only when Akanksha was born in 1996 that Kusum and he realized the need to build a financial buffer.

Mr Talwar booked his first fixed deposit (FD) within a few days of Akanksha's birth. Over the years, FDs remained his preferred investment. The Talwars also kept buying gold, whenever possible, as jewellery for Kusum. Gold not only conformed to traditional wisdom (about it being a reliable store of value) but would also come handy when it was time for Akanksha to get married. Some of his colleagues would invest in stocks, but between 1991 and 2004 the Indian stock market was characterized by regular share price rigging scams, and Mr Talwar saw investors in stocks as punters. Like most well-educated Indians, he saw the stock market as an unknown area of darkness. In fact, he had seen most of his friends losing significant amounts of money every now and then in the stock market.

In 1999, Mr Talwar bought his first flat in Noida. This was more on the insistence of his parents who had scored a hat trick by pushing him into the three big decisions of his life—marriage, children and now the house! It was a matter of pride for them that their son owned a house at thirty-two years of age because they were only able to afford it in their fifties. The house was purchased using a home loan. In those days, interest rates were as high as 13 to 14 per cent. The monthly instalments forced the Talwars to live a hand-to-mouth existence for years. They had to break their FDs to buy the house. As a result, through their thirties all their savings were invested in real estate.

Thankfully, interest rates came down over the years and Mr Talwar's salary increased. As the burden of the monthly instalments eased, the family breathed easier. It allowed the Talwars to start saving again and they turned to their old friend—fixed deposits. But this time, Mr Talwar was a little more aggressive. In the post-2000 India, he bought stocks. This was based on the collective wisdom of a small group of stock investors in his office. In those days, stock investing meant trading. There was no concept of holding a stock for the long term. One bought a stock, watched it like a hawk and sold it once the price went up. Being able to exit a stock at a high point was considered an art and gave one bragging rights in the office. Mr Talwar loved the highs of stock investing. However, for reasons he could not understand, his portfolio did not grow much. The high brokerage, which is the commission charged by the broker, and the frequent churn in Mr Talwar's portfolio—driven as it was by office gossip—

meant that it was the broker who made all the money. The brokerage used to be in excess of 1 per cent of the transaction value in those days!

Then came the Bull Run! While his stock portfolio was meagre, the value of his house appreciated by leaps and bounds as both equity and real estate prices increased multifold in that period. But this did not mean much in terms of cash flow as he was staying in the house and had no intention of selling it. But it felt good to be a *crorepati*! Like some of his wealthier friends, he also started lending funds to real estate builders through a private network hidden from the taxman. At 2.5 per cent per month interest, it beat any other investment Mr Talwar had made in his life, and he kicked himself for not doing this earlier. The money always came back and there were always more builders to lend to.

Mr Talwar loved real estate as an asset class. All around the country people were buying property and getting richer; he didn't want to miss out. The willingness of the banks to grant home loans of up to 90 per cent of the property value meant that an appreciation of 50 per cent in the value of the property (which, as per Mr Talwar, was a given) was actually a 500 per cent return on investment. So, other than the flat he lived in Aviral Housing Society, he booked another flat in a luxury high-rise complex called Empire Apartments that was under construction in Noida. The National Capital Region was witnessing a boom—one could actually see the growth as the high-rises in Noida and Gurgaon reached for the sky. Mr Talwar was now hopeful. Finally, he thought, India had stopped whining and started shining.

One day the gravy train stopped. First came the stock market crash of 2008—between January and November of 2008—when the Nifty fell 55 per cent. The crash almost entirely wiped out Mr Talwar's stock portfolio since most of the stocks were speculative investments made on the basis of tips from colleagues and his stockbroker. However, he remained optimistic as most of his wealth was invested in real estate. In fact, after seeing the stock market sink, Mr Talwar was completely convinced about the infallibility of the Indian Real Estate—after all, as his friend Mr Kalra put it, a house was a real asset bound to go up in value in a country with a housing shortage whereas stocks were only pieces of paper with no certain value. Mr Talwar swore never to invest in stocks and doubled down on real estate in the form of paying the next instalment for the flat he had booked in Empire Apartments.

However, soon the real estate engine too started sputtering. The first signs were the plateauing of house prices in 2013. Indian investors had seen property prices going up almost on a monthly basis and a continuous price appreciation was taken for granted. While the stagnation in prices upset Mr Talwar, he wasn't alarmed as yet as the press said that this was just a temporary demand slowdown. The real estate pundits (i.e. property developers and property brokers) who were featured on the financial news channels said that it was a matter of time before house prices picked up again.

Unfortunately, the slowdown in demand continued from 2013 to 2017 and prices continued correcting in some form or the other. The real estate developers started defaulting on loans from 2015 as they ran out of customers who would pay for their overpriced flats. Mr Talwar was now dealt with a double blow. The money that he had lent to the builders was stuck and so was the flat that he had booked in Empire Apartments. The flat, which was supposed to be delivered in three years, was now in its sixth year of construction and still a long way from completion. The builder had drawn down more than 95 per cent of the price of the flat and still did not have money to finish the project. Unfortunately, there were scores of such cases in Noida. Apart from a long court battle with the builder, which he was pursuing with his fellow house-buyers, there was nothing else that Mr Talwar could do. Thus, his dalliance with the stock market and real estate had ended in severe financial reverses even as the clock ticked down on his career.

He poured himself another peg and switched on the TV. A one-day international match that India had won against Pakistan five years ago was being telecast. But Mr Talwar's mind was somewhere else. He was fifty years old now and had another ten years of working life ahead of him. Apart from his investment in property, he had some savings in FDs and in gold. He had also taken a few insurance policies whose worth he never got around to assessing fully. Assuming that after his retirement he and Kusum lived for another thirty years, they would need at least Rs 30 lakh per annum post tax to enjoy a comfortable life. An amount of Rs 30 lakh per annum over thirty years was a lot of money. 'I need at least Rs 9 crore. Where will I get that sort of money from?' thought Mr Talwar.

Like the Indian innings on TV, his career was also entering its final ten overs, and he had to make it count. How could he make the most of it? The Indian team had held Mahendra Singh Dhoni back for the big hits in the slog overs. Who would bat for Mr Talwar in the slog overs of his career? The question kept troubling him.

Just as he was about to pour himself another peg, Kusum entered the room and said, 'Shouldn't we call it a day? Sitting alone in the dark with a glass of Scotch is not going to help. Let's get some sleep and have a chat over a hot cup of coffee tomorrow morning.' Mr Talwar sighed. His wife had always been a more level-headed person than him.

Mr Talwar's life chart: A typical senior executive's lifeline

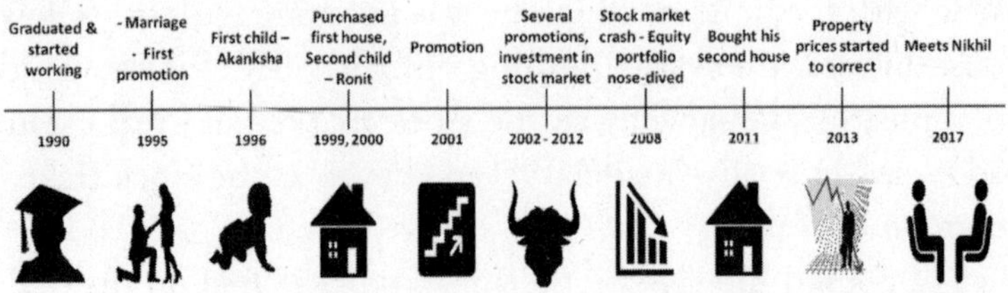

Mr Sanghvi has the same troubles as Mr Talwar but with more zeroes!

Noida is not just home to thousands of successful executives like Mr Talwar but also houses close to 2500 manufacturing businesses. Amongst the 700-odd textile firms in Noida, Mukesh Sanghvi's firm was one of the oldest. The Sanghvi family had run textile plants for generations. While their pot of wealth had grown over the generations, their business was now facing acute competition from Bangladesh (where wages are a third of what they are in India). On top of that, the Sanghvi family was dealing with unfavourable labour and tax regulations. The firm had also taken on a lot of debt lately and the Sanghvis—two brothers and a sister—had decided to put the business into liquidation.

Each sibling wanted to pursue a new line of business/profession, but Mukesh Sanghvi was clear that at fifty-five years of age, he wanted to take it easy and live off his accumulated wealth. It was by no means meagre—according to a rough estimate he had Rs 25 crore spread across assets like residential and commercial properties, gold, FDs, stocks and a significant amount of cash he would receive from the liquidation.

However, he was aware that his existing lifestyle meant that he would require a very large annual surplus to support it. He had two sons and a daughter. The oldest, Sujay, was twenty-five years old and worked as a manager in Mr Sanghvi's friend's pharmaceutical firm. The other two children, Nirmesh (aged twenty-three) and Komal (aged twenty), were studying in the US and the UK respectively. The family liked the good things in life. They went for three overseas holidays every year and changed their luxury (German) cars every other year. Given that Mr Sanghvi had let go of the business, he was nervous and unsure about whether his corpus would be enough to meet his family's requirements. After all, the family's annual financial outgo was Rs 1.5 to 2 crore, and if he had to sustain that for another thirty years, he needed a corpus of at least Rs 50 crore.

So far, the sole source of income for Mr Sanghvi was the dividends he received from the company and the large salary he drew as the firm's director. His wife had bought a lot of jewellery over the years and they had a few commercial properties. He was very active in the local Hundi circuit where people lent each other unsecured loans for as much as 25 per cent per annum on an annualized basis (without declaring anything to the taxman).

Over the years, Mr Sanghvi had had multiple trysts with the stock market. He was a punter by nature and liked making aggressive bets. In fact, Mr Sanghvi dealt in the Futures and Options market and took leveraged positions in stocks. At the peak of the Bull cycle in January 2008, he was worth Rs 150 crore, but by November 2008 his net worth had fallen so much that he was teetering on the brink of bankruptcy, all thanks to the margin calls that his brokers had made on him. He had sworn to never make that mistake again and hence missed out on the 145 per cent rally in the Nifty between March 2009 and November 2010. Seeing his friends make money over that period had made Mr Sanghvi envious. So, when Narendra Modi took over as the Prime Minister of

India in May 2014, Mr Sanghvi decided it was high time that he reentered the markets.

That was then. Now, with the business liquidated and the dividends gone, Mr Sanghvi was scratching his head to figure out how to finance the rest of his retirement, his family's lifestyle and his children's education on a paltry corpus of Rs 25 crore.

Mr Sanghvi's life chart: A typical small business owner's lifeline

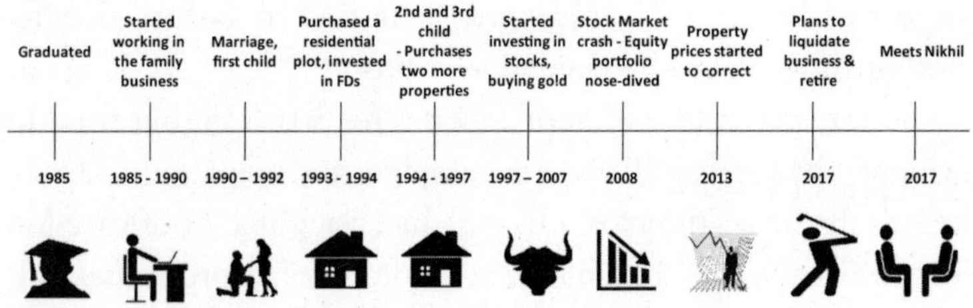

Enter the Adviser: Nikhil

Over steaming cups of masala chai, poha and fruits the next morning, Kusum understood what was worrying her husband. She told him that their neighbours, the Krishnans, had found it useful to see a financial adviser from a wealth management firm. She called the Krishnans over for breakfast and they pointed the Talwars towards Nikhil Banerjee, a senior relationship manager with a reputed wealth management firm. When Nikhil came to meet Mr Talwar, he carried a laptop with a 'financial planning' software package. The meeting lasted more than three hours and the results were a revelation for Mr Talwar.

Nikhil told Mr Talwar that the key was to quantify everything since reality is different from perception and hard numbers help differentiate one from the other. The first thing they did together was to quantify the Talwars' net worth.

Exhibit 1: Mr Talwar's personal balance sheet

	Assets	Value in Rs lakhs	Remarks
1	House #1	250	Primary residence in Noida
2	House #2	150	Flat booked in Empire Apartments
3	Loan made to developers	85	Only 50 per cent probability of this being repaid
4	Gold	60	Jewellery used by Mrs Talwar
5	Fixed Deposits	25	
6	Insurance Sum Assured	12	Across seven policies
7	Cash	5	
8	Stocks	5	
	Total Assets	**592**	

	Liabilities	Value in Rs lakhs	Remarks
1	Loan for House #2	130	Loan taken at 9.5 per cent
2	Car Loan	11	Loan taken at 12 per cent
	Total Liabilities	**141**	
	Net Assets	**451**	(Total Assets—Total Liabilities)

Source: Ambit Capital

Next, they calculated the return his portfolio had generated for him over the past twenty-seven years. They segmented the numbers methodically so that Mr Talwar could see the returns that each asset class generated for him (see Exhibit 2). The results stunned Mr Talwar. On a weighted average basis, he had earned a return of only 4 per cent per annum over these twenty-seven years.

Exhibit 2: Mr Talwar's portfolio and the annualized returns each asset class generated for him since 1990

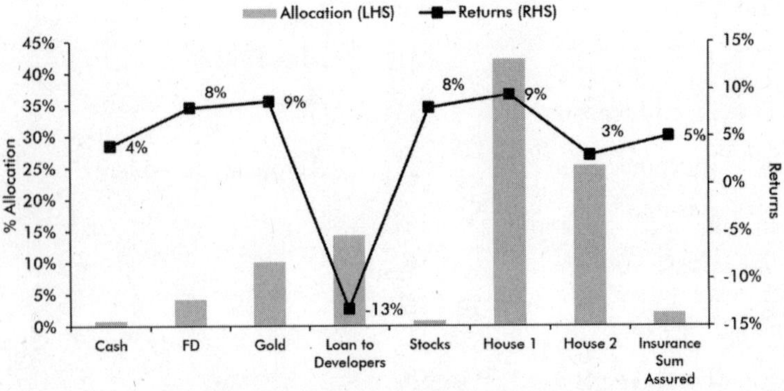

Source: Ambit Capital. Returns for house #2 are on the basis of its current value in the resale market.

Mr Talwar held his head in his hands. The past had to be left behind, Nikhil comforted Mr Talwar. But at the same time, Nikhil said that if Mr Talwar did not learn from his mistakes, he was staring at a very uncertain future. It was important for Mr Talwar to assess the kind of returns that he would need from his portfolio. The required returns were actually a function of the financial goals he had in the coming years. Mr Talwar, guided by Nikhil, wrote down his primary financial goals (see Exhibit 3).

Exhibit 3: Mr Talwar's financial goals along with the current equivalent cost

	Goal	Cost in Rs lakhs [at today's prices]	Year of Goal
1	Akanksha's higher education	80	2021
2	Ronit's higher education	80	2025
3	Akanksha's wedding	70	2024
4	Ronit's wedding	70	2028
5	Buying a holiday home	100	2027
6	Buying a car	10	Every three years
7	International vacation	5	Every year

Source: Ambit Capital

When Nikhil uploaded these goals on the financial planning software, he had to account for an important adjustment—inflation. The current cost was compounding at the rate of inflation and becoming uncomfortably high at the time of actual occurrence. For example, Akanksha's wedding, which would cost Rs 70 lakh now, would cost Rs 1.2 crore in 2024, assuming an inflation rate of 8 per cent.

The software showed the devastating effect inflation would have on Mr Talwar's cash flow. It showed that at the current rate of savings (income minus expenses) and returns on his investments, his standard of living would come drastically down once he retired at the age of sixty. The cost of his goals was going up considering an inflation rate of 8 per cent per annum whereas his portfolio, in its current shape, having grown at 4 per cent per annum for the last twenty-seven years, was only likely to grow at 6 to 8 per cent per annum. Therefore, to meet the goals shown in the preceding table, Mr Talwar would need to dig deep into his meagre retirement corpus, which in turn would severely compromise the quality of life he and his wife would be able to lead after retirement.

On the first iteration, the software showed that his portfolio had to return 21 per cent per annum on a post-tax basis from now if he had to meet all his financial goals. This sort of return was absolutely out of reach for Mr Talwar. Nikhil then went over the exercise again after bringing down the frequency of vacations, changing cars and excluding the goal of buying a holiday home. The required return came down to 16 per cent per annum. Given that there was only so much he could expect from his salary and bonuses over the years, his future depended on how well he invested his savings hereon.

He had seen a time when he had earned returns as high as 80 per cent on his investments, but in the end those returns had averaged out to a disappointing 4 per cent. He was at his wit's end; he didn't believe there was anything that could deliver a post-tax return of 16 per cent per annum over the next ten years.

The solution for Mr Talwar: Use the power of equity

Nikhil told Mr Talwar that it was a mistake to not invest in equity. Mr Talwar had burnt his fingers with stocks and now considered it as risky as betting. After all, he had never made money in equity investing. Nikhil told him that this was because he was making the classic mistakes. One, he was trading heavily. They calculated that, over the years, Mr Talwar's average holding period was four months and up to 80 per cent of his stock investments had never lasted more than a year. Mr Talwar's high turnover was a broker's delight. In fact, he was paying up to 7 per cent of his portfolio value each year as brokerage. There was no way, Nikhil told him, that he could have generated any returns with such investment practices.

The other mistake, Nikhil told him, was that he was an irregular investor who was always trying to time the market. Instead of being invested, he came in and went out as he saw 'opportunities'. This meant that he effectively ended up entering the stock market when the market was peaking and exiting when the market was bottoming out. Nikhil told Mr Talwar that equity markets had high volatility and the only way to consistently make returns was to stay invested. For the uninitiated, volatility refers to the amount of risk and uncertainty with regard to the size of changes in the value of a share. This broadly means that the price of the share could change dramatically over a short period of time in either direction.[1] Nikhil's message to Mr Talwar was clear. More often than not, stocks appreciate when one least expects them to. And they do not appreciate evenly.

Thankfully, Nikhil told Mr Talwar that he still had time to correct his course. He had ten years to go before retirement and hence there was enough time for equity to work its magic. Since its inception in 1979, the BSE Sensex has delivered a compounded annual return of 15.8 per cent. Judicious stock pickers had delivered far more in this time period. This 15 per cent return (net of tax since stocks have zero long-term capital gains tax) compared favourably with the pre-tax return of 4 per cent that Mr Talwar had historically earned on his portfolio.

To highlight the difference and show the power of compounding, Nikhil showed him the final value from each

---

1 'Volatility', Investopedia, http://bit.ly/1H51f4r.

asset class had Mr Talwar invested Rs 1 lakh in 1990, the year he started his career (see the exhibit below).

Exhibit 4: Value in 2017 of Rs 1 lakh invested in 1990 in various asset classes (pre-tax)

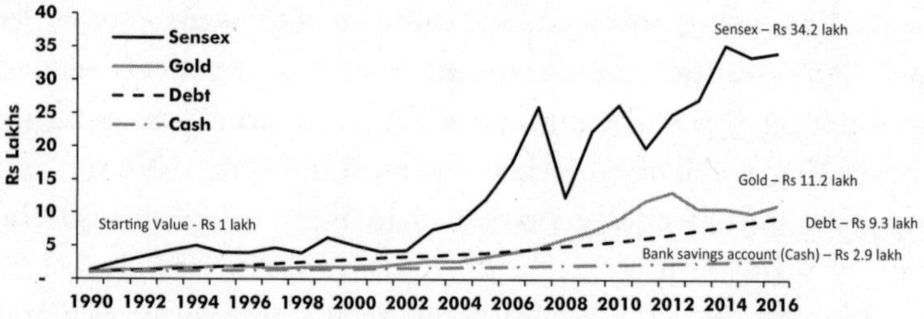

Source: Ambit Capital

At the end of the meeting, Mr Talwar was a convert. He realized the mistakes he had made and understood the long-term benefits of equity investment. He swore to become a patient and disciplined equity investor, which Nikhil assured, gave him the best chance of undoing the damage that he had done to his net worth over the years. Mr Talwar agreed to invest 80 per cent of his overall corpus (up from almost nil) into a long-term equity portfolio. In the final chapter of the book, we will examine in detail Nikhil's plan to help Mr Talwar meet his goals and have a reasonably comfortable retirement corpus.

Nikhil meets Mr Sanghvi

Nikhil ran the same financial planning exercise for Mr Sanghvi. Due to his aggressive style of investing, Mr Sanghvi had not only been taken to the cleaners in the stock market, he had also amassed a clutch of commercial properties that were largely vacant now. The promised rents never came, and it was now difficult to exit these properties. His loans in the Hundi circuit were stuck because of the recent slowdown in the economy that impacted small and medium enterprises across varied industries (including his own textile business). The slowdown in real estate after 2013 had jammed the flow of most financiers in the city, which meant that these loans were not getting refinanced and there was no exit.

In fact, Mr Sanghvi rarely made money on his investments and hence needed a big course correction. Nikhil painstakingly explained to him the benefits of patient long-term investing. More specifically, Nikhil highlighted that investing in equity markets for the long term could create significant wealth for Mr Sanghvi and help him and his family sustain their lifestyle post retirement. The conversation was surprisingly similar to the one Nikhil had had with Mr Talwar even though Mr Talwar and Mr Sanghvi were like chalk and cheese as far as their financial status was concerned. In the final chapter, we will examine Nikhil's plan to help Mr Sanghvi meet his goals.

We all make mistakes

Common to Mr Talwar and Mr Sanghvi are some very basic investment mistakes that have led to either wealth erosion or sub-optimal returns. Listed below are the seven basic investment mistakes most of us make.

No clear investment objective/plan: If you don't know where you are going, you will probably end up in the wrong place. This is one of the biggest mistakes that most investors tend to make while starting investments—they do not have their life objective/goals in mind when they invest. Most of their investing is usually random and based on market rumours/tips. It is extremely important to list one's life goals and make a financial plan to meet those objectives. The longer you postpone getting your objectives baked into a financial plan, the harder it will become for you to meet these. For Mr Sanghvi, his portfolio had, for most of his life, been just a pot of money to be used for making aggressive gambles. It was only after he sold his company that he realized that his portfolio needed a purpose and objective, namely, to sustain him and his family through his retirement.

Trading too much, too often: Too many people trade too much, too often and do not reap the benefits of long-term investing and sensible asset allocation. Repeated trading and modification in investments usually lead to lower returns and higher transaction costs (which are a source of income for brokers and most financial advisers). Buying and selling investments may be fun, but if you want to benefit from long-term wealth creation, patience is the key. Mr Talwar realized that he was losing a large part of the return due to the high churn that enriched his broker.

Lack of diversification: Different assets carry different kinds of risk and return potential. Hence, diversifying your portfolio is very important to insulate yourself from shocks in a particular asset class. More specifically, adequate diversification across different asset classes can help in sustained long-term wealth creation. Mr Talwar's concentrated investments in property (both buying property and lending to developers) meant that when the tide turned against real estate, he was left high and dry. That being said, excessive diversification and exposure to too many stocks/funds can also negatively impact the returns of the portfolio.

High commissions and fees: Paying a higher fee on your investments over the long term can have a significant impact on the performance of your portfolio. The money you pay as fees and brokerage every year compounds along with your investment returns over time. Many advisers will often recommend high-cost funds or high-cost advisory services to you—don't let these high costs eat away your returns. It is extremely important to choose funds that have reasonable expense ratios. Mr Talwar ended up with a much lower corpus from his insurance schemes because most of them had extremely high expenses.

Chasing short-term returns: Most investors chase higher returns or yields on their investments without really knowing the risk attached to them. A high yielding asset is a very tempting proposition but past returns and/or current high yields are no assurance of higher returns in the future. It is important to focus on the whole picture and not disregard the risk you carry on your investments. Both Mr Talwar and Mr Sanghvi got greedy and chased short-term returns through developer and Hundi lending respectively. When the music stopped, they suffered massive erosion in their investments.

Timing the market: Markets do not move linearly and are inherently volatile. Whilst there are indicators of various kinds that reflect the market trend at any given point of time, this does not mean that one can accurately determine when to enter or exit the markets. The belief that one can catch the top and bottom is a myth. Mr Sanghvi ended up losing crores in trying to time the market. The market taught him, as it teaches all of us, that you only end up losing money in this game.

Ignoring inflation and taxes: Most investors focus on absolute returns instead of looking at real returns. To arrive at actual returns from your investments, you need to adjust for (or subtract) the impact of inflation and taxes. Mr Talwar was losing most of his equity returns because his holding period was less than a year and that meant that even if he made money on stocks, the taxman took away 15 per cent of his gains. Also, both these gentlemen held gold believing it to be a great asset. But on an inflation-adjusted basis, gold did not deliver much for them—in the twenty-seven years since he started working in 1990, gold delivered an inflation-adjusted return of just 2 per cent per annum for Mr Talwar.

Exhibit 5: Gold has hardly delivered any returns adjusted for inflation (invested amount of Rs 1 lakh)

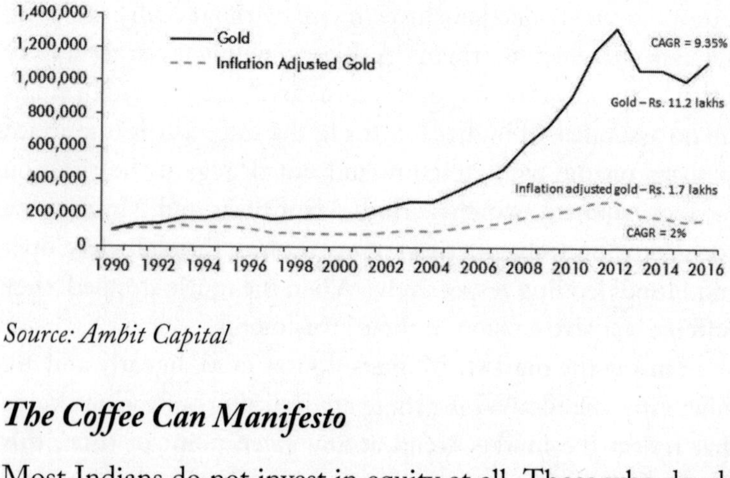

Source: Ambit Capital

The Coffee Can Manifesto

Most Indians do not invest in equity at all. Those who do, do so in a very haphazard manner. The result is that the long-term gains from what is a very powerful asset class have eluded the majority of affluent Indians.

Granted equity carries more volatility, but the rewards more than compensate for this. Also, volatility is sometimes overrated. For a saver looking to build up a corpus for the next twenty to thirty years, two to three-year spurts in volatility do not matter. The longer the time horizon for your investments, the higher should be your investment portfolio's equity exposure. It, thus, sounds counterintuitive for investors when they are told, for example, that they should increase their equity exposure from 5 per cent to 75 per cent. Yet, over a span of twenty years while the volatility seems like an afterthought, the difference in returns becomes staggering. An investor holding Rs 5000 in equity and Rs 95,000 in debt (assuming 15 per cent and 7.5 per cent compounded annualized returns respectively) will end up with a corpus of Rs 4.85 lakh in twenty years. If, on the other hand, the equity component was 75 per cent (i.e. Rs 75,000 in equity and Rs 25,000 in debt) the same investor would have a corpus of Rs 13.3 lakh in twenty years!

In the course of the next few chapters, we will lay out a very different way to make money and generate serious wealth in India without taking untoward risks and making your broker or financial intermediary rich. Most of these practices are quite intuitive and yet are followed by only a few.

In **Chapter 2**, we will demonstrate how to build a Coffee Can Portfolio using consistency of historical revenue growth and return on capital employed. Such a portfolio beats benchmarks across all time periods and also performs admirably well during stressful periods (like the Lehman crisis in 2008) when the overall stock market nosedived. If invested for over a decade with no churn, this portfolio generates returns that are substantially higher than the benchmark stock market index in India, the Sensex.

In **Chapter 3**, we study the impact of expenses on the value of the portfolio. We also witness the evolution of mutual funds—globally and in India. Along with this, we also learn the difference between active and passive funds. Globally, we are seeing a massive shift in investment flows from active funds to passive funds because active funds are no longer giving the outperformance they used to and passive funds are far cheaper. In India, we see that large-cap mutual funds outperformance vis-à-vis the Sensex has more or less vanished. However, they still continue to charge high fees compared to their global counterparts. In this chapter, we also learn about the introduction of 'direct' mutual funds and the concept of 'advisory' vs 'distribution'.

In **Chapter 4**, we take a look at real estate, the asset class which accounts for the lion's share of most Indian investors' portfolios. We study, in contrast to popular perception, how residential real estate has given very poor returns to investors over long periods of time. We also show the other disadvantages of this asset class—high transaction costs, illiquidity and sub-optimal taxation. Along with that, the bubble-like valuations in the residential real estate in India forebodes sustained underperformance in this asset class in the foreseeable future. Commercial real estate, on the other hand, appears to be a far more promising asset class in India.

In **Chapter 5**, we analyse the potential of smaller companies to outperform large-caps in India. The NDA-led government's multi-pronged attack on black money is resulting in the active diversion of savings away from physical assets to financial assets, which in turn benefits smaller businesses disproportionately (relative to the large household names that dominate the stock market). Against this backdrop, we analyse two key drivers of outperformance of smaller companies—they have the potential to grow their profits much faster than large companies and, secondly, as small companies grow in size they are 'discovered' by the stock market.

In **Chapter 6** we demonstrate how patient investing (i.e. holding stocks for longer than a year) in high-quality stocks helps an investor generate outstanding returns with low levels of volatility. While intuition suggests that shorter investment horizons are akin to speculative investing, where investors do not need to focus too much on the quality of the company, our analysis shows that even for short time horizons, high-quality stock picking is central to generating healthy returns.

In **Chapter 7**, we put our learnings to work to build good-quality investment portfolios for Mr Talwar and Mr Sanghvi. We study the importance of financial planning as an exercise to match investments with life goals. By combining Coffee Can Portfolios, Exchange Traded Funds, small-cap funds and liquid funds, we help Mr Talwar and Mr Sanghvi look forward to a financially secure future.

Finally, in **Chapter 8**, we put our takeaways from the preceding chapters to work to create a financial plan for you using the Ambit Financial Planning tool.

Three takeaways from this chapter:

1. It is critical for an investor to nail down objectives and bake them into a financial plan. The exercise helps match the investor's financial goals with the kind of risk that needs to be taken in the portfolio.
2. It is important to not adhere to the age-old wisdom of investing heavily in fixed deposits, real estate and gold. These assets have unperformed equity by significant margins over long periods of time. In fact, these assets have often given returns lower than inflation over long periods of time and thus damaged investors' wealth.
3. Equity remains the most powerful driver of long-term sustainable returns. However, investors need to be patient and systematic with equity investments. They also need to keep their brokerage and financial intermediation fees low.

CHAPTER 2

Coffee Can Investing

'For indeed, the investor's chief problem—and even his worst enemy—is likely to be himself.'

—Benjamin Graham, *The Intelligent Investor* (1949)[1]

Framing the investment problem properly

Sir Isaac Newton was one of the smartest people ever. But being a smart physicist is not necessarily the same thing as being a smart investor. Unfortunately, Newton learned this the hard way. In an updated and annotated text of Benjamin Graham's classic, *The Intelligent Investor*, Jason Zweig included an anecdote about Newton's adventurous investing in the South Sea Company:

> Back in the spring of 1720, Sir Isaac Newton owned shares in the South Sea Company, the hottest stock in England. Sensing that the market was getting out of hand, the great physicist muttered that he 'could calculate the motions of the

1 Benjamin Graham, *The Intelligent Investor*, Harper Business, 2013 edition.

> heavenly bodies, but not the madness of the people'. Newton dumped his South Sea shares, pocketing a 100 per cent profit totalling £7,000. But just months later, swept up in the wild enthusiasm of the market, Newton jumped back in at a much higher price—and lost £20,000 (or more than $3 million in [2002–03's] money). For the rest of his life, he forbade anyone to speak the words 'South Sea' in his presence.

Sir Isaac Newton's experience back in the eighteenth century is not too dissimilar to what most stock market investors have faced in India. Newton obviously wasn't unintelligent. Neither is Mr Talwar, nor is Mr Sanghvi. Newton invented calculus and conceptualized the path-breaking laws of motion. But this little episode shows that he wasn't a smart investor because he let his emotions get the best of him and was swayed by the irrationality of the crowd.

Successful equity investing largely hinges around answering two simple questions: *Which stocks should I buy?* and *For how long should I hold the stocks I bought?* These questions are simple but not easy to answer.

In a typical social gathering in Mumbai, the most common topic of discussion is: *Which stocks should one look to buy or sell?* The people answering this question usually make the following statements: *I had bought XYZ stock twelve months ago and it has almost doubled since then*, or, *You should buy XYZ stock today since it is likely to do well over the next six months.*

Such discussions on investing, however, helped neither Mr Talwar nor Mr Sanghvi nor Sir Isaac Newton when it came to figuring out answers to questions regarding which stocks to buy and for how long to hold these.

For the vast majority of equity investors in India, investment becomes a complicated affair, not only because they are surrounded by sub-standard advisers, but also because they imbibe (or are fed) incorrect investment theories—the most common one being that *to make higher returns from the stock markets, one must take higher risks.* Such misconceptions in the minds of investors blur the demarcation between 'punting' and 'investing' as investors respond to ephemeral events which corrode their capital and enhance the wealth of intermediaries.

Punters (who incorrectly think and call themselves investors) buy shares in a company because a friend of a friend says that they have heard the stock price could go up. Or they trade in small-cap stocks, cyclical stocks or beaten down stocks without really knowing what the company does, how honest and capable the promoter is and what the risks associated with the investment are. These punters not only have no advantage over other investors in the market, they actually have less information compared to professional fund managers. Hence, in all likelihood, they end up losing more money than they make in the long run. Sir Isaac Newton, Mr Talwar and Mr Sanghvi are all punters destined to be taken to the cleaners by stockbrokers feeding off their vulnerability.

Investment philosophies from the legends

'An investment in knowledge pays the best interest.'
—Benjamin Franklin (1706–90)

So, if we leave the punters behind and listen to those who have methodically thought through how to stay patient and make a great deal of money in the stock market, what can we learn?

In Berkshire Hathaway's 2007 letter to shareholders,[2] Warren Buffett explains that the kind of companies he likes to invest in are 'companies that have a) a business we understand; b) favourable

[2] Warren E. Buffett, annual report for Berkshire Hathaway Inc., 2007, http://www.berkshirehathaway.com/letters/2007ltr.pdf.

long-term economics; c) able and trustworthy management; and d) a sensible price tag. A truly great business must have an enduring "moat" that protects excellent returns on invested capital. The dynamics of capitalism guarantee that competitors will repeatedly assault any business "castle" that is earning high returns. Business history is filled with "Roman Candles", companies whose moats proved illusory and were soon crossed. Our criterion of "enduring" causes us to rule out companies in industries prone to rapid and continuous change. Though capitalism's "creative destruction" is highly beneficial for society, it precludes investment certainty. A moat that must be continuously rebuilt will eventually be no moat at all. Long-term competitive advantage in a stable industry is what we seek in a business'.

On the subject of *For how long should an investor hold the shares they buy*, Warren Buffett, in 1988's Berkshire Hathaway's letters to shareholders stated, 'When we own portions of outstanding businesses with outstanding managements, our favourite holding period is forever. We are just the opposite of those who hurry to sell and book profits when companies perform well but who tenaciously hang on to businesses that disappoint. Peter Lynch aptly likens such behavior to cutting the flowers and watering the weeds.'

Roger Lowenstein's 1995 book, *Buffett: The Making of an American Capitalist*, states that 'Buffett's style of investing was "perfectly learnable". However, there is a duality there. Part of the duality was that people confused "simplicity" with "ease". Buffett's methodology was straightforward, and in that sense "simple". It was not simple in the sense of being easy to execute. Valuing companies such as Coca-Cola (Berkshire Hathaway's largest investment in the late 1980s) took a wisdom forged by years of experience; even then, there was a highly subjective element. Most of what Buffett did, such as reading reports and trade journals, the small investor could also do. He felt very deeply that the common wisdom was dead wrong; the little guy ***could***[3] invest in the market, so long as he stuck to his Graham-and-Dodd knitting. But many people had a perverse need to make it complicated.'

Akash Prakash, founder and CEO of Amansa Capital, a Singapore-based foreign institutional investor which focuses on investing in India, explained his philosophy in Saurabh's first book, *Gurus of Chaos* (2014), as, 'Our view has always been that we need to invest in companies where we can trust in the people who are running the company. Trust, in turn, is driven by capital allocation. Where you get shafted by entrepreneurs, other than through theft and bad accounting by crooks, is capital allocation. In an environment like India, where you always have so many "perceived good opportunities", if you invest in poor capital allocators, you will never get a return. Secondly, our firm belief is that good management teams create optionality for you . . . in an environment like India, smart managers can create a lot of wealth. Therefore, even more important than the "buy" decision is how long you let that position run. At Morgan Stanley, at its peak, we owned 14 per cent of Infosys, and I was responsible largely for that position. I don't think we deserve great credit for buying Infosys. What's creditworthy is that we held on to it for so long. Unless a stock reaches an absurd valuation or if something fundamental has changed in the business environment for that company or something critical has changed in the company's growth outlook, we prefer not to sell stocks that we own. Our view is that there are a limited number of companies in India where everything lines up . . . good business, capable and ethical management, you have access to the management: such combinations do not come that often.'

---

[3] The emphasis in bold has been added by us.

Our learning from legendary investors like Warren Buffett, Akash Prakash, Sanjoy Bhattacharyya and K.N. Sivasubramanian is that to consistently generate healthy returns from equity investing, one has to invest in high-quality companies and then sit tight for long (often very long) without losing sleep about where the share price is going.[4]

The Coffee Can Portfolio: Robust returns with a low degree of uncertainty

Headquartered in Los Angeles, Capital Group is one of the world's largest asset management firms with assets under management in excess of US$1.4 trillion. In the late 1960s, Capital Group set up an entity called Capital Guardian Trust Company whose aim was to provide traditional investment counselling services to wealthy individuals. Robert Kirby joined Capital in 1965 as the main investment manager in Capital Guardian Trust, where his job involved advising high net worth clients on investments and managing their portfolios. Nearly twenty years later he wrote a remarkable note which introduced to the world the concept of the 'Coffee Can Portfolio'.

Kirby, in a note written in 1984,[5] narrated an incident involving his client's husband. The gentleman had purchased stocks recommended by Kirby in denominations of US$5000 each but, unlike Kirby, did not sell anything from

---

4 For more detailed insights from India's greatest investors on this subject, please read *Gurus of Chaos: Modern India's Money Masters* (2014).

5 Robert G. Kirby, 'The Coffee Can Portfolio', 1984, https://thetaoofwealth.files.wordpress.com/2013/03/the-coffee-can-portfolio.pdf.

the portfolio. This process (of buying when Kirby bought but not selling thereafter) led to enormous wealth creation for the client over a period of about ten years. The wealth creation was mainly on account of one position transforming to a jumbo holding worth over US$8,00,000 which came from 'a zillion shares of Xerox'. Impressed by this approach of 'buy and forget', Kirby coined the term 'Coffee Can Portfolio', a term in which the 'coffee can' harks back to the Wild West, when Americans, before the widespread advent of banks, saved their valuables in a coffee can and kept it under a mattress.

Although Kirby made the discovery of the Coffee Can Portfolio sound serendipitous, the central insight behind this construct—that in order to truly become rich an investor has to let a sensibly constructed portfolio stay untouched for a long period of time—is as powerful as it is profound. After all, the instinctive thing for a hard-working, intelligent investor is to try and optimize his portfolio periodically, usually once a year. It is very, very hard for investors to leave a portfolio untouched for ten years. A retail investor will be tempted to intervene whenever he sees stocks in the portfolio sag in price. A professional investor will feel that he has a fiduciary responsibility to intervene if parts of the portfolio are underperforming. But Kirby's counterintuitive insight is that an investor will make way more money if he leaves the portfolio untouched.

Five years ago, inspired by Kirby's 1984 note on 'Coffee Can Portfolio', analysts at Ambit decided to recreate the Coffee Can Portfolio for Indian equity investors.

The Coffee Can Portfolio comes to India

In the Indian context, we have built the Coffee Can Portfolio using a simple construct: we use straightforward investment filters to identify ten to twenty-five high-quality stocks and then leave the portfolio untouched for a decade. Both in back-testing and in the live portfolios that we manage for our clients, we have found that this simple approach delivers consistently impressive results. In particular, the portfolio not only outperforms the benchmark consistently, it also delivers healthy absolute returns and, more specifically, it performs extremely well when the broader market is experiencing stress.

Before we detail the returns delivered by the Coffee Can Portfolio, let's explain the simple investment filters that we employ. To begin with, of the approximately 5000 listed companies in India, we will limit our search to companies with a minimum market capitalization of Rs 100 crore, as the reliability of data on companies smaller than this is somewhat suspect. There are around 1500 listed companies in India with a market cap above Rs 100 crore. Then, we look for companies that over the preceding decade have grown sales each year by at least 10 per cent alongside generating Return on Capital Employed (pre-tax) of at least 15 per cent.

Why Return on Capital Employed (ROCE)? A company deploys capital in assets, which in turn generate cash flow and profits. The total capital deployed by the company consists of equity and debt. ROCE is a metric that measures the efficiency of capital deployment for a company, calculated as a ratio of 'earnings before interest and tax' (EBIT) in the numerator and capital employed (sum of debt liabilities and shareholder's equity) in the denominator. The higher the ROCE, the better is the company's efficiency of capital deployment.

Why use a ROCE filter of 15 per cent? We use 15 per cent as a minimum because we believe that is the bare minimum return required to beat the cost of capital. Adding the risk-free rate (8 per cent in India) to the equity risk premium[6] of 6.5 to 7 per cent gives a cost of capital broadly in that range. The equity risk premium, in turn, is calculated as 4 per cent (the long-term US equity risk premium) plus 2.5 per cent to account for India's credit rating (BBB-as per S&P). A country's credit rating affects the risk premium as a higher rating (e.g. AAA, AA) indicates greater economic stability in the country which lowers the risk premium for investing in that country and vice versa.

Why use a revenue growth filter of 10 per cent every year? India's nominal GDP growth rate has averaged 13.8 per cent over the past ten years. Nominal GDP growth is different from real GDP growth as unlike the latter, nominal GDP growth is *not* adjusted for inflation. In simple terms, it is (GDP) evaluated at current market prices (GDP being the monetary value of all the finished goods and services produced within a country's borders in a specific time period). A credible firm operating in India should, therefore, be able to deliver sales growth of at least that much every year. However, very few listed companies, only nine out of the 1300 firms run under our screen, have managed to achieve this. Therefore, we reduce this filter rate modestly to 10 per cent; i.e. we look for companies that have delivered revenue growth of 10 per cent every year for ten consecutive years.[7]

For financial services stocks, we modify the filters on ROE and sales growth as follows:

---

[6] The equity risk premium denotes the additional return that an investor expects, over and above the risk-free rate of return, for investing in equity.

[7] It is important to note that we are *not* looking for companies that have grown sales over a ten-year period at a compounded annualized rate of at least 10 per cent. Instead we *are* looking for companies which have grown sales every single year for ten consecutive years by at least 10 per cent.

ROE of 15 per cent: We prefer Return on Equity[8] over Return on Assets[9] because this is a fairer measure of banks' (and other lenders') ability to generate higher income efficiently on a given equity capital base over time.[10]

Loan growth of 15 per cent: Given that nominal GDP growth in India has averaged 13.8 per cent over the past ten years, loan growth of at least 15 per cent is an indication of a bank's ability to lend over business cycles. Strong lenders ride the down-cycle better, as the competitive advantages surrounding their ability to source lending opportunities, credit appraisal and collection of outstanding loans ensure that they continue their growth profitably either through market share improvements or by upping the ante in sectors that are resilient during a downturn.

Now, let's look at the results. Detailed back-testing of the Coffee Can Portfolio based on data going back to 1991 shows that *such a portfolio beats benchmarks across all time periods.* The portfolio also performs admirably well during stressful periods (like the Lehman crisis in 2008) when the overall stock market nosedived. If invested for over a decade with no churn, this portfolio generates returns that are substantially higher than the benchmark (median compounded annualized outperformance of 11.9 per cent points).

---

8 Return on Equity (ROE) is the profit earned (after paying corporate taxes) as a percentage of the shareholders' equity.

9 ROA gives a sense of how efficient a management team is at using its assets to generate earnings. ROA is calculated by dividing a company's annual profits (after paying corporate taxes) by its total assets.

10 The assets of a bank are its equity plus the amount of money the bank has borrowed. Therefore by looking at ROE, rather than ROA, we are not only able to measure a bank's ability to lend money profitably but also measure its ability to gauge exactly how much money the bank should borrow.

Exhibit 6: The CCP has outperformed benchmark indices over all its seventeen iterations

Kick-off	No. of Stocks	CCP Start		CCP End		CCP TSR*	Sensex TSR*	Outperformance
Year	#	Date	Value (Rs)	Date	Value (Rs)	CAGR	CAGR	relative to Sensex
2000	5	Jul-00	500	Jun-10	3831	22.6%	16.0%	6.6%
2001	6	Jul-01	600	Jun-11	9798	32.2%	20.5%	11.7%
2002	8	Jul-02	800	Jun-12	7631	25.3%	20.2%	5.1%
2003	9	Jul-03	900	Jun-13	10,117	27.4%	20.2%	7.2%
2004	10	Jul-04	1000	Jun-14	16,880	32.7%	19.7%	12.9%
2005	9	Jul-05	900	Jun-15	6659	22.2%	16.1%	6.0%
2006	10	Jul-06	1000	Jun-16	6376	20.4%	11.4%	9.0%
2007	15	Jul-07	1500	Jun-17	9030	19.7%	9.3%	10.3%
2008	11	Jul-08	1100	Jun-17	6471	21.8%	11.8%	10.0%
2009	11	Jul-09	1100	Jun-17	5657	22.7%	11.5%	11.2%
2010	7	Jul-10	700	Jun-17	2621	20.8%	10.1%	10.7%
2011	14	Jul-11	1400	Jun-17	3105	14.2%	10.3%	3.9%
2012	22	Jul-12	2200	Jun-17	6650	24.8%	13.8%	10.9%
2013	18	Jul-13	1800	Jun-17	5709	33.5%	13.7%	19.7%
2014	17	Jul-14	1700	Jun-17	3424	26.3%	8.2%	18.1%
2015	20	Jul-15	2000	Jun-17	2772	17.7%	6.5%	11.2%
2016	17	Jul-16	1700	Jun-17	2009	18.1%	15.3%	2.8%
2017**	12	Jul-17	1200	NA	NA	NA	NA	NA

*Source: Bloomberg, Capitaline, Ambit Capital. Note: Portfolio at start denotes an equal allocation of Rs 100 for the stocks qualifying to be in the CCP for that year. The portfolio kicks off on 1 July every year. CAGR returns for all the portfolios since 2007 have been calculated until 30 June 2017. *Both CCP returns and Sensex returns in this table are computed using TSR, i.e. Total Shareholder Returns, which include dividends for both CCP as well as for the Sensex.*

*** 2017 iteration started on 1 July 2017 and hence its returns could not be computed*

In the next exhibit we have analysed the performance of these seventeen historical iterations of the Coffee Can Portfolio with each portfolio lasting for up to ten years of holding period, i.e. 125 years of cumulative portfolio investments. The median portfolio return[11] (compounded and annualized) has remained robust at around 24 to 25 per cent historically, regardless of whether the investor's holding period has been as short as three years or as long as ten years. Moreover, the Coffee Can Portfolio also delivers an extremely low level of volatility in these annualized returns for all holding periods—a necessary condition for investors to hold large exposure to equities in their net worth.

In more technical terms, analysing the numbers behind the table above shows that over the past seventeen years, the Coffee Can Portfolio's returns within two standard deviations (i.e. the 95 per cent probability interval) have been positive for all holding periods of three years or more, and have been in excess of 9 per cent per annum for all holding periods of five years or more. In simple terms, it means that historical data suggests the Coffee Can Portfolio offers more than a 95 per cent probability of generating a positive return as long as investors hold the portfolio for at least three years. If held for at least five years, there is more than 95 per cent probability of generating a return greater than 9 per cent.

---

11 Median denotes the midpoint of returns, such that there is an equal probability of falling above or below it.

Exhibit 7: Coffee Can Portfolio returns have been robust across various holding periods (x-axis), with limited volatility in these returns, as depicted by the height of vertical bars which measure two standard deviations (95 midpoint confidence interval) of returns

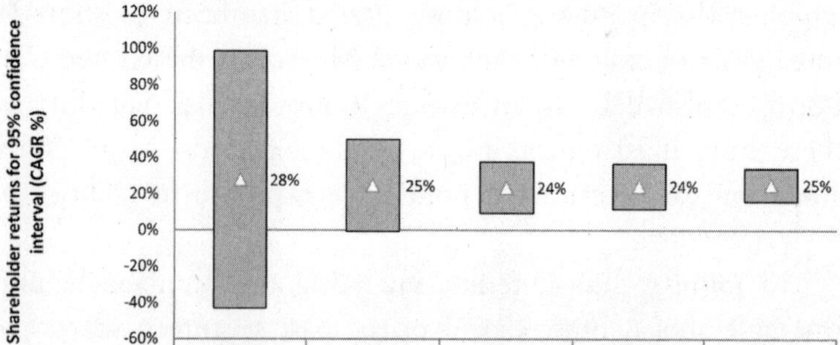

	1 Year	3 Year	5 Year	7 Year	10 Year
Upper Bound of 95%	99%	50%	38%	37%	34%
Median	20%	24%	23%	24%	25%
△ Mean	28%	25%	24%	24%	25%
Lower Bound of 95%	-43%	-1%	9%	12%	16%

Source: Ambit Capital, Bloomberg

Note: Period under consideration is July 2000–June 2017. The investment horizons are calculated on a weekly rolling basis. For instance, the standard deviation of one-year return is the standard deviation of returns generated by considering 6008 one-year periods (for all the CCP iterations) including 01/07/2000 to 01/07/2001, 08/07/2000 to 08/07/2001 and so on.

Just to emphasize the importance of 24 to 25 per cent midpoint CAGR portfolio returns, a run rate of 26 per cent return per annum results in the portfolio growing in size to ten times in ten years, 100 times in twenty years and 1000 times in thirty years.

Why does the Coffee Can Portfolio perform so well?

> 'The ancient Romans were used to being defeated. Like the rulers of history's great empires, they could lose battle after battle but still win the war. An empire that cannot sustain a blow and remain standing is not really an empire.'
>
> —Yuval Noah Harari, *Sapiens: A Brief History of Humankind* (2011)[12]

Many historians are of the view that the 'greatness' of a kingdom or an empire should be measured by its longevity. How long did the empire last? How durable was it? By this measure the first great empire was arguably the Persian Empire. Founded around 550 BC, it lasted for around 200 years until Alexander the Great's rise in 330 BC after defeating King Darius III. However, if longevity is the measure of a great empire, then the Roman Empire is possibly the greatest empire the world has ever seen. Whilst the first Roman republic, headquartered in Rome, lasted from 100 BC to 400 AD, the imperial successor to the Republic lasted for a staggering 1400 years before falling to the Ottoman Turks in 1453. So ubiquitous is the influence of this empire that the language in which we are writing this book, the legal system which underpins the contract between the publisher and the authors of this book, the mathematical concept of compounding which underpins much of this book, all of them come more or less directly from the Roman Empire!

When it comes to investing in stock markets, greatness is defined as 'the ability of a company to grow whilst sustaining

---

[12] Yuval Noah Harari, *Sapiens: A Brief History of Humankind*, HarperCollins, 2015.

its moats over long periods of time'. This then enables such great companies to sustain superior financial performance over several decades.

The Coffee Can philosophy of investing is built using the twin filters to identify great companies that have the DNA to sustain their competitive advantages over ten to twenty years (or longer). This is because 'greatness', which the Coffee Can Portfolio seeks, is not temporary and definitely not a short-term phenomenon. Greatness does not change from one quarterly result to another. In fact, great companies can endure difficult economic conditions. Their growth is not beholden to domestic or global growth—they thrive in economic down cycles as well. Great companies do not get disrupted by evolution in their customers' preferences or competitors or operational aspects of their business. Their management teams have strategies that deliver results better than their competition can. These great companies effectively separate themselves from competition using these strategies. Over time, they learn from their mistakes and increase the distance between themselves and their competition. Often, such companies appear conservative. However, they do not confuse conservatism with complacency. They simply bide their time before making the right move. These traits are rarely found outside great companies.

Why choose revenue growth and ROCE as the financial metrics to measure 'greatness'?

Charlie Munger, vice chairman of Berkshire Hathaway, stated in his lecture at the University of Southern California in 1994, 'Over the long term, it's hard for a stock to earn a much better return than the business which underlies it earns.'

Munger meant that the returns generated by any company's share price in the long term cannot be significantly more than the return on capital employed generated by the company in its day-to-day business.

He explained this with an example, 'If the business earns 6 per cent on capital over forty years and you hold it for those forty years, you're not going to make much different than a six percent return—even if you originally buy it at a huge discount. Conversely, if a business earns 18 per cent on capital over twenty or thirty years, even if you pay an expensive looking price, you'll end up with one hell of a result.'

Whilst there are several factors affecting short-term share price performance, as shown in the exhibit below, earnings is the biggest driver of stock market returns in the long run.

Exhibit 8: Sensex returns have mirrored earnings growth over long periods of time

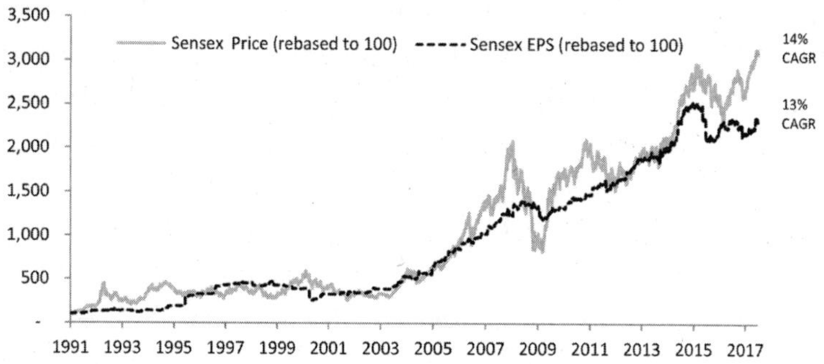

Source: Ambit Capital, Bloomberg, Ace Equity

Having established earnings as the biggest driver of share prices, the next question to be answered is: *What drives earnings growth?* Intuitively, one might imagine that 'earnings growth' is an independent metric—the more products or services you can sell, the more revenues you book and the more profits you deliver!

Rather than considering earnings growth as an independent metric by itself, it is more useful to see earnings growth to be an outcome of two independent parameters—growth in Capital Employed in a business and the firm's ability to generate a certain Return on the Capital Employed (ROCE). As a result, 'earnings growth' can be achieved either by growing capital employed whilst maintaining ROCE, or by growing ROCE through enhanced operating efficiencies whilst maintaining the firm's capital employed.

On similar lines, Warren Buffett in his 2007 letter to shareholders defined three categories of businesses based on Return on Capital:

High earnings businesses with low capital requirements: The first example refers to a business like See's Candies, a chain of candy and chocolate stores in California that Mr Buffett owns. These businesses can't, for any extended period, reinvest a large portion of their earnings internally at high rates of return. However, in light of the firm's pricing power, See's Candies' earnings keep growing without needing incremental capital, thus steadily delivering a high return on (rather low) capital employed. Typically, for such companies, two factors help minimize the funds required for operations. First, the product is sold for cash, which eliminates the need to wait for the customer to pay up and thus reduces accounts receivables. Second, the production and distribution cycle is short, which minimizes inventories. Such a business eventually becomes like a cash machine, allowing investors to use that steady stream of cash to buy other attractive businesses. In the Indian context, Hindustan Unilever is an example of this type of business.

Businesses that require capital to grow and generate decent ROCE: Buffett says that the businesses described above are extremely difficult to find. Typically, companies require additional capital to keep growing their earnings. That's because growing businesses have both working capital needs, which increase in proportion to sales growth, and significant requirements for fixed asset investments. Such businesses also form a decent investment option as long as they enjoy durable competitive advantages that can lead to attractive return on the incremental capital employed. An example of this type of business is HDFC Bank. As described by Saurabh Mukherjea in his bestselling book *The Unusual Billionaires*, 'A rupee invested in HDFC Bank at its IPO in March 1995 is worth Rs 134 now (April 2016), implying a CAGR of 26 per cent. At the heart of this outstanding performance there have been a) a risk-aware culture that focused on generating healthy returns without taking high risks; b) an internal architecture that has consistently allowed the bank to innovatively rethink the core process flows that characterize the central offering of the banking sector in areas like cash management and low-cost deposits; and c) the strength of the iconic HDFC brand.'

Businesses that require capital but generate low Returns on Capital: Finally, Buffett talks about the worst sort of businesses, which grow rapidly, require significant capital to engender growth and then earn little or no money. The Indian telecom sector over the past decade has been a good example of this, wherein building durable competitive advantages has proven to be elusive for all the players. The telecom industry in India has grown exponentially over the past decade (41 per cent CAGR in the number of telecom subscribers over FY02–17 from seven million subscribers in FY02 to

1200 million in FY17), industry leader Bharti Airtel has maintained its market share (by number of subscribers) at 20 to 24 per cent. Such exponential growth has been fuelled by heavy capital investments. Over FY07–17, Bharti's standalone business (which largely includes its Indian telecom revenues) had higher 'cash outflows from investing' (i.e. capital investments) than its operating cash flows. Despite these investments and exponential growth in its subscriber base, the firm delivered only 13 per cent revenue CAGR for its Indian telecom business, with its earnings declining from Rs 40 billion in FY07 to a loss of Rs 99 billion in FY17. As a result, pre-tax ROCE declined from 28 per cent to 7 per cent over the decade (using standalone financials). Such businesses' demand for capital is insatiable and investors who have chased growth of such companies have ended up destroying wealth over long periods of time. Bharti Airtel's share price in August 2017 is 2 per cent lower than what it was ten years ago.

Page Industries: A case study of 'greatness'

Page controls the master franchise of Jockey (innerwear and leisurewear) and Speedo (swimwear) in India. As shown in the exhibit below, over the past fifteen years (FY02–17), the firm has consistently achieved revenue growth in excess of 10 per cent per annum and ROCE in excess of 15 per cent each year. In compounded annualized terms, over the past fifteen years, Page's revenues have grown at 31 per cent CAGR, earnings have grown at 40 per cent CAGR and ROCE has averaged a staggering 55 per cent.

Exhibit 9: Page's ROCE and revenue growth has remained very consistent over the past fifteen years

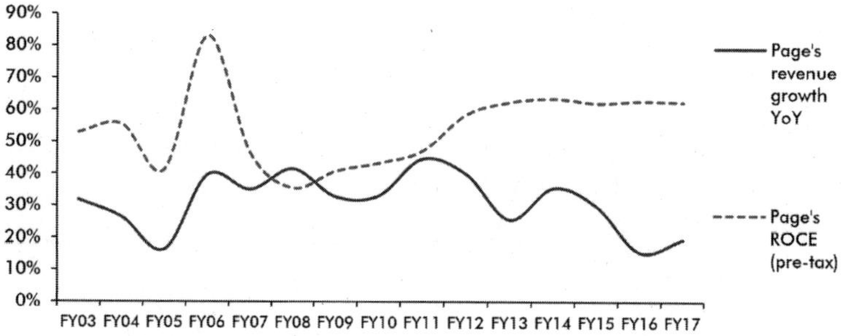

Source: Ambit Capital, Company, Bloomberg

As per Warren Buffett's categorization of businesses, Page Industries is a perfect example of a business that requires capital to grow and generates decent ROCE. Over the past ten years, Page has, on an average, reinvested around 50 per cent of its operating cash flows back into the core business via fixed asset investments to expand its manufacturing capacity. Despite this, the firm has either maintained or improved its ROCE over time, implying that it has successfully and consistently generated healthy ROCE on the reinvested capital as well.

Exhibit 10: Page Industries has allocated capital steadily towards capex and dividends over the past decade

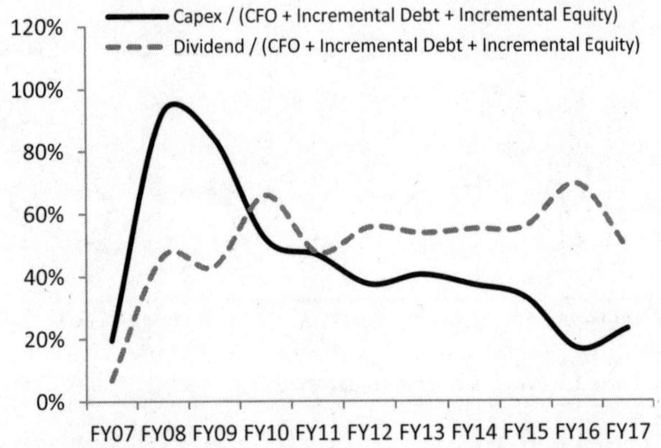

Source: Company, Ambit Capital. CFO = Cash Flow from Operations

Exhibit 11: Page Industries has maintained a prudent dividend payout ratio and debt/equity ratio over the past decade

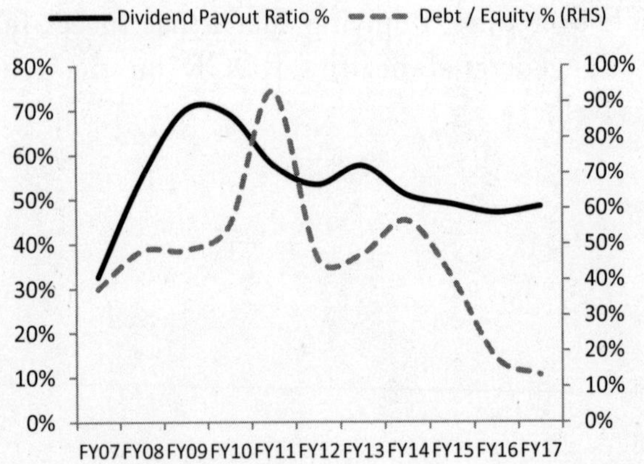

Source: Company, Ambit Capital

Consequently, Page's share price has compounded at 45 per cent per annum over the past decade (July 2007–July 2017). More importantly, although the stock's trailing P/E multiple re-rated from 27 times in 2007 to 70 times in 2017 (a CAGR of 10 per cent in the P/E multiple), the firm has delivered 32 per cent earnings CAGR over this decade. Hence, almost 80 per cent of Page's share price performance can be attributed to its earnings growth and only the balance 20 per cent to P/E multiple re-rating. Simply put, Page's share price performance is largely attributed to its healthy earnings trajectory, rather than the re-rating of its P/E multiple.

So, how has Page delivered such earnings growth over fifteen years despite operating with only a single brand in a single category, with competitors ranging from domestic incumbents like Associated Apparels (which had operated Jockey's master franchise in India during the 1960s), VIP, Rupa, TTK Tantex, Triumph, Enamor and Lovable Lingerie to international players like Hanes, Benetton, Fruit of the Loom, USPA, FCUK, La Senza and Tommy Hilfiger?

One would think that making innerwear isn't rocket science. And given that innerwear is neither on display (at least not in India as yet) when worn by users or widely spoken about in everyday conversation, the presumption would be that 'brand' can't possibly be that important. But think about this: comfortable innerwear is much more important than the clothes we wear over it. Innerwear also has to be strong and durable. As if all this wasn't enough, difference in physiques, weather-related factors and consumer preferences of comfort in India are not entirely similar to those abroad. Consequently, the product design, fit and fabric composition of an undergarment stock keeping unit (SKU) has to be indigenized in order to be successful in India. This is a curse if you get it wrong and a boon if you get it right.

If a consumer accepts a particular style and brand, it is highly likely that she/he will stick to it. Therefore, consistency of product quality and design over a period of time across geographies is critical for a brand to avoid losing a satisfied consumer. Finally, a steady stream of new products keeps distributors and retailers active and interested. Selling the same product year after year does get boring. The 'feel good' factor of consumer purchase in innerwear is driven by a combination of fresh introduction of designs across sub-segments of innerwear and fresh introduction of colours within existing styles. Very few clothing brands have got all these factors right in India.

The firm has been very focused on deepening its moats for a very long time. Page's journey with Jockey goes back to 1959. Four generations of the Genomal family (the promoters of Page) have focused on the undergarment business and have no intention of diverting to anything else. As a result, unlike many other promoters in India, who end up diluting their firm's ROCE by misallocating surplus capital, Page has maintained strict capital allocation discipline over the past two decades. Page has been judicious while balancing the source of funding—between equity and debt—for its growth (see exhibits below). Page makes capex decisions based on assessment of business growth and expansion. This assessment includes understanding subjects like market expansion and penetration, leveraging new technologies to reduce cost of production, investment in software, backward integration for cost advantages, etc.

Exhibit 12: Sources of funds for Page from FY07–17—large internal accruals

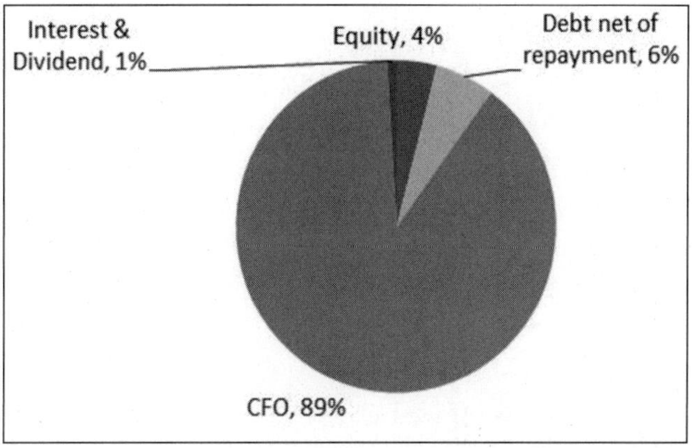

Source: Company, Ambit Capital. CFO: Cash Flow from Operations

Exhibit 13: Application of funds for Page from FY07–17—capex + dividends

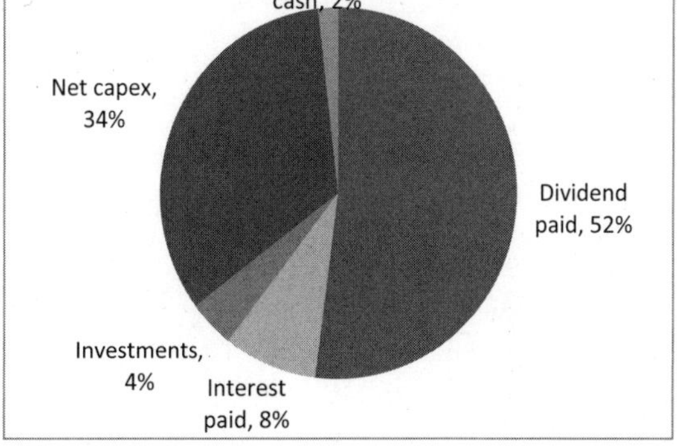

Source: Company, Ambit Capital

Exhibit 14: Page has not retained unallocated cash on its balance sheet

Particulars	FY09	FY10	FY11	FY12	FY13	FY14	FY15	FY16	FY17
Cash Equivalent (Rs mn)	103	30	26	31	56	35	44	86	727
as a % of net worth	*11.9%*	*3.0%*	*2.1%*	*1.9%*	*2.1%*	*1.2%*	*1.1%*	*1.6%*	*3.1%*
as a % of capital employed	*8.0%*	*1.9%*	*1.1%*	*1.4%*	*1.5%*	*0.8%*	*0.8%*	*1.4%*	*2.8%*
Dividend (incl. DDT*) as % of PAT	70%	69%	58%	53%	58%	51%	49%	47%	48%

Source: Company, Ambit Capital

** DDT is dividend distribution tax.*

In its twenty-three years of operation, Page has consistently widened the gap between itself and competition and achieved steady market share gains without compromising on its pricing power. Central to this success has been the firm's deepening of its moats through the following factors:

'Manufacturing prowess' is Page's biggest competitive advantage. Innerwear is a highly labour-intensive industry with limited scope for automation. This calls for astute labour management as the business grows. Whilst several of Page's competitors have suffered from labour unrest or annual workforce attrition level as high as 100 per cent, Page has maintained this figure at only 12 to 13 per cent. This has been achieved through: a) measured capacity expansion with no more than 1500 labourers in a single factory, which reduces the risk of unionization; b) focus on hiring women (who historically have been less prone to unionization than Indian men); and c) lifestyle support provided to the workforce. This workforce is regularly trained to ensure high efficiency levels. These aspects have been supported by use of operational efficiencies and R&D to help it produce a high-quality product.

Page has also built a very strong front-end with innovative marketing, retail and distribution. Unlike a wholesale-based distribution channel for larger competitors like Rupa, Page has built a strong network of exclusive distributors who are well-incentivized to create a push-based demand[13] at mom-and-pop stores. In addition to this, Page has also rolled out a wide network of over 350 exclusive brand outlets (targeting to cross 1000 outlets by 2020) which help introduce new product launches to customers when mom-and-pop shops are reluctant

[13] Push-based demand implies that the distributors get involved in pushing the product actively to the retailers rather than only fulfilling the incoming demand for products from the retailers.

to stock such new launches until they become popular with consumers. The firm also regularly invests in IT infrastructure to forecast demand, improve working capital cycles and respond to evolution in consumer preferences.

Page's approach to advertising has been unique on several fronts—high-impact advertising campaigns, significant emphasis on in-store advertising, consistent use of Caucasian models in its advertisements (which firmly entrenched its brand recall as an 'international brand') and strict pricing discipline (no discounts).

The Genomals' relationship with Jockey International, USA, is Page's biggest strategic asset. For Jockey USA, Page Industries is now its biggest franchisee. For the Genomals, India remains a large market growing in size (more consumers aspiring to buy Jockey products) and expanding in depth (new segments like leggings for women and underwear for children). Accessing Jockey's innovations in the US and bringing them to a steadily growing market like India is a formula that has worked since 1995 for Page and should continue in the foreseeable future.[14]

Back to the Coffee Can Portfolio: The case against churn

A critical feature of the Coffee Can Portfolio is that not only does it use the twin filters (ROCE above 15 per cent and revenue growth of 10 per cent) to identify great companies, but it also then holds these companies for ten years. In fact, during that decade the Coffee Can Portfolio does not make any changes to the portfolio. That might strike several readers to be strange to the point of irresponsible.

We believe that there are very compelling reasons to not touch investment portfolios for long periods of time. In fact,

---

[14] If you want to understand more about this remarkable company, please refer to Chapter 5 of *The Unusual Billionaires*.

churn in a portfolio goes against the basic philosophy of long-term investing, which is a cornerstone of Robert Kirby's original Coffee Can construct. Here are four compelling factors that go against churn in a portfolio composed of great companies:

Higher probability of profits over longer periods of time: As is well understood, equities as an asset class are prone to extreme movements in the short term. For example, whilst the Sensex has returned over 15 per cent CAGR returns over the last twenty-five years, there have been intermittent periods of unusually high drawdowns. In 2008, for instance, an investor entering the market near the peak in January would have lost over 60 per cent of value in less than twelve months of investing. Thus, whilst over longer time horizons, the odds of profiting from equity investments are very high, the same cannot be said of shorter time frames. In his book, *More Than You Know*,[15] celebrated American strategist Michael Mauboussin illustrates this concept using simple maths in the context of US equities. We use that illustration here and apply it in the context of Indian equities.

The Sensex's returns over the past thirty years have been 14.5 per cent on a compounded annualized basis, whilst the standard deviation of returns (which is a measure of volatility) has been 28.6 per cent. Now using these values of returns and standard deviation and assuming a normal distribution of returns (admittedly a simplifying assumption), the probability of generating positive returns over a one-day time horizon works out to 51.2 per cent. As the time horizon increases, the probability of generating positive returns goes up as the economic and business cycle turns. The probability of generating positive returns goes up to 70 per cent if the time horizon increases to

---

[15] Michael J. Mauboussin, *More Than You Know: Finding Financial Wisdom in Unconventional Places*, Columbia University Press, 2006.

one year; the probability tends towards 100 per cent if the time horizon is increased to ten years (see the exhibit below).

Exhibit 15: Probability of gains from equity investing in India (Sensex) increases disproportionately with increase in holding horizons (This study is for the thirty-year period from March 1987 to March 2017.)

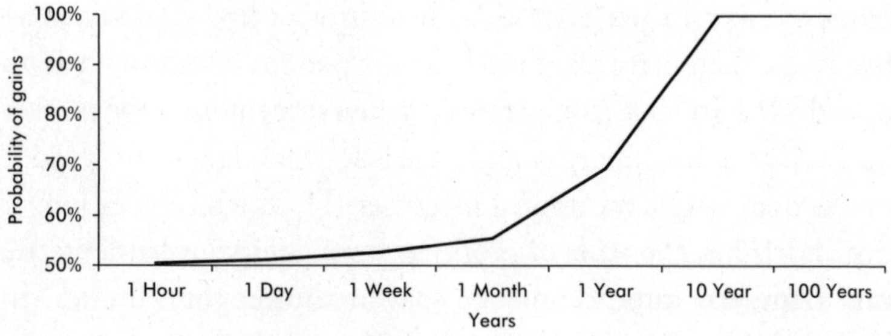

Source: Bloomberg, Ambit Capital

Note: This chart has been inspired by similar work done by Michael Mauboussin in the context of the US stock market.

The power of compounding: Holding a portfolio of stock for ten years or more allows the power of compounding to play out its magic. Over the longer term, the portfolio comes to be dominated by the winning stocks whilst losing stocks keep declining to eventually become inconsequential. Thus, the positive contribution of the winners disproportionately outweighs the negative contribution of losers to eventually help the portfolio compound handsomely. We will illustrate the point here using simple mathematics. Let's consider a hypothetical portfolio that consists of only two stocks. One of these stocks, A, grows at 26 per cent per annum whilst the other, say stock B, declines at the same rate, i.e. at 26 per cent per annum. Overall, not only do we assume a 50-50 strike rate, we also assume symmetry around the magnitude of positive and negative returns generated by the winner and the loser respectively.

In the exhibit below, we track the progress of this portfolio over a ten-year holding horizon. As time progresses, stock B declines to irrelevance while the portfolio value starts converging to the value of holding in stock A. Even with the assumed 50 per cent strike rate with symmetry around the magnitude of winning and losing returns, the portfolio compounds at a healthy 17.6 per cent per annum over this ten-year period, a pretty healthy rate of return. This example demonstrates how powerful compounding can be for investor portfolios if only sufficient time is allowed for it to work its magic.

Exhibit 16: A hypothetical portfolio with 50 per cent strike rate and symmetry around positive and negative returns

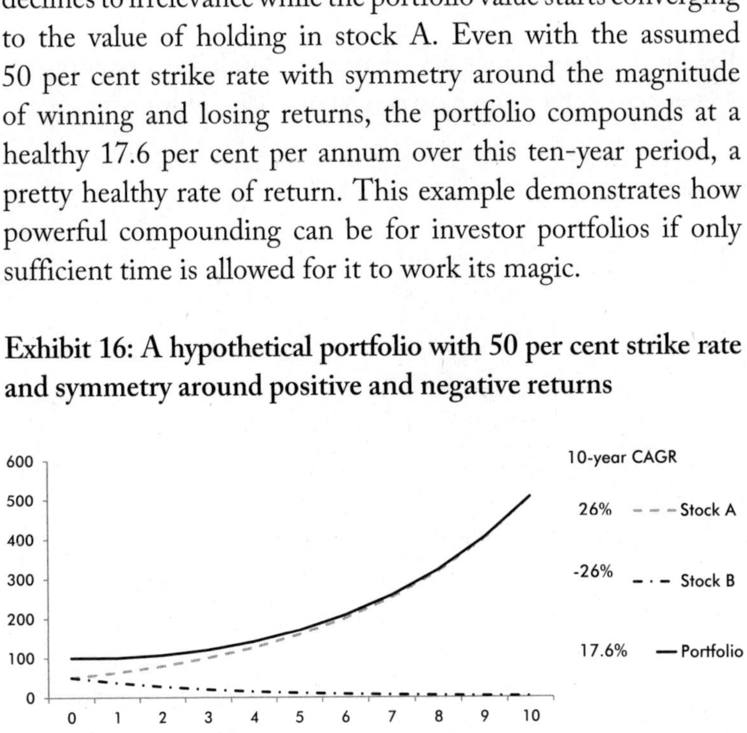

Source: Ambit Capital

Neutralizing the negatives of 'noise': Investing and holding for the long term is the most effective way of killing the 'noise' that interferes with investment decisions. Often, deep-rooted psychological issues outweigh this commonsensical advice. It is easy to say we should ignore noise in the market but quite another thing to master the psychological effects of that noise. What investors need is a process that allows them to reduce the noise, which then makes it easier to make rational decisions. As an example, we highlight how, over the long term, Page's stock price has withstood short-term disappointments to eventually compound at an impressive 45 per cent CAGR since March 2007 to June 2017 (see the exhibit below).

Exhibit 17: Page's stock price has compounded at an impressive 45 per cent per annum between March '07 and June '17

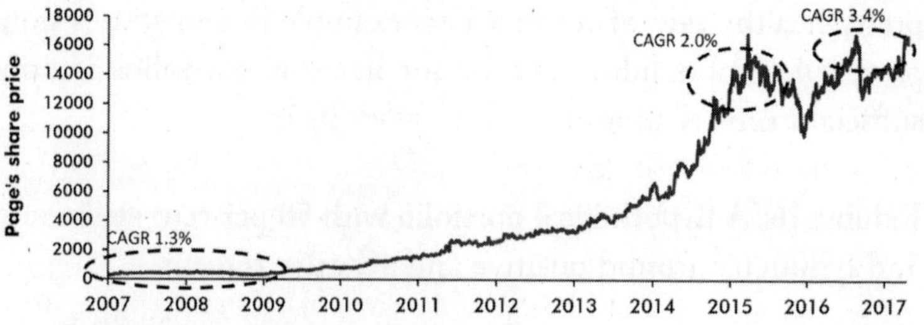

Source: Bloomberg, Ambit Capital

However, the chart above also highlights that over the past ten years, there have been several extended time periods when Page's share price did not generate impressive returns (circled in the exhibit above). In spite of being flat over these periods, Page has performed so well in the remaining period that the ten-year compounded annualized investment return from the stock (from March 2007 to June 2017) is 45 per cent. At its simplest, this is why the concept of investing for longer time horizons works—once you have identified a great franchise and you have the ability to hold on to it for a long period of time, there is no point trying to be too precise about timing your entry or your exit. As soon as you try to time that entry/exit, you run the risk of 'noise' rather than fundamentals driving your investment decisions.

Transaction costs: By holding a portfolio of stocks for over ten years, a fund manager resists the temptation to buy/sell in the short term. This approach reduces transaction costs that add to the overall portfolio performance over the long term. We illustrate this with an example. Assume that you invest US$100 million in a hypothetical portfolio on 30 June 2006. Assume further that you churn this portfolio by 50 per cent per annum (implying that a typical position is held for two years) and this portfolio compounds at the rate of Sensex Index. Assuming a total price impact cost and brokerage cost of 100 bps for every trade done over a ten-year period, this portfolio would generate CAGR returns of 13.3 per cent. Left untouched, however, the same portfolio would have generated CAGR returns of 14.5 per cent. This implies that around 9 per cent of the final corpus (around US$35 million in value terms) is lost to churn over the ten-year period. Thus, a US$ 100 million portfolio that would have grown to US$382 million over the ten-year period (30 June 2006–30 June 2016) in effect grows to US$347 million due to high churn. The shortfall in the return is obviously the returns that the broking community earns for helping the investor churn his portfolio.

What about valuations? Isn't buying and selling at the right price the greatest skill in investment?

Given the way price multiples have expanded for high-quality companies over the last decade, should investors be concerned about the sustainability of stock returns from such companies if they buy at current levels? Our answer is a resounding NO. As we show in Appendix 5 of this book, whether we look at the last three, five or ten years, whether we look at bull market phases of the Indian stock market or bear market phases, all the evidence points in one direction—starting-period valuations have very little impact on long-medium run investment returns in India.

The lack of correlation between starting-period valuations and long-term holding period returns seems to be specific to India.

Eugene Fama and Kenneth French, Nobel Prize winning economists and professors at the University of Chicago's Booth School of Business, defined a term 'value premium' in 1992 as the outperformance of value stocks over growth stocks[16] when measured using risk-adjusted returns. By this definition, a low P/E multiple stock achieves a higher risk-adjusted return compared to a high P/E multiple stock.

However, our analysis above suggests that in the Indian stock market, a low P/E multiple-based investing approach does NOT improve the return profile of an investor.[17] Given this analysis of value investing, it's clear that investors in Indian stock market should stick with high-quality franchises for the long haul without giving undue importance to valuations.

Some readers might say that 'OK, I understand that buying cheap stocks is not a very clever idea. But surely, selling expensive stocks when they become expensive is a good idea.'

To probe this issue, we analysed the impact of valuation-driven 'selling' in a high-quality portfolio and whether it generates incremental returns over and above the 'buy and

---

[16] A value stock is a stock that tends to trade at a lower price relative to its fundamentals (e.g. dividends, earnings and sales) and is thus considered undervalued by a value investor. A growth stock is a share in a company whose earnings are expected to grow at an above-average rate relative to the market. Source: http://www.investopedia.com/terms/.

[17] The reason that value investing (i.e. buying stocks with low P/E and P/B multiples) works in the US but not in India is because: a) accounting quality is highly variable in India and often the companies with low P/E have fake earnings, which makes their P/E optically low; and b) since there is no market for 'corporate control' in India (due to the way takeover laws have been framed in the country), underperforming management teams with low P/E multiples do not get booted out in India.

hold' strategy. We use our Coffee Can Portfolios of the last seventeen years as a proxy for 'high-quality' portfolios for this analysis. We then set an upper and lower limit on the market by using the Nifty's trailing P/E multiple which triggers a SELL or BUY decision on the portfolio. Details of this analysis are discussed in Appendix 3.

We find that such an investment philosophy (which SELLs the Coffee Can Portfolio when the Nifty is trading at above a certain P/E multiple and BUYs the Coffee Can Portfolio when the Nifty is trailing below a certain P/E multiple) does not generate any outperformance relative to the 'buy and hold' style.

The findings above make sense when one realizes that the firms that do make it to the Coffee Can Portfolios enjoy sustainable competitive advantages over their competitors and reflect this in their share price performance. Specifically, the franchises which featured most often in Coffee Can Portfolios tend to have three common characteristics: a) obsessive focus on the core franchise instead of being distracted by short-term gambles outside the core segment; b) relentless deepening of competitive moats and; c) sensible capital allocation. Thus, trying to time the market using valuations as a guide (especially to make 'SELL' decisions) can prove to be counterproductive—companies which possess the three characteristics mentioned in the preceding sentence are not only very rare in India, they will also continue to outperform 99.5 per cent of listed companies year after year on fundamentals.

The Coffee Can Portfolio is skewed towards specific themes by design

Given the desire for longevity and consistency of performance around ROCE and revenue growth, the Coffee Can Portfolio is oriented towards the following themes:

More B2C (Business to Consumer) than B2B (Business to Business) sectors: By definition, a B2C firm is one which sells its products or services directly to the end-consumer unlike a B2B firm which sells to another business, which in turn sells it forward after adding more value to it. Most B2C businesses are in sectors like consumption (in the broadest sense of the word), banking and pharma. Within B2C, the Coffee Can portfolio attracts businesses with smaller ticket size and repeat purchase of products and services (i.e. excluding infrequent large ticket consumption areas like residential real estate) where the companies can leverage on loyalty built with consumers during frequent customer interactions as one of its competitive advantages.

Due to its proximity with the end-consumer, a great B2C firm is better able to respond to or drive an evolutionary trend of its end-consumer. Hence, a portfolio construct chasing consistency of performance over long periods is likely to end up focusing more on B2C businesses than B2B businesses. Over the past seventeen years, Ambit's Coffee Can philosophy has seen an average of 75 per cent allocation to sectors like consumption (including autos, home-building materials, staples consumption and discretionary consumption), banking, pharma and IT.

More structural rather than cyclical plays: An analysis of BSE200 companies (ex-financial services) shows that historically the only ten-year periods when cyclical stocks[18] outperformed structural (non-cyclical) stocks were when the commodities cycle was roaring. Hence, a long-term investor who wants to be successful at investing in cyclical stocks needs to second-guess the commodities cycle in order to identify a turnaround for cyclicals. We are not good at this and most investors that we know are not very good at this either. On

[18] A cyclical stock is a share whose price is affected by ups and downs in the overall economy.

the other hand, a long-term investor who wants to successfully invest in structural stocks needs to follow a thorough bottom-up analysis of the stock and sector under consideration.

Avoiding companies that borrow lots of money to grow: Leverage on the balance sheet is beneficial to the extent that it either improves capital efficiency (for example, a cash-generative textile company deciding to raise debt through the Government of India's subsidy on loans under Technology Upgradation Funding Schemc) or helps a company fund a sudden increase in capital expenditure required to fulfil strategic initiatives like M&A or capacity expansion. However, we avoid companies which need leverage to grow revenues, e.g. power, steel and real estate sectors. This is because the illiquidity of their asset base reduces the flexibility required to evolve the company over longer periods of time. This illiquidity arises because of the specialized nature of these assets and their specific use; in cases requiring immediate change of business direction, these assets cannot be sold immediately. Also, changes to the supply of credit in the economy can adversely affect their ROCE. As a result, there is a risk that time and again the focus of the management teams of leveraged companies gets diluted as a large part of their bandwidth gets utilized in trying to service or refinance vast amounts of debt sitting on the balance sheet.

Prefer companies with intangible strategic assets: Strategic assets are those that give a firm a platform over which it can build a stack of initiatives like raw material procurement, product development, marketing strengths, great distribution, pricing power, supply chain, etc., and hence sustain competitive advantages. For most good (but not 'great') companies, strategic assets are only tangible in nature—access to natural resources, strategically positioned real estate, one good CEO, or surplus capital on the balance sheet.

The Coffee Can philosophy, however, prefers companies whose strategic assets are a combination of such tangible strengths alongside intangibles and hence difficult to replicate no matter how much money a competitor is willing to spend. Such intangible assets can either include intellectual property (patents or proprietary know-how), licences or culture-oriented aspects like: a) hiring, incentivizing, empowering and retaining top-quality talent; b) using IT (technology) investments not just as a support function, but as a backbone of the organization to ensure all aspects of the business are process-oriented and hence efficient; or c) proactively looking after the company's channel partners, vendors and employees at times when they undergo personal or professional crises.

Creating your Coffee Can Portfolio today

Having discussed the virtues of the Coffee Can Portfolio, if today (in August 2017) one were to screen the entire spectrum of listed companies with market cap greater than Rs 100 crore using our twin filters of revenue growth (or loan book growth for banks) and profitability every year over FY07–17, we get a list of twelve stocks mentioned in the exhibit below.

Exhibit 18: The Coffee Can Portfolio for 2017

Company Name	Amount Invested (Rs)	Mcap (Rs cr)*	Mcap ($ mn)*
HDFC Bank	100	4,55,427	71,160
HCL Technologies	100	1,21,180	18,934
Lupin	100	44,633	6974
LIC Housing Finance	100	33,505	5235
Page Industries	100	19,581	3059

(*Cont.*)

Company Name	Amount Invested (Rs)	Mcap (Rs cr) *	Mcap ($ mn) *
GRUH Finance	100	18,486	2888
Amara Raja Batteries	100	13,355	2087
Abbott India	100	9054	1415
Astral Poly	100	8204	1282
Dr Lal PathLabs	100	6682	1044
Repco Home Finance	100	4064	635
Muthoot Capital Services	100	729	114

Source: Ambit Capital, Bloomberg

* *This data is as of 30 August 2017.*

As discussed in the preceding pages, a Coffee Can Portfolio constructed today needs to be invested equally in all the stocks mentioned in this list. This portfolio should be left untouched for the next ten years regardless of how well or badly it does in a short-term period within this ten-year holding period.

The three key takeaways from this chapter:

1. **Intermediaries make equity investing a complicated affair:** For the vast majority of equity investors in India, investment becomes a complicated affair, not only because they are surrounded by substandard advisers, but also because they imbibe (or are fed) incorrect investment theories. The most common one is: *to make higher returns from the stock markets, one must take higher risks.* Such misconceptions in the minds of investors blur the demarcation between 'punting' and 'investing' as investors respond to ephemeral

events which corrode their capital and enhance the wealth of intermediaries. Our learning from legendary investors like Warren Buffett, Akash Prakash, Sanjoy Bhattacharyya and K.N. Sivasubramanian is that to consistently generate healthy returns from equity investing, one has to invest in high-quality companies and then sit tight for long (often very long) without losing sleep about where the share price is going.

2. **The Coffee Can Portfolio of great companies:** In the Indian context, we have built the Coffee Can Portfolio using a simple construct: we look for companies above Rs 100 crore market capitalization, which over the preceding decade have grown sales each year by at least 10 per cent alongside generating Return on Capital Employed (pre-tax) of at least 15 per cent each year. Detailed back-testing of the Coffee Can Portfolio in India, based on data going back to 1991, shows that *such a portfolio beats benchmarks across all time periods*. The portfolio also performs admirably well during stressful periods (like the Lehman crisis in 2008) when the overall stock market nosedived. If invested for over a decade with no churn, this portfolio generates returns that are substantially higher than the benchmark.[19]
3. **Why does the Coffee Can Portfolio perform so well?** The Coffee Can philosophy of investing is built to identify great companies that have the DNA to sustain their competitive advantages over ten to twenty years (or longer). This is because 'greatness', which the Coffee Can Portfolio seeks, is not temporary and is surely not a short-term phenomenon. In fact, great companies can endure

[19] More often than not, the Coffee Can Portfolio has produced annualized outperformance (relative to the Sensex) of 11.9 percentage points.

difficult economic conditions. Great companies do not get disrupted by evolution in their customers' preferences or competitors or operational aspects of their business. Their management teams have strategies that deliver results better than their competition can. Often, such companies appear conservative. However, they do not confuse conservatism with complacency. These traits are rarely found outside great companies.

CHAPTER 3

Expenses Matter

'Beware of little expenses. A small leak will sink a great ship.'

—Benjamin Franklin (1706–90)

Mr Talwar's expensive investment products

Mr Talwar was a broker's delight as he primarily focused on gross returns—be it returns from stocks or the long-term returns that his Unit Linked Insurance Plans (ULIPs) promised. Gross return is not a true reflection of a portfolio's performance because it is inclusive of fund managers' and brokers' fees. Investors should instead look at net returns (net of the fund managers' and brokers' fees and commissions). Had Mr Talwar looked at his portfolio more keenly, he would have realized that his basic purpose of investing money was being defeated by very high expenses. At 1 per cent (or more) brokerage (or fees) per transaction and due to the frequent churn, he ended up paying up to 7 per cent per annum of his stock portfolio as commissions.

ULIPs were even worse. They have three components—insurance, investment and expenses—and their tenors run into decades. However, what Mr Talwar did not realize was that he would end up paying up to 60 per cent of his first-year premium as fees. Such a high fee significantly reduces the principal left for actual investments. This is like starting a run chase in a one-day cricket match with four wickets down! Obviously, the impact is huge but is camouflaged by the complexity of this multi-decadal product.[1]

Expenses, expenses and more expenses

In the investment world, there are primarily three types of expenses that the investor, knowingly or unknowingly, pays for:

---

[1] ULIPs, or Unit Linked Insurance Plans, unlike plain vanilla Term Insurance plans, also have an investment portion. There is interplay between how much goes into covering mortality (the insurance part) and how much goes into investment. These can be easily tweaked by the manufacturer to give attractive optics to customers, but the reality is that ULIPs are 'push' products and thus require huge brokerage commissions to be sold. The fact that the tenors run into decades allows the manufacturer to implicitly charge the customer hefty upfront brokerage commission and yet promise good absolute returns to the client. Over the years, the brokerage has come down significantly from 40 to 60 per cent of the first-year premium to less than 5 per cent now. However, ULIPs continue to be far more expensive than mutual funds. Also, mutual funds allow investors to choose the best in class fund managers while ULIPs' investment performance tracking is far less transparent.

Halan, Sane & Thomas document that Indian investors lost more than Rs 1.5 lakh crore (approximately US$23 billion) on these products because of lapsing. Also, the India Household Finance Committee report (2017) acknowledges the mis-selling of ULIPs where investors were not informed about the compulsory investment required in subsequent years. That allowed insurance companies to confiscate investors' funds when the investor did not make payments in subsequent years (Source: http://www.igidr.ac.in/pdf/publication/WP-2013-007.pdf).

Transaction fees: Also called brokerage, it is the fee you end up paying every time you enter a transaction. More typical to the stock portfolio, these expenses look small in themselves; however they have a devastating effect when the portfolio turnover or the churn goes up. If a broker charges you a 0.5 per cent fee for a stock purchase, it may not seem like much. If, however, in the course of a year you bought and sold five times, your total fee as a percentage of your portfolio becomes 5 per cent!

Annual fees: This is more typical of funds (like mutual funds and PMS) wherein the fund manager charges an annual fee which can actually be paid on a monthly or quarterly basis as well. Additionally, there may be a performance fee as well where the fund manager is entitled to a share of the profit that he is able to generate for investors. The performance fee is typically settled annually.

Hidden fees: In insurance products and structured products, it is not easy for investors to understand exactly what fees are being charged. In structured products,[2] for example, the investor could be given a formula for the return on his principal but that is really the net return in his hands. He is not told what the actual gross return generated from that product is. The difference between the two is what the manufacturer and the distributor cream from the buyers of structured products. Such hidden charges are also embedded in complex products like ULIPs.

---

[2] Structured products are financial notes (similar to bonds or debentures) issued by institutions which typically offer capital protection and some participation in equity markets. Thus they allow the investor to benefit from an appreciation in the stock market while staying insulated from significant downside.

Most literature on finance is about investing money wisely to generate stellar returns. As a result, investors tend to focus largely on gross returns without realizing that high expenses can be just as damaging to their long-term financial health as weak returns. The financial services industry realizes that expenses are a blind spot for most investors and, hence, clever brokers and intermediaries have created different ways to skim investors. In this chapter, we highlight investment methods that minimize expenses.

Fund expenses compound too!

Most of us invest in the markets through the managed fund route. These could be mutual funds, PMS or AIFs.[3] While these are different types of investment structures, they are more or less similar as they pool investors' money and then nominate a fund manager to manage the corpus. The investor pays certain expenses for this fund management as well as other operational expenses. In Chapter 2, we mentioned the power of compounding. Unfortunately for investors, expenses too can compound over time! As an illustration, let us compare two mutual funds with the same gross return of 15 per cent per annum. The first has an expense ratio of 2.5 per cent per

---

[3] MFs, PMS and AIFs are all funds or pooling vehicles to invest in securities. MFs, the oldest category, have a minimum investment of Rs 5000 and are popular among retail investors. For the same reason, they are the most stringently regulated. PMS (Portfolio Management Schemes) have a minimum investment size of Rs 25 lakh and allow more customized and focused strategies designed for HNWs. The third category, AIF (Alternate Investment Funds) was launched in 2013 and allows for a minimum investment of Rs 1 crore. AIFs follow far more sophisticated and complex investment strategies and are meant for Ultra HNWs.

annum while the second has an expense ratio of 0.1 per cent per annum. Let us now see the impact of these expense ratios on the long-term returns generated from investing Rs 1 lakh in each of these mutual funds (see the exhibit below).

Exhibit 19: Expenses drag down returns significantly (initial corpus of Rs 1 lakh)

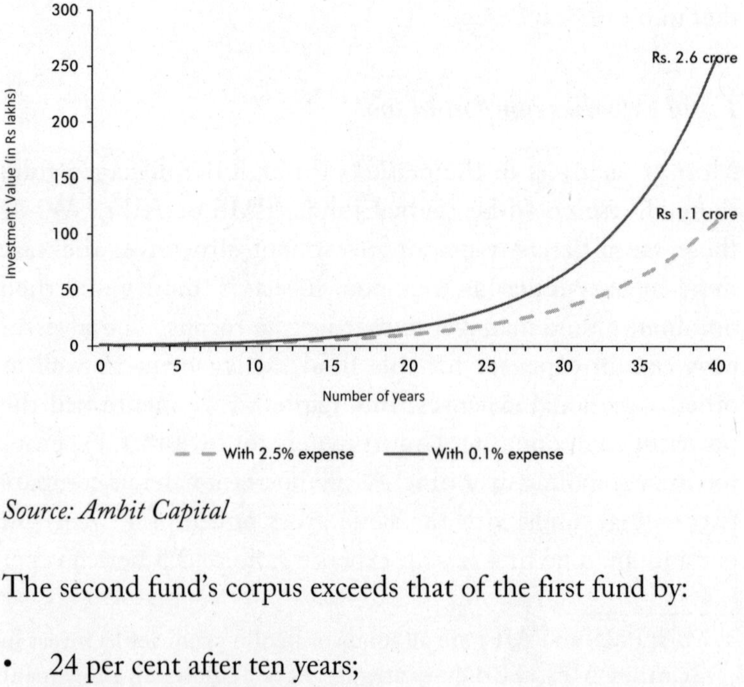

Source: Ambit Capital

The second fund's corpus exceeds that of the first fund by:

- 24 per cent after ten years;
- 53 per cent after twenty years;
- 89 per cent after thirty years; and
- 133 per cent after forty years.

A twenty-year-old who invests Rs 1 lakh when he/she starts working will get Rs 1.11 crore when they retire (at sixty) from the first fund which has a 2.5 per cent expense ratio. From the second fund, which has a 0.1 per cent expense ratio, he/she will get Rs 2.58 crore. That's more than double the corpus from the first fund!

These are not assumptions which we have plucked from thin air. Presently, most equity mutual funds have an annual management fee of 2.5 per cent. In contrast, in an ETF (Exchange Traded Fund), the fee is approximately 0.1 per cent.

Most investors tend to focus on gross returns alone and, as a result, they chase the best performing mutual fund. In doing so they forget that performance is not guaranteed—it can go up and down. But the expenses are bound to be charged. Apart from death and taxes, you can now add expenses as the only certainties in life! Given the effect of these expenses over long periods of time, they often become the single biggest driver of returns, especially in a world where fund managers with broadly similar capabilities (and similar access to information) are slugging it out daily in the stock market.

Past, present and future

Like all other industries, the portfolio management industry has also evolved over the past hundred years. The industry grew rapidly in the US in the early part of the twentieth century and in India in the 1990s. In that pioneering era, excellence did not matter. Almost all fund managers outperformed the index in those days. However, with rising competition and greater regulatory oversight, first in developed markets and now in India over the last ten years, it has become much harder for Indian mutual fund managers to generate outperformance. This squeezed the profit margins for the mutual funds and for their distributors.[4] That, in turn, brought modern technology to the forefront as enterprising fund houses started using algorithms to run funds at very low costs.

We cover this transformation in the industry through three central themes:

1. The 'Alpha Squeeze' in actively managed funds,
2. The introduction of inexpensive fund options and direct schemes in mutual funds, and
3. The advisory-led offering versus the distribution-led offering.

But first, a little bit of history.

Evolution of mutual funds

A mutual fund by definition is an investment vehicle made by collecting funds from various investors for the purpose of investing in assets like stocks, bonds, etc. Such funds are managed by an expert manager who seeks to provide returns/gains to the investors.

Mutual funds are believed to have originated in the Netherlands. In 1774, a Dutch merchant named Adriaan van Ketwich pooled money from a number of subscribers to form an investment pool and named it *Eendragt Maakt Magt*, which means 'unity creates strength'. By early 1775, the fund was fully

[4] Distributors are brokers and agents who sell a mutual fund scheme to the investor and in return get commissions from the fund house. Amongst the top distributors in India are NJ Wealth, HDFC Bank and IIFL Wealth Management.

subscribed, and the shares became tradable on the Amsterdam Exchange.

Ketwich's model of fund pooling gained popularity across Europe through the 1800s and eventually reached America. These early mutual funds were mainly close-ended and issued only a fixed number of securities.[5] The first modern-day mutual fund, Massachusetts Investors Trust, was created in the United States in 1924. It was an open-ended mutual fund and allowed for continuous issue and redemption of shares. By the end of 1929, there were about twenty open-ended mutual funds and more than 500 closed-ended mutual funds in the US.

The mutual fund industry in India was born in 1963 when the Unit Trust of India (UTI) was formed through an Act of Parliament. For almost twenty-five years, the UTI was the only entity offering mutual funds in India, and the first scheme it launched was Unit Scheme 1964. In the 1970s and 1980s, the UTI launched many more products to cater to various investment needs. By the end of 1987, it was managing approximately Rs 6700 crore in assets under management. In 1987, for the first time, non-UTI public sector entities were permitted to enter the

---

[5] To this day, mutual funds are offered in two variants—open and closed-ended. Open-ended funds allow investors to enter and exit anytime. There may be exit loads applicable, but the investor has the option to exit any day at the prevailing net asset value (NAV). Closed-ended funds, on the other hand, are typically new offerings which give back money at the end of the tenor. Investors cannot redeem the fund in between at the prevailing NAV. Since SEBI mandates that all closed-ended funds be listed, technically the investor can sell the fund in the exchange for exit. However, liquidity (the number of available buyers and sellers on exchange) is typically absent for such funds (i.e. there are very few buyers and sellers of closed-ended funds) unless a distributor or the investor can get a prospective buyer himself. A Fixed Maturity Plan (FMP) is an example of a closed-ended fund.

industry and this marked the entrance of various other public sector entities like the State Bank of India, Canara Bank, Punjab National Bank, LIC and GIC. By 1993, the total industry assets under management were close to Rs 50,000 crore.

The year 1993 marked the entry of private sector companies in the sector. Kothari Pioneer (now Franklin Templeton) was the first private sector mutual fund to be registered in 1993. The number of mutual funds registered with SEBI kept increasing through the 1990s with many foreign mutual funds setting up shop in India. By the end of 2003, there were more than thirty mutual fund houses with more than Rs 1 lakh crore worth of assets under management.

The Indian mutual fund industry now has more than forty fund houses offering approximately 2500 schemes across various asset classes like equity, debt, hybrid and commodities (gold). The industry now manages more than Rs 20 lakh crore (i.e. Rs 20 trillion or approximately US$ 315 billion) in AUM, of which about Rs 6 lakh crore is in equity. Over the past eighteen years, the industry's total assets under management have grown at 19.4 per cent per annum whereas total equity assets under management have grown at 17.7 per cent per annum.[6] The tax efficiency of the product (mutual fund investments enjoy tax benefits as they are eligible for taxation at concessional rates), the growth of the distribution industry (wherein third parties like banks, brokerages and financial advisers can sell mutual funds) and the continual rise in India's national income have been the key drivers of this stellar growth.

---

[6] Assets under Management (AUM) is the sum total of all monies invested across asset classes and managed by the Mutual Fund whereas equity assets under management refers to that portion of AUM which is invested in stocks.

Exhibit 20: The evolution of mutual funds in India

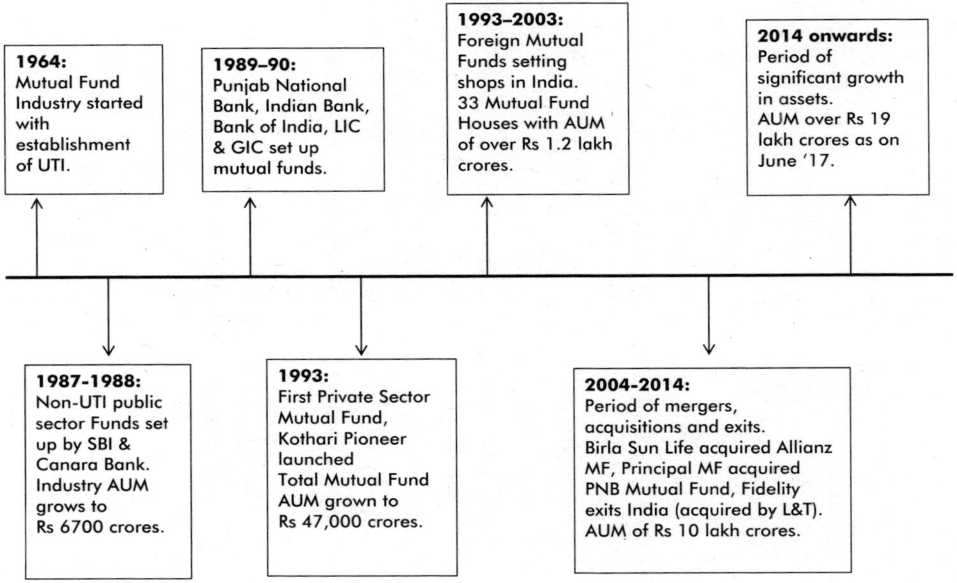

Source: AMFI

The early years of mutual funds: An era of high expenses

Fund expenses are the financial cost of investing in a fund. Typically, there are three types of costs that investors have to bear: entry load, exit load and recurring expenses. Recurring expenses include the fund management fee and various other operational costs like broking, custody, fund accounting, compliance and marketing fees. Entry and exit loads are the additional expenses that funds can charge the investor. A decade ago, mutual funds used to charge 2.25 per cent as upfront fees or entry loads. While SEBI has abolished entry loads in mutual funds, exit loads are still being charged. Most of the equity funds charge a 1 per cent exit load if investors redeem in less than a year.

The American mutual fund industry is around forty years older than ours and, hence, both more mature and more competitive. In the US, fund management fees have come down significantly. In fact, as shown in Exhibit 21, total expenses in the US (expressed as a percentage of assets under management) have fallen cumulatively by 40 per cent in the last two decades (left axis of the chart). In contrast, in India, expenses continue to be high (right axis of the chart). Apart from SEBI abolishing the upfront fees, it would appear that little has changed with respect to fund management charges.

Exhibit 21: Equity mutual fund expenses in the US and India

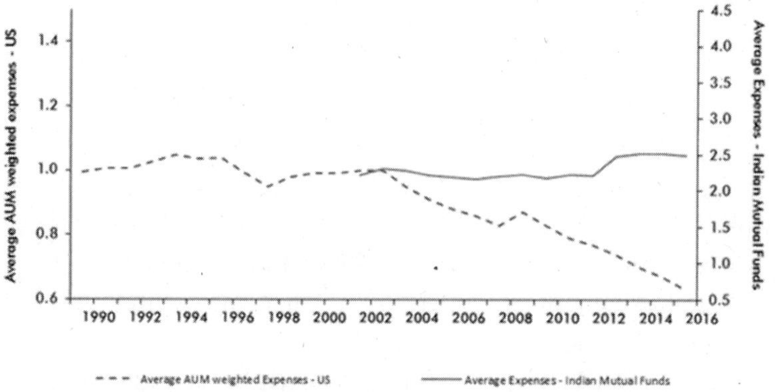

Source: Morningstar, Investment Company Institute, AMFI, Ambit Capital. US data is asset weighted average of Equity MFs. India data is average of all existing open-ended diversified Equity MFs.

Part of the reason why expenses have remained high in India is that so far it has been easy for the funds to get away with high expenses. Funds have managed to generate significant outperformance in India, especially in bull markets, which has meant high returns, net of fees, for the investors. For example, between July 2003 and January 2008, the leading mutual funds in India gave compounded annualized returns of 58 per cent compared to 48 per cent from the Sensex. Those years were the golden period for mutual funds as well as the distribution industry.

Reminiscing about that era, a veteran private banker told us, 'Money was pouring in from everywhere. The funds used to charge 2.25 per cent as upfront expense, all of which went straight to the distributors who sold those funds to investors. There was also an exit load. With the markets moving up on almost a daily basis, relationship managers were churning portfolios like mad, citing profit booking as the grounds for moving investors from one fund to another. They were earning as much as 5 to 10 per cent annually from the upfront commissions alone.'

Another veteran private banker also has fond memories of the 2003 to 2008 era: 'We were on a roll. Every three months, some mutual fund or the other used to take our sales teams to foreign locations. I personally saw at least fifteen different countries thanks to them. These trips were lavish and no expenses were spared to indulge the distribution team. This, in turn, was driving the sales behaviour.' Such lavish entertainment for mutual fund distributors is still the norm. Exhibit 22 shows two such 'contests' recently hosted by manufacturers to incentivize their distributors to sell more—the more they sell, the nicer their all-expenses-paid holidays.

Exhibit 22: Mutual fund houses offer distributors a range of incentives

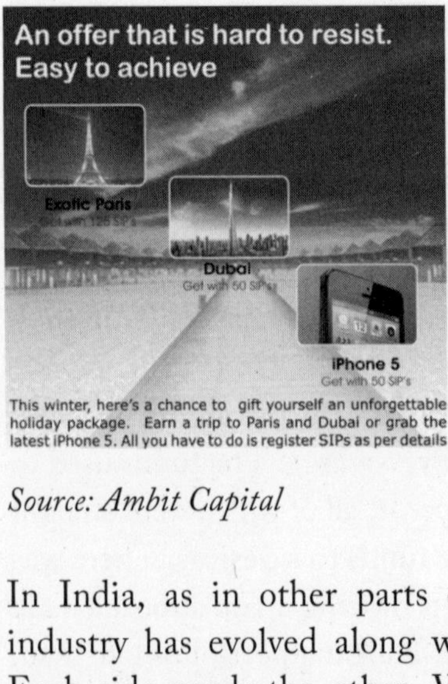

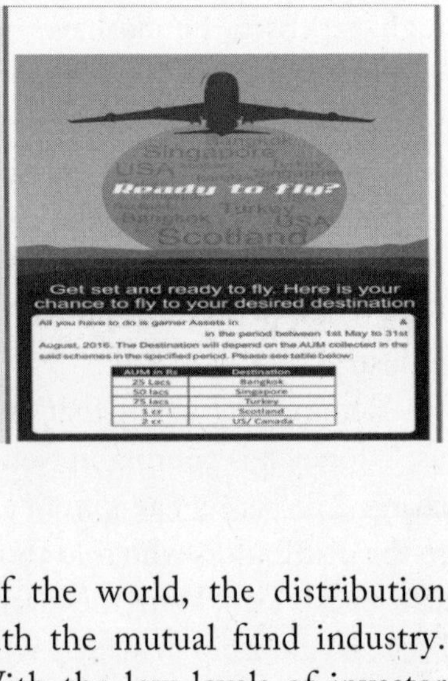

Source: Ambit Capital

In India, as in other parts of the world, the distribution industry has evolved along with the mutual fund industry. Each side needs the other. With the low levels of investor education and awareness (only 5 per cent of household assets are invested in financial assets; see Exhibit 23), for the fund manufacturer it is not enough to just have a good fund in place. It is critical to reach out and 'push' people to invest and that's where the distributors come into the picture. Since most mutual fund houses do not want to invest in a large in-house sales team, they remain dependent on their distributors to reach out to investors.

Exhibit 23: Allocation of household assets in India shows dismal holding in financial assets

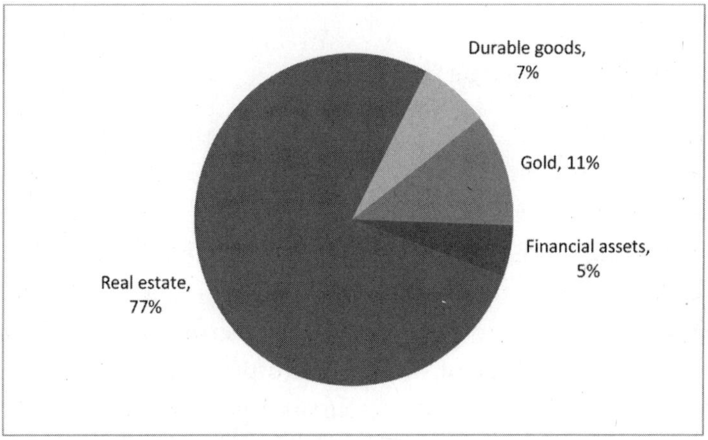

Source: Household Finance Committee Report, 2017

As shared earlier, a distributor is a broker who sells a mutual fund scheme to the investor and gets commissions from the fund house in return. These commissions come in two forms: upfront and annual. In 2009, the SEBI banned upfront commissions which used to be the entire entry load of 2.25 per cent (which was collected by the fund house and passed on to the distributor). The annual commission (or 'trail' in industry jargon) was and remains typically at 1 per cent. The biggest distributors are the banks—both multinational and Indian—which use their branch networks as staging grounds to 'push' investment products. If you visit the branch of a typical private sector bank on a Saturday afternoon, you will see dozens of investors being subjected to sales pitches from their 'relationship managers' whose bonus depends on persuading the investor to buy the product.

Over time, however, a second category of equity funds with lower expenses have emerged. These funds do not need a fund manager and thus do not incur fancy fund management charges. These funds are called passive funds.

Active versus passive funds

An expense borne by the fund house is ultimately a fee that you as an investor will pay. To a consumer of a service, as long as the service is making sense, the expenses are not a problem. In the case of mutual funds, the service is the 'outperformance' that the fund manager is able to generate for you. Note that our focus is on outperformance and not just the performance of the fund. Outperformance, which is also called 'alpha', is the incremental performance that the fund manager generates vis-à-vis a benchmark (such as the Nifty or the Sensex).

There are ETFs, or exchange traded funds, which fully replicate a benchmark. For example, a Nifty ETF is a fund that invests in all the fifty Nifty companies in the same proportion as they are in the index. This ensures that the value of the fund moves exactly like Nifty.

ETFs as a rule have very minimal expense ratios since they do not offer 'active' fund management and hence do not have to employ highly paid fund managers. An ETF is almost like a technology platform. Since an ETF does not have to pay a fund manager, it is able to charge fees which are lower than actively managed funds. Most index ETFs today charge fees ranging from 0.05 to 0.15 per cent whereas most active equity funds in India charge in excess of 2 per cent.

In an actively managed fund, a fund manager manages the money using his judgement and discretion and thus charges a fee. At the other end, passively managed funds have no input from a human manager. Passively managed funds come in two types: funds with brains and funds without. In the former (also called 'Smart Beta' funds), the fund is run based on a preset strategy or an algorithm. For example, there are mutual funds which invest in a mix of Nifty and government bonds. The weightage of each asset class is determined by the Price/Earnings (or P/E)[7] of the Nifty. In other words, based on an allocation table, the fund invests more in the Nifty when markets are cheap and less when markets are expensive. Since the decision making is based on a predetermined formula, there is little contribution from the fund manager except executing the trade. The second category of passively managed funds is index funds (just like Index ETFs). They are simply built to replicate an index like the Nifty or the Sensex and have minimal human input.

In every country, the fund management industry starts with actively managed funds. Then, as that market becomes more competitive, more perfect, it first becomes more difficult and then almost impossible for funds to outperform the broader market. That is when passively managed funds and ETFs (with low expenses) start gaining market share. Let us understand what a perfect market is.

---

7 Price Earnings ratio is the ratio of a company's current share price to its earnings per share.

A perfect market: It is all in the price

In a perfect market, all buyers and sellers have exactly the same information. There is no information asymmetry or, in other words, there is nothing that one single market participant knows which others don't. Information is power in an imperfect market, and if you know something about a stock, e.g. the sales numbers in this quarter, before anybody else, you can trade favourably in that stock before that information is known to everyone else. Then, once that piece of information is available to everybody else, the stock will move in the direction that favours you.

The perfect market assumes that all available information is reflected in the stock price. Sure, Company XYZ has lowered its revenue projection over the next few quarters, but everybody knows that. The stock has already been sold to that extent to absorb that information. Sure, Company LMN has hit upon a new patent and has a rosy future. But again, it has been bought enough by the market participants, and the price already reflects that.

No market can be absolutely perfect or imperfect. But the developed markets in the US and Europe are nearly there after over two centuries of evolution. As a result, in these markets, actively managed funds have no edge over index ETFs. According to Morningstar's July 2017 report, only 10 to 20 per cent of active US equity funds beat their benchmarks over the ten-year period ending December 2016.

India is an example of a market that is moving in the direction of the American and European markets. There is still information asymmetry, but it is reducing gradually. From massive outperformance a decade ago, actively managed funds in India struggle to eke out meaningful outperformance today.

And even that little bit of outperformance is under threat as SEBI, the market regulator, ramps up its vigilance.

To be more specific, the Indian market regulator now has sharper teeth compared to the pre-SEBI era where stock manipulation was rampant. According to Pawan Agarwal, a veteran stock broker, 'The nexus of brokers had its heydays in the late 1990s and early 2000s. Money was being made and lost by rigging up prices all the way up and then down. While brokers, in cahoots with the promoters were making a lot of money, innocent investors were burning their hands. These shady practices are one of the reasons why stock market investing never took off among Indian retail investors.'

The 'Alpha Squeeze' in Indian mutual funds

Ambit Capital has delved deep to quantify the outperformance or 'alpha' that the large-cap equity mutual funds have generated in the past. To test the hypothesis of whether alpha in India has fallen over time (as it did in the West), we divided the performance across two time periods: the long past (1991–2009) and the recent past (2010 to 2017).

Exhibit 24 shows the outperformance of the large-cap equity funds between January 1991 and December 2009. Large-cap funds have given meaningful outperformance in this period. On a median basis, there is an Alpha of 4.7 per cent per annum in the five-year and 1.1 per cent per annum in the ten-year rolling periods.

Exhibit 24: Large-cap equity mutual fund outperformance between January 1991 and December 2009

	Rolling Five Year		Rolling Ten Year	
	Equity MFs	BSE 100[8]	Equity MFs	BSE 100
Average Returns[9]	17.4%	14.3%	17.4%	13.3%
Median Returns[10]	14.5%	9.8%	15.8%	14.7%
Standard Deviation[11]	14.4%	14.0%	7.1%	4.8%

Source: www.mutualfundindia.com, Ambit Capital. There are 2659 and 1405 data points used to calculate the return parameters for five- and ten-year holding horizons above. Each data point is the past five- and ten-year annualized return as on that date.

However, when we did the same exercise for the period January 2010 to February 2017, the script changed dramatically (Exhibit 25). In this seven-year period, there is hardly any alpha left. Given that the index does not carry the effect of dividend returns, actively managed large-cap equity funds in India have

---

8 BSE 100 is an index designed to measure the performance of the 100 largest and most liquid Indian companies within the S&P BSE large mid-cap.

9 Average return is the simple mathematical average returns of a series of returns generated over a period of time.

10 Median return is the middle number return in a sorted list of returns.

11 Standard Deviation is a measure of volatility. Mathematically speaking it is the dispersion of a set of data from its mean.

actually underperformed the index between 2010 and 2017. So there is actually a negative alpha!

Exhibit 25: Large-cap equity mutual fund outperformance between January 2010 and August 2017

	Rolling Five Year[12]		Rolling Ten Year	
	Equity MFs	BSE 100	Equity MFs	BSE 100
Average Returns	12.1%	10.5%	15.6%	15.4%
Median Returns	12.7%	10.2%	16.7%	16.2%
Standard Deviation	5.4%	5.9%	3.5%	3.9%

Source: www.mutualfundindia.com, Ambit Capital. There are 1922 data points used to calculate the return parameters for five- and ten-year holding horizons above. Each data point is the past five- and ten-year annualized return as on that date.

The more visual representation of the 'alpha squeeze' is shown in Exhibit 26.

12 Rolling returns are fixed period returns calculated at predetermined frequency, e.g. five- or ten-year returns calculated on a daily basis.

Exhibit 26: Alpha of average large-cap MF performance over Nifty total return index

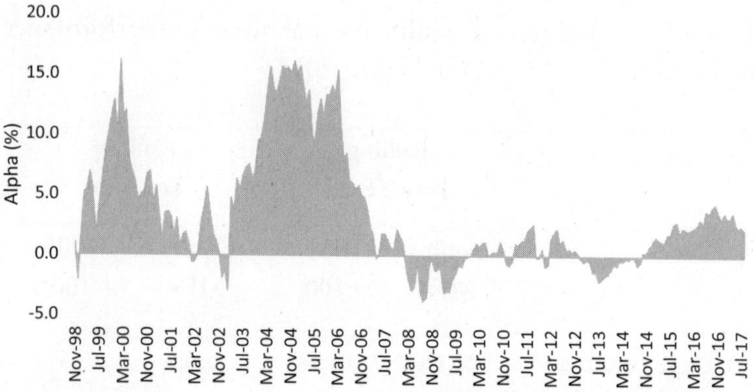

Source: MFI Explorer, Ambit Capital. Each data point is annualized alpha of large-cap funds over Nifty Total Return Index for the last three years as on that date. There are 225 such data points spread over nineteen years.

We can almost hear those championing the cause of active large-cap equity fund management saying, 'Even if large-cap equity mutual funds as an asset class cannot deliver alpha, surely there are a handful of truly great fund managers who can. Let's focus on giving them money to manage.' Unfortunately, even this argument does not hold true.

Inconsistency in mutual fund performance

Another issue plaguing most large-cap equity fund managers is the inconsistency in the performance of the fund. Ambit Capital's analysts have used data from mutualfundindia.com to quantify this issue.

Exhibit 27: The leading mutual funds lack the consistency to keep outperforming peers

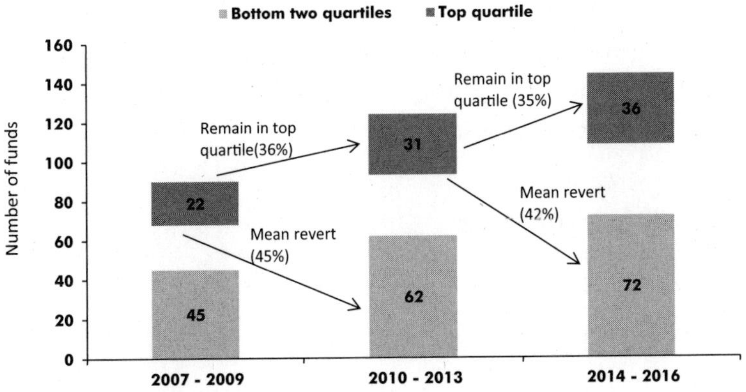

Source: www.mutualfundindia.com, Ambit Capital

Of the twenty-two funds that were in the top 25 per cent (or a quartile) in terms of their performance between FY2007–09, only 36 per cent (approximately one-third) remained in the top quartile over the subsequent three-year period, FY2010–13. Almost half of them (45 per cent) ended up in the bottom two quartiles of performance or in the bottom 50 per cent.

The same story played out in the next phase. Approximately one-third (35 per cent) of the top performing funds in FY2010–13 retained their place in the top quartile over FY2014–16. Around 42 per cent again ended up in the bottom two quartiles. This indicates that, of the twenty-two funds, only two to three maintained consistency in their performance over FY2007–16.

We can thus conclude that not only has the outperformance of large-cap equity mutual funds as an asset class more or less vanished, but there is randomness even in the relative performance of mutual funds. The inconsistency in the mutual funds' relative performance also shows us why the past performance of a fund does not indicate future outperformance. All this is compelling evidence that the Indian market is becoming more efficient. In such a scenario, it is difficult to see how these funds will be able to keep attracting investors if they keep charging such high fees.

Costs dictate the flows

The Americans were the first to fall in love with passive funds

In America, investors seem to be totally convinced about the 'Alpha Squeeze' and the need for low-expense ratios. In the calendar year 2016, active funds in the US saw a net outflow of $326 billion compared to passive funds which reported a net inflow of $429 billion.

This shift has not been one-off. In fact, in the last ten calendar years from 2007–16, only twice (2009, 2010) has the active funds inflow been more than passive funds. According to Morningstar, four out of these last ten years have seen net outflow from active funds.

Even within active funds, the outflow is not uniform. American investors have taken out the maximum monies from high-cost funds. According to Morningstar, if we were to divide the active funds into two categories—the cheapest 20 per cent and the remaining 80 per cent then, from year 2007 to 2016, the cheapest 20 per cent have seen net outflows only once while the remaining 80 per cent have seen net outflows on six out of ten occasions.

Thanks to these tectonic shifts in investor preference, passive funds have gained significant AUM from active funds. From less than 10 per cent at the turn of the century, passive funds today command 37 per cent of the total fund industry AUM in the US. Morningstar estimates that passive funds' AUM will be close to 50 per cent or half of industry assets by CY 2021.

Developments in India

In the 1990s and 2000s, the trend of upfront commission[13] and upfronting of trail commission to intermediaries accelerated. This not only reduced investors' returns (net of fees) but also encouraged unethical selling practices. Over the years, SEBI has intervened repeatedly and successfully brought down expenses. It has now capped the expense ratio of equity mutual funds and debt mutual funds to 2.5 per cent per annum and 2.25 per cent per annum respectively. In 2009, SEBI abolished entry loads, which meant that the fund houses could not charge the client any upfront fees. This also reduced to a large extent the distributors' incentive to churn.

Mutual funds continued to incentivize distributors by giving them exorbitant upfront commissions from their own pockets. In CY 2013, for example, mutual funds offered between 5 and 8 per cent upfront commissions to distributors to sell closed-ended equity funds. It resulted in total equity mutual fund sales of Rs 7000 crore, most of which were into such closed-ended schemes.

In response, SEBI, through AMFI—the mutual fund industry's trade body—introduced the 'best practice guidelines' in 2015. The guidelines stated that the upfront commission that a fund pays to a distributor cannot be more than 1 per cent.

---

[13] Upfront commission is the commission paid to the broker or mutual fund distributor at the time the customer purchases the mutual fund investment for the first time. Upfronting of trail commission is when the mutual fund pays the distributor the trail commission of a future date at the time of the first purchase of the mutual fund.

The guidelines also placed restrictions[14] on trail commission and mandated that for subsequent years it should not be higher than that of the first year. SEBI also made it mandatory to disclose the commissions paid to distributors in the account statement to investors. Thanks to mutual fund selling practices coming under such scrutiny, by 2015, distributors had shifted to hard selling more lightly regulated products—PMS schemes and AIFs.

Direct schemes: SEBI's knockout punch

Direct schemes were launched by SEBI in 2007. A direct scheme of a mutual fund has the least expense possible because mutual funds cannot give commissions to any broker. Direct code investments give investors an option to deal directly with the fund house without any intervention by intermediaries like distributors, agents, financial planners, banks, etc. The process to buy the scheme remains the same, except that the investor keeps the broker code field empty in a mutual fund application form.

There was minimal awareness of these direct schemes in the investing community because it was against the interest of the fund-house-distributor nexus to market these schemes. In fact, most of the fund houses never launched the direct option for their popular schemes.

Then, in 2013, SEBI mandated that all mutual funds had to have a direct option for all schemes. This meant that an investor now did not have to limit his/her investment universe if they wanted to go direct.

Direct plans are much cheaper, by 0.5 to 1 per cent per annum in equity and 0.05 to 0.5 per cent per annum in debt. These fees were almost half the expenses charged by

---

[14] A trail commission is paid over the lifetime of the product until the investment is withdrawn.

conventional mutual funds, which remain in the vicinity of 2 to 2.5 per cent in equity and 0.5 to 2.25 per cent in debt. The difference in fees is obviously due to the distributor or broker being disintermediated by direct schemes.

The results have been game-changing (see Exhibit 28) and SEBI deserves a lot of credit for that. Already, 38 per cent of the industry's Rs 20 lakh crore of assets under management is in direct code (June 2017). The effect of direct schemes has been most pronounced in debt funds[15] with 61 per cent of assets under management now under direct code. In equity funds,[16] 13 per cent of assets under management are now under direct code. These numbers will keep rising as the trend towards direct is now irreversible. Given the limited value addition from distributors in mutual funds, investors are increasingly choosing the direct schemes.

Exhibit 28: Direct schemes are pulling away assets under management from distributors

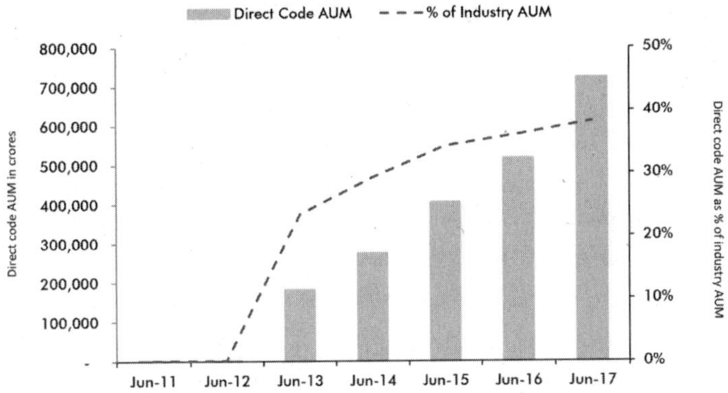

Source: Ambit Capital, AMFI

---

15 A mutual fund scheme in which core holdings are fixed-income investments like bonds, debentures, etc.

16 A mutual fund scheme that invests primarily in equity instruments.

Let us revisit the effect of compounding of expenses and show below the difference in return in direct versus regular schemes, assuming 1.5 per cent annual expenses in the former and 2.5 per cent in the latter. We have again assumed 15 per cent annual returns from the underlying investment product.

Exhibit 29: Direct fund returns far exceed funds with higher expense (initial corpus of Rs 1 lakh)

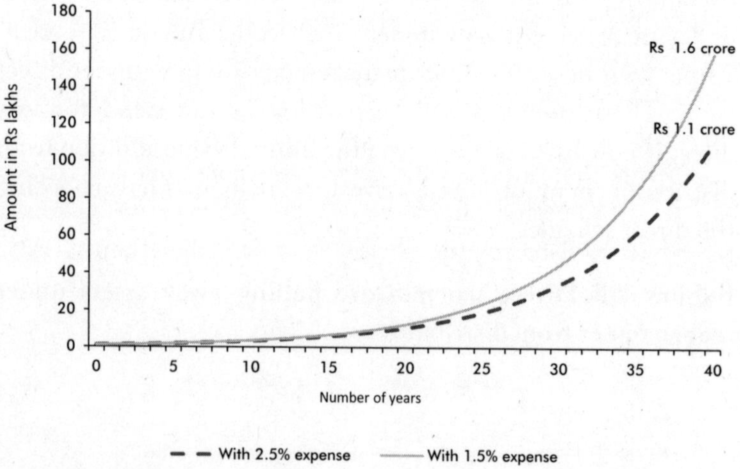

Source: Ambit Capital

A twenty-year-old who invests Rs 1 lakh at the start of his career will get Rs 1.6 crore at the age of sixty from his investment in the direct fund (which has no involvement with any distributor). In contrast, he will only get Rs 1.1 crore in the regular scheme. As much as Rs 50 lakh, or a staggering 31 per cent of his returns, are taken away by the distributor from whom he bought the fund forty years ago. So, if you are an investor prone to using brokers and distributors to buy fund management products, you might want to investigate how many crores you end up paying to them.

Next stop: Advisory only

Thankfully for the Indian investor, SEBI continues to intervene forcefully in his/her favour. The regulations announced in 2013 state that an intermediary can only be an adviser or a distributor—he cannot be both. Thus, a distributor cannot be seen as recommending a mutual fund scheme. He can only execute the transaction on the client's behalf when asked to. Similarly, an adviser can only advise on which funds to invest; he cannot be a broker for that transaction. This solution from SEBI could eliminate the conflict of interest inherent in mutual fund distribution where the broker or distributor of mutual funds has historically been the investor's main adviser.

Given that in the new regulatory construct an adviser cannot earn anything from the schemes he is recommending, his advice will be for the client's benefit rather than chasing the most remunerative schemes for himself. He earns an advisory fee (which typically varies between 0.1 per cent and 1 per cent of assets advised) directly from the client, which is part of the contract between him and the client. This contract and fee construct now align the investor's interests with that of the adviser. Why? Because the client now invests in direct schemes and the distributor does not get any commission from the product he is recommending. He then naturally advises the investors to buy the funds most suitable for them.

Conclusion: The future is looking brighter for Mr Talwar

The old model of manufacturing and distributing mutual funds is broken at every level in India. Firstly, it is no longer obvious that actively managed large-cap equity mutual funds in India consistently generate outperformance thanks to the greater levels of transparency and competition in the Indian stock market. This has created a large opportunity for passively managed equity mutual funds in India that charge fees which are significantly lower than actively managed equity mutual funds (0.1 per cent vs 2 per cent).

Secondly, thanks to regulatory intervention and technological advances, investors no longer have to rely on the broker or the distributor to provide access to mutual funds; investors can now directly buy mutual funds from the fund manufacturers at the click of a button. Furthermore, since the new construct removes the distributor from the picture, it results in expenses almost halving for the investor, which in turn means significantly higher returns.

Finally, SEBI has created a new regulatory construct which forces intermediaries to declare whether they are a fund distributor, and will therefore have their interests aligned with the fund manufacturers, or an 'adviser' whose fees will be paid by the ultimate investor and whose interests are fully aligned with the investor. The combination of hiring a good adviser and then purchasing sensibly priced funds directly from the fund houses gives investors a higher chance of generating healthy returns whilst keeping risk under control.

Over the next decade, the vestiges of the old system will give way completely to the new order and the investor will be the biggest beneficiary.

The three key takeaways from this chapter:

1. Fund expenses are often ignored but are deceptively important. Given their compounding over long periods, they have the ability to drag down investor returns drastically. For example, Rs 1 lakh invested for forty years and assumed to grow at 15 per cent per annum becomes Rs 1.11 crore and

Rs 2.58 crore at annual expenses of 2.5 per cent and 0.1 per cent.

2. Unlike earlier years, the alpha (or outperformance) in large-cap equity mutual funds is now negligible. In this scenario, it makes much more sense to invest in passive funds or ETFs. Already, in the US, active funds have started seeing massive outflows, which are becoming inflows for passive funds.
3. A broker suggesting funds to an investor leads to a conflict of interest. Driven by SEBI, the country has already moved on to an 'only advisory' or 'only broking' model. Thus, an investor is better off paying a certain percentage as advisory and investing in the most inexpensive funds (as opposed to the traditional practice of using an intermediary who is remunerated by the fund manufacturers).

CHAPTER 4

The Real Estate Trap

'He is not a full man who does not own a piece of land.'

—Hebrew proverb

'Many of the truths we cling to depend greatly on our point of view.'

—Obi-Wan Kenobi, legendary Jedi Master

(Star Wars: Episode VI—*Return of the Jedi*, 1983)

For most Indian investors, as for Mr Talwar and Mr Sanghvi, real estate remains the biggest asset by value in their portfolios. Both these gentlemen initially earned rich dividends from their investments in property but eventually faced major setbacks.

Its large transaction size and value have meant that real estate has remained one of the largest components in most investors' portfolios. Most Indians associate property with safety, status and prestige, given the feudal traditions of our country. And yet, whilst real estate has traditionally been perceived as the safest asset class, it is anything but that. In this chapter, we will share how real estate becomes the biggest investment trap for investors.

The residential real estate quagmire

For Indians, owning a house is seen as one of the prime necessities of life: *roti, kapda aur makaan* are critical priorities as far as Indians are concerned. However, while the first two are affordable, the makaan has an element of aspiration packed into it because of the high prices of urban residential real estate. Until the mid-1990s, owning a house was restricted to very few well-heeled families. This was an era where most jobs were either with the government or public sector companies. The employees stayed in the quarters offered by these companies. In that era, people typically built houses when they retired. A house was something which was built for staying, never as an investment.

Fast forward ten to fifteen years. In the opening decade of the new millennium, we saw a paradigm shift in the way retail investors started viewing residential real estate. For most of 2003–13, house prices seemed to be on steroids with prices moving up almost on a monthly basis. Along with the price rise, the other factor that led to a massive interest in this asset class was affordability. Interest rates came down significantly over these years (see Exhibit 30). Along with this, an increase in Loan to Value[1] (from 65 to 70 per cent in the 1990s to up to 95 per cent in 2004) and an increase in household income, along with tax incentives from the government, meant that buying a house was within the reach of the more affluent middle-class households.

---

[1] The maximum ratio of a loan's size to the value of the property, which secures the loan.

Exhibit 30: State Bank of India's one-year deposit rates are a proxy for interest rates in India

Source: Bloomberg

The 2003–13 real estate boom established residential real estate as an asset class by itself. This is why Mr Talwar ended up buying another house in Noida even though he owned the spacious flat in which he and his family were residing. In spite of the positive publicity given to this asset class in weekend newspaper supplements, in spite of the regular TV shows on investing in real estate and despite the pitch from the 'friend' who has made a fortune with his third flat in Mumbai, real estate is a uniquely dangerous asset class for investors for the following reasons:

Investment size: You can buy a stock for Rs 500 and a mutual fund for Rs 5000, but you need to have a few lakhs with you for investing in the cheapest of properties. This makes real estate a rich man's asset class where high ticket sizes prevent widespread adoption of the asset class.

Liquidity: Compared to financial assets such as stocks and bonds, and even compared to physical assets such as gold and silver, real estate is an illiquid asset class. You can sell a stock on the exchange, sell gold to buyers, or even barter a goat, but it is very difficult to sell a plot or a house. It takes several months, sometimes years, to arrange a buyer. In fact, as sellers in many parts of the National Capital Region and Mumbai have discovered after 2014, finding a buyer can be impossible at times.

Transaction costs: Stamp duty, registration and other transaction charges associated with buying property now exceed 10 per cent of the cost of the property. More often than not, the developer or the housing society also charges transfer fees. These costs make residential real estate the most expensive asset class to trade by a long margin. Added to that the taxation—short-term capital gains taxes on real estate are at the marginal rate for the income-tax payer and the long-term capital gains tax is 20 per cent. This implies that most of the gains from investing in real estate are lost via transaction costs and taxation.

Non-standard assets: An ounce of 24-carat gold will appreciate at the same pace in your hand as it will in the hands of another investor. An Infosys stock will give you the same appreciation as it will to anybody else who holds it. However, real estate is very non-standard. It varies across macro markets (like Mumbai versus Delhi), micro markets (Bandra versus Lower Parel) and even across streets and neighbourhoods. This makes it a very unpredictable asset class and returns are driven as much by luck as by thought-out investment decisions.

A murky sector: Residential real estate is one of the least clean sectors in India. The multitude of regulatory clearances required to buy land, develop it and then sell residential apartments make real estate an ideal sector for bribe-seeking politicians and civil servants. Over time, and over repeated transactions, rather than having a transactional relationship, many real estate developers have realized that they might as well work in partnership with the politicians, regulators and civil servants. It is these people who are first in the queue to cream the gains from real estate. The middle-class investor, no matter how affluent he/she may be, is the last to benefit from any upside associated with real estate development in India.

The above peculiarities are specific to the 'residential' side of the real estate industry. As we will discuss further in this chapter, commercial real estate is quite a different animal.

Why do so many investors get trapped in residential real estate?

In spite of the drawbacks in residential real estate as an investment class, it remains the single biggest asset class for affluent Indians. The biggest portion of most people's net worth is invariably in one or more of the houses they own. There are several reasons for this:

A head start: Until the stock market came to the fore over the past decade, buying a house, buying land or buying gold was the only known way to save and invest money. Compared to the familiarity of buying land or gold, investment in any form—either in mutual funds or in stocks or bonds—is alien to most Indian investors (see the exhibit below). According to the RBI's Household Finance Committee Report (2017), only 5 per cent of India's household savings is invested in financial assets as against 77 per cent in real estate. As a result, residential real estate occupies a much larger mind share for Indian investors than any other asset class.

Exhibit 31: The allocation of household assets in India shows significant skew towards real estate

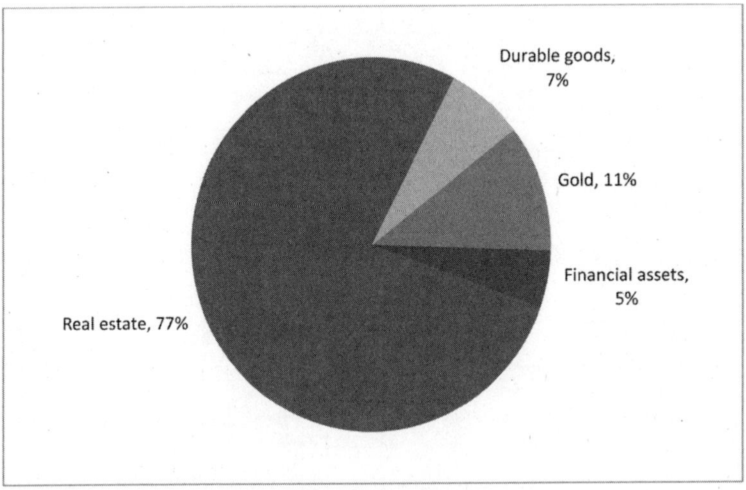

Source: The RBI's Household Finance Committee Report, 2017

'House prices only go up': Unlike other asset classes like equity and debt, which can have a cycle of three to five years (i.e. price movements change their trend every three to five years), real estate runs into super cycles of more than ten years. So, most people who made significant profits in the bull cycle of 2003–13 don't have any experience or memory of a downward cycle. As a result, they get caught in the belief that real estate prices can only go up. The fact that there are no reliable real estate price indices helps to propagate this myth in India (one that is held by millions of Indians). However, veterans who saw the real estate crash of the late 1990s know better. Thanks to an article published in the *India Today* in August 1997, we have some data on how prices crashed in that era.

Exhibit 32: Price correction in major Indian cities between 1995 and 1997

MUMBAI				BANGALORE			
RESIDENTIAL*	1995	1996	1997	RESIDENTIAL*	1995	1996	1997
South Mumbai	20.0	18.0	16.0	Indiranagar	2.5	2.0	1.5
Bandra/Khar (W)	10.0	8.0	7.5	Koramangala	2.0	1.5	1.2
Goregaon - Borivilli	3.0	2.2	2.0	R.T. Nagar	1.2	0.9	0.7
COMMERCIAL*	1995	1996	1997	COMMERCIAL*	1995	1996	1997
South Mumbai	22.0	18.0	16.0	M.G. Road	7.0	6.0	4.5
Central Mumbai	13.0	11.0	8.5	Indiranagar	2.5	2.0	1.5
Bandra (W)	14.0	11.0	8.5	Jayanagar	1.3	1.1	1.0
DEHLI				CHENNAI			
RESIDENTIAL*	1995	1996	1997	RESIDENTIAL*	1995	1996	1997
Central Delhi	8.0	7.0	6.7	Egmore/Kilpauk	3.0	2.5	2.1
Vasant Vihar/G.K.	4.0	3.1	3.0	T. Nagar	3.0	2.5	2.4
West Delhi	1.6	1.3	1.2	Mandveli	2.9	2.3	2.1
COMMERCIAL*	1995	1996	1997	COMMERCIAL*	1995	1996	1997
Connaught Place	17.0	13.0	11.0	Mount Road	7.0	6.0	5.8
Bhikaji Kama Place	9.0	8.0	7.5	N.H. road	6.0	5.0	5.0
Nehru Place	7.0	6.0	5.8	T. Nagar	3.0	2.5	2.4
PUNE				AHMEDABAD			
RESIDENTIAL*	1995	1996	1997	RESIDENTIAL*	1995	1996	1997
Koregaon park	3.2	3.0	2.8	Gulbai Tekra	12.0	11.0	8.0
Erandwane	2.8	2.7	2.5	Satellite	10.0	8.0	6.0
Aundh	1.6	1.5	1.5	Shahibaug	10.0	8.0	6.0
COMMERCIAL*	1995	1996	1997	COMMERCIAL*	1995	1996	1997
Cantonment	8.0	6.0	5.0	C.G. Road	2.0	1.8	1.5
Deccan Gymkhana	5.5	5.0	5.0	Ashram Road	1.6	1.4	1.3
Boat Club Road	3.2	3.0	2.8	Drive-in-road	1.4	1.2	1.1
*(Rs'000/sq ft)							

Source: India Today *(4 August 1997)*[2]

The lure of magnificent returns: One of the reasons even the most hardnosed investors find it hard to ignore real estate is that the asset class made a tremendous amount of money over 2003–13 as house prices in most locations went up by

[2] V. Shankar Aiyar, 'The crash of '97', *India Today*, 4 August 1997, http://indiatoday.intoday.in/story/real-estate-business-in-india-faces-unprecedented-crisis-as-prices-plummets/1/276369.htmlThis.

as much as five to ten times. For example, property prices in Gurugram's Sector 49 rose 6.4 times from Rs 1360/square feet to Rs 8670/square feet during this golden decade. Elsewhere, in Lower Parel (Mumbai), a flat selling for Rs 4500/square feet in 2003 sold for Rs 35,000/square feet in 2013, going up 7.7 times.

For most buyers of such properties, who used a mortgage, the return on the amount invested (or RoE) is mindboggling.[3] More importantly, outsized gains on this scale leave a lasting imprint on not just those who made the gains but also on their friends and relatives—envy is a powerful emotion. However, as we learnt subsequently, 2003–13 was the best period for residential real estate in India and, in all likelihood, it will be a long time before we see another such period of price appreciation. In fact, in a downward pricing spiral, investors in an illiquid and tax-unfriendly asset class such as real estate can really get squeezed on their mortgages as their modest equity is wiped out by the drop in the price of the property (a phenomenon known as 'negative equity').

Absolute returns versus compounded returns: All investment decisions have to be considered relative to their opportunity costs.[4] Most real estate investors are usually satisfied simply because they look at absolute returns in isolation. Thus, an investor may have a very fond memory of his property going up by five times in the last twenty years. But the compounded annualized return that property has generated over the last

---

3 Whilst this is true, for a home buyer who lives in this property this gain is illusionary as it will cost him more to buy or rent another house if he sells this property.

4 Opportunity cost is the difference between the asset returns against the returns you would have generated had you invested in the best available alternative.

twenty years is just 8.3 per cent. In that same period, the Indian stock market's benchmark index is likely to have risen at 15 per cent per annum which, compounded over twenty years, translates to a sixteen-times return! We have lost count of the number of real estate millionaires we met in India who have never done this 'opportunity cost' comparison.

The Coffee Can in real estate: Investors also invest in real estate because most of them burn their fingers in stocks. They usually see real estate investments as being safer than their stock investments. What they don't realize is this is because of the inadvertent Coffee Can style of investing that they adopt in real estate as against the trading style in their stock portfolios, i.e. when it comes to real estate, investors are happy to buy and hold for long periods of time. As a result, they end up holding their properties through thick and thin, which is why they are able to see an appreciation in the value. In contrast, in equity, investors typically end up buying at the peak, trade frequently and then exiting at the bottom. The harshness of most investors' experience of the stock market versus their happier experience in real estate is, therefore, in part self-inflicted rather than being due to the underlying nature of these asset classes.

Chalk and cheese: Commercial real estate versus residential real estate

Commercial real estate also has two sets of buyers: the end-users and the investors. With end-users, it is a simple equation. For them, real estate is simply a capital expenditure or a cost which has to be incurred, and these costs have to be seen relative to the return that the business generates. If businesses don't want to incur the heavy upfront cost associated with real estate, they end up renting the premises or moving to a cheaper location. On the other hand, for investors, commercial real estate is a really interesting asset class as it offers a mix of rental yield and capital appreciation.

For most affluent investors, investment in commercial real estate is in the form of shops, office units and small warehouses. This mimics their residential realty investment style in the size and locality of investments. Ultra HNW investors also have access to what are called the 'Grade A' office buildings. Grade A offices are large, modern and top-of-the-line buildings, typically built in the most prime locations. These are typically occupied by blue-chip Indian corporates or multinationals and are the benchmark of commercial realty in any country. Thus, one would measure growth in a Grade A property area to ascertain how commercial property as an asset class is doing. However, the ticket sizes associated with such deluxe office buildings are large—in Mumbai it is upward of Rs 10–20 crore for a single floor plate.[5] Hence, the key investors in these types of properties are large Indian developers (like Raheja, Embassy, Prestige Estates and DLF) or very large foreign funds (like GIC, Blackstone, Brookfield and Canadian Pension Plan Investment Board). In fact, foreign players are the largest investors in Grade A property in India with Blackstone alone holding 70 million square feet in the country. With even single floor plates at times costing upward of Rs 10–20 crore, only a few ultra HNWs have the capacity to invest in such projects. For others, investment in Grade A properties has been through real estate funds, which are actually pooling vehicles (for clubbing together many dozens of investors).

---

[5] A floor plate is an entire floor of a large building. The areas of such floor plates run into thousands of square feet.

Rental yields from commercial properties are a function of property prices and the underlying interest rates in the country. At 7 to 9 per cent today, these gross yields are far higher than the 1.5 to 3 per cent yields that residential real estate has to offer. Whilst an investor in commercial real estate also hopes for capital appreciation over time, given that the capital appreciation associated with this asset class forms a lower proportion of the overall gains, commercial properties are far safer investments than residential real estate (where capital appreciation is pretty much the only source of gains). Commercial real estate prices have been less volatile in India than residential real estate prices primarily because of the interplay between two forces. Firstly, the end-users of commercial real estate have been businesses. For these businesses, it is imperative to make profits and if the cost of a particular building or location is too high, they will consider moving to some other building or location. This rational frame of mind is very different to the mindset of the residential real estate investor who invests in an overvalued asset and still expects future price appreciation (irrespective of the current cost of the property). These contrasting mental frameworks have created a remarkable anomaly in the Indian real estate market. For example, in Mumbai's Lower Parel, which is now a thriving central business district, commercial property prices are half that of residential properties. Given that land costs and quality of construction are more or less the same for both sets of properties,[6] it is baffling why commercial properties (which give rental yields that are five to six times that of residential real estate) should be

[6] We know because we have seen most of these properties rise in front of us from the windows of Ambit House in Lower Parel.

selling at half the price. This again shows the absurdity in the residential real estate asset class and warrants extreme caution from investors.

How can investors access this asset class?

As described above, for investors, real estate is no longer just about buying physical properties. Today an investor can participate in the sector through multiple ways other than simply buying a property.

Real Estate Private Equity Funds

Real Estate Private Equity funds give funds to developers in exchange for equity. The funding (and hence the equity) could be at the developer's holding company level or for specific projects. When it is for a specific project, it is also known as SPV (Special Purpose Vehicle) funding. An SPV is typically a company that the developer incorporates only for execution of one or more specific projects. Since it is an equity investment, the investor gets full participation in the SPV's/Fund's profits. However, the flip side is that the equity investor has to bear the downside as well. While prices usually don't crash, projects typically get delayed. This increase in the duration of the project means that the equity investor's return plummets (as the return comes much later than the investor expected).

For example, an investor may get Rs 150 back on an investment of Rs 100. If the money comes back in two years, it is a compounded annualized return of 22 per cent. However, if the same money comes back in five years (maybe because the local government took longer than expected to give the 'occupancy certificate'), the investor's compounded annualized return drops to a paltry 8 per cent. Investors who get an 8 per cent return from investing in real estate will justifiably feel hard done by as they might have made more money from investing in a fixed deposit than in a high-risk venture like a real estate project.

Private equity funds burst into the scene in 2005–06 and saw many launches in the next few years. These funds typically had a tenor of five to seven years. However, almost a decade later, many of them are yet to return money, and almost none of them gave the kind of returns they were aspiring for. In that sense, the first outing of Real Estate Private Equity funds in India has been nothing short of a disaster.

Rental Yield Funds

These funds emerged in 2008 with the objective of investing in commercial property and earning the high yields that were offered. These funds were typically of lower tenure than the private equity funds since they were investing in ready properties. In that sense, they also did not carry the development risk. These funds hoped to also earn capital appreciation apart from the annual rental yield which was supposed to make the overall internal rate of return (IRR) very attractive.

Again, like private equity funds, these funds also failed to deliver. To be fair, rental yield funds have had fewer disasters than private equity funds. While the thesis for rental yields played out, the lack of exit opportunities meant that these funds dragged on far longer than their intended tenures and sometimes had to sell their assets at a discount to the price to be able to give money back to investors.

Non-convertible Debentures / Real Estate Debt Funds

Around 2009, when interest rates were very low in India (liquid funds were giving 6 per cent per annum returns), Real Estate Non-convertible Debentures (NCDs) emerged, offering very high returns. NCDs are similar to bonds issued by borrowers which promise to pay a certain coupon along with the principal back within a predetermined tenure. They were issued by real estate developers, typically at a project SPV level. The high interest rates offered—anywhere between 18 and 25 per cent—was because these projects could not get funding from banks and often, while the collateral was the project, the end-use was buying land elsewhere. Unlike private equity and rental yield funds, there was no capital appreciation expectation and thus, technically, the investor was assured of his compounded annualized return. This made NCDs extremely popular among investors and led to massive issuances from developers (see the exhibits below). This was soon followed by funds which pooled investors' money and invested it in multiple NCDs. They offered diversification which made the investments seem less risky.

Exhibit 33: NCD issuance has rocketed in the last few years

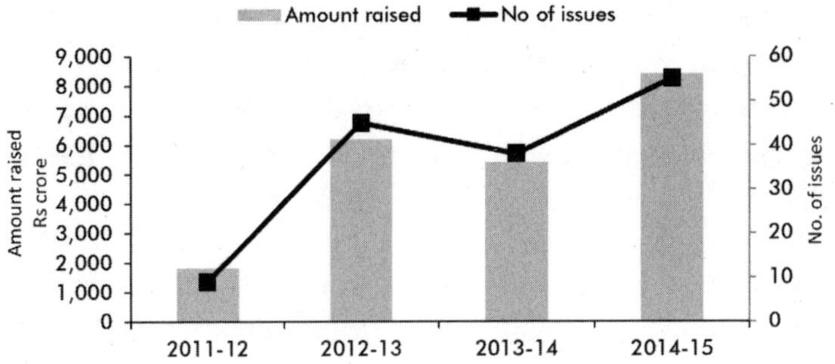

Source: Crisil

Exhibit 34: Risk associated with NCDs has risen manifold as reflected in the yields being offered

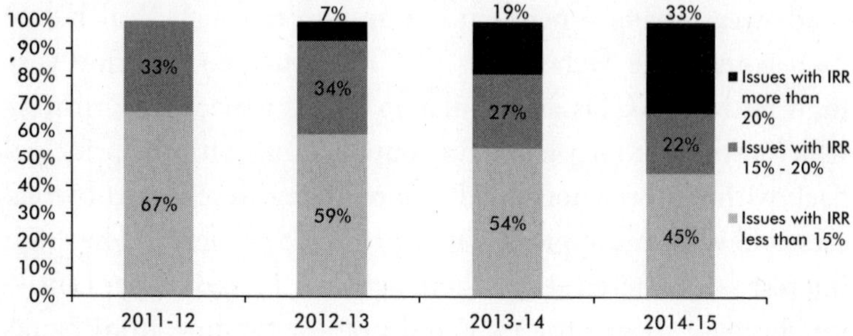

Source: Crisil

The party continued for a few years, but it was soon clear that debt with such high servicing costs was unsustainable and builders desperate enough to borrow at such high costs were not in a position to return money to clients. Then the musical chair of refinancing this high cost debt started. It meant issuing a fresh three-year NCD to take care of the maturity of the existing one. Assuming an 18 to 20 per cent per annum cost of interest servicing, the profitability of the real estate project had long gone out of the window and the objective was to somehow prevent or postpone default as long as possible.

The NCD market is now at a stage where refinancing has slowed and we are seeing defaults in various projects. The reduced appetite for residential real estate, demonetization and the widespread crackdown on black money has not helped.

REITs

REITs, or Real Estate Investment Trusts, are structurally similar to mutual funds in that they pool investors' monies and invest in real estate projects. However, there are a few differences between REITs and mutual funds. Most importantly, REITS are allowed to invest in income-bearing assets only and mandated to return more than 90 per cent of the rents they get as annual income to investors. The pooling gives an excellent opportunity to investors with small ticket sizes who cannot afford to invest in a single property. It also diversifies the risk across multiple projects and is tax efficient.

REITs are extremely popular in developed markets. Their evolution is an indicator of the potential and the future path of real estate investment in India.

While the Indian regulator, SEBI, and the government have been keen to bring REITs to India, progress has been extremely slow. The last hurdles in taxation are being cleared only now. InVITs, similar to REITs but with the underlying assets being in the infrastructure space, have already been launched and are traded in the Indian stock market. REITs should follow soon. This will bring far more transparency and broader retail participation in the real estate market. Several large foreign funds that have invested heavily in commercial real estate are expected to monetize their assets through REITs in the coming years.

Busting the myth: Real estate as an asset class is safe as a house

Lessons from the world

Investors across the world, especially in English-speaking countries, have a fascination for real estate as an asset class and for reasons not too different from what we discussed earlier in this chapter. However, we have far more comprehensive data for the developed markets than for India and, thus, it becomes far easier to apply cold logic to these markets. In the US, for example, data is available from the early years of the twentieth century and throws up some startling findings. Since 1900, real estate in the US has given an annual compounded return of 0.4 per cent as against an annual return of 5 per cent from the Dow Jones, the standard benchmark of the US stock market.

Exhibit 35: Dow Jones vs real estate returns in the US since 1900

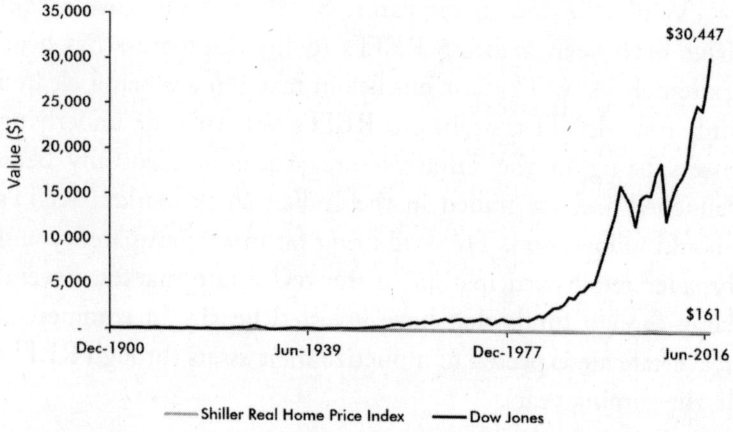

Source: Real house price index for the United States, Robert J Shiller

$1 invested in the Dow in 1900 would have become $30,447 in 2017. This compares to only a return of $161 if the dollar was invested in real estate. The story is not unique to the United States. As can be seen in the exhibit below, real estate hardly gives returns over long periods of time. Since 1980, American and German real estate have given compounded annualized returns of 3.8 per cent and 2 per cent respectively while Japanese investors have hardly made any money at all from real estate.

Exhibit 36: Real estate returns in developed markets

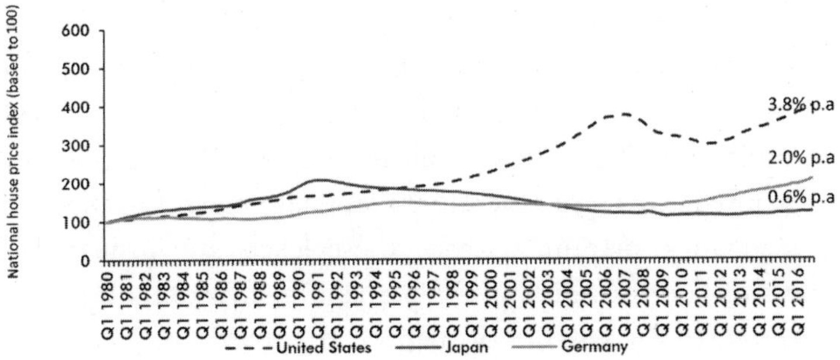

Source: Seasonally adjusted nominal house price index, OECD

In fact, real estate has time and again gone through boom-bust cycles across the world. Unfortunately, because these cycles are long, investors tend to forget the previous bust when they are in the middle of a boom, and the length of these cycles (alongside poor data availability in an emerging market like India) prevents them from developing a deeper understanding of this tricky asset class.

Exhibit 37: Real estate crashes in recent history

Country	Quarter of Peak	Quarter of Trough	No. of Quarters	Peak to Trough (%)
USA	Q2' 2007	Q2' 2011	16	-16.3
Denmark	Q1' 2007	Q2' 2009	9	-17.0
Spain	Q1' 2008	Q3' 2011	14	-18.2
Sweden	Q1' 1991	Q3' 1993	10	-20.9
Switzerland	Q4' 1989	Q1' 2000	41	-25.2
Norway	Q1' 1988	Q1' 1993	20	-25.8
Netherlands	Q2' 1978	Q2' 1982	16	-32.8
Finland	Q3' 1989	Q2' 1993	15	-36.9
Ireland	Q3' 2007	Q3' 2011	16	-44.2
Japan	Q1' 1991	Q3' 2011	82	-49.1

Source: Central Bank of Ireland

In India, most residential real estate is unaffordable

Adjusted for earnings, Indian property is easily among the most expensive in the world. The exhibit below shows the price of one square metre of residential property as a multiple of GDP per capita. Judging by this simple measure of affordability, India is the most expensive residential real estate market in the world by a gigantic margin. Clearly, these levels are unsustainable unless of course India's GDP per capita skyrockets tomorrow morning. In the absence of such GDP growth, residential real estate prices in India have nowhere to go but down.

Exhibit 38: Affordability as measured by price/square metre as a multiple of GDP per capita [2016][7]

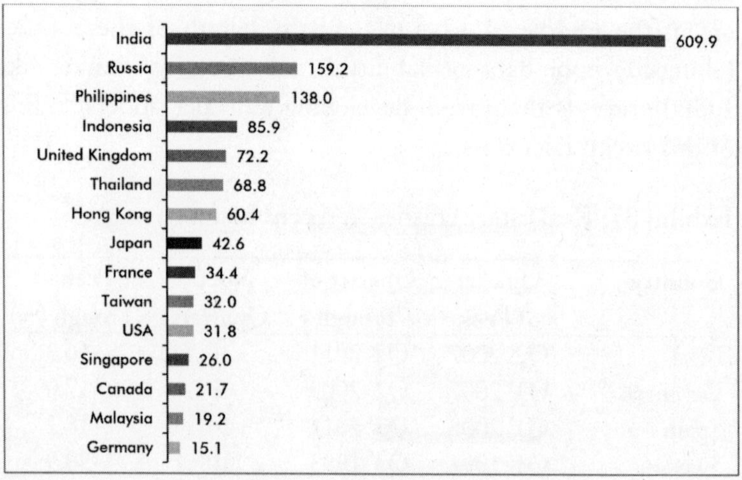

Source: Global Property Guide

[7] For India, even if we use urban GDP per capita instead of national GDP per capita (which is pulled down by Indian poverty), the price per square metre as a multiple of GDP per capita would still be significantly higher than that of Russia.

Another measure of affordability is rental yields, i.e. the rent from the property divided by the price of the property. The exhibit below shows that at 2.4 per cent, Indian rental yield is among the lowest in the world. A 2.4 per cent rental yield means that for a property worth Rs 1 crore, the annual rent that the house owner gets is Rs 20,000 per month or Rs 2.4 lakh per annum. While commercial rental yields have always been higher, residential yields have been traditionally lower because of an in-built expectation of property appreciation.

This also has to be seen in the context of underlying interest rates in the countries. For most developed countries, rental yields are far higher than their policy or ten-year government bond rates. In India, it is the reverse. Ten-year bond yields vary in the range of 6 to 7 per cent in India compared to the 2.4 per cent rental yield.

Exhibit 39: Indian rental yields are amongst the lowest in the world (2016)

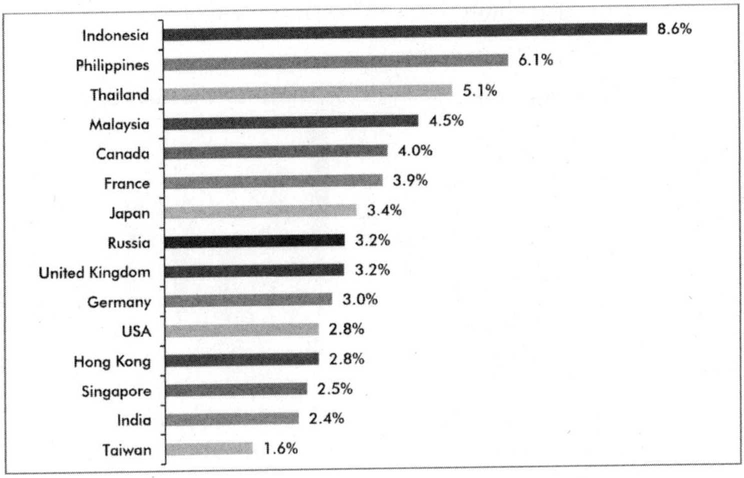

Source: Global Property Guide

Almost by any yardstick, the residential property market in India is significantly overvalued. Some of the micro markets are stretched to a bubble proportion. Today, a small house in the suburbs of Mumbai costs anywhere between Rs 1.5 and 2 crore. The equivalent monthly instalment (EMI) for a loan of that amount is roughly Rs 1.5 to 2 lakh per month. To be able to afford a Rs 2 lakh EMI, a professional has to earn at least Rs 3.5 lakh per month. This corresponds to a pre-tax salary of about Rs 60 lakh per annum. As per Income Tax returns filed for FY17, there are only 1.7 lakh people in the country earning more than Rs 50 lakh annually. So, it is not clear who exactly will buy these tens of thousands of flats in the suburbs of Mumbai, New Delhi or Bengaluru.

Not surprisingly, prices have already corrected. As can be seen in the exhibit below, prices have come down significantly in a few cities and have stagnated for other cities (except Navi Mumbai and Hyderabad). Even for Navi Mumbai, the annual compounded return is only 5.2 per cent. This compares with Sensex's annualized return of 12 per cent in the same period (September 2013–March 2017).

Exhibit 40: Price change in the last four years (absolute)

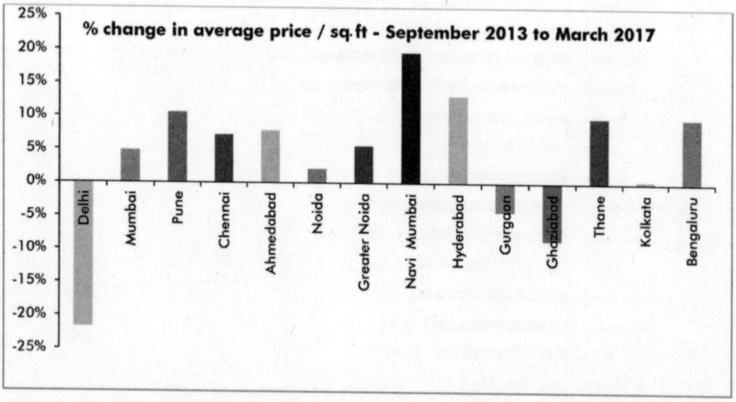

Source: Magic Bricks

In spite of a significant decline in the number of new launches (see Exhibit 41), sales have been sluggish and have led to massive inventory build-up across all cities in India with the situation most acute in the National Capital Region. On an average, at the current consumption rate, it will take eleven years just to clear the inventory.

Exhibit 41: New launches have come down significantly

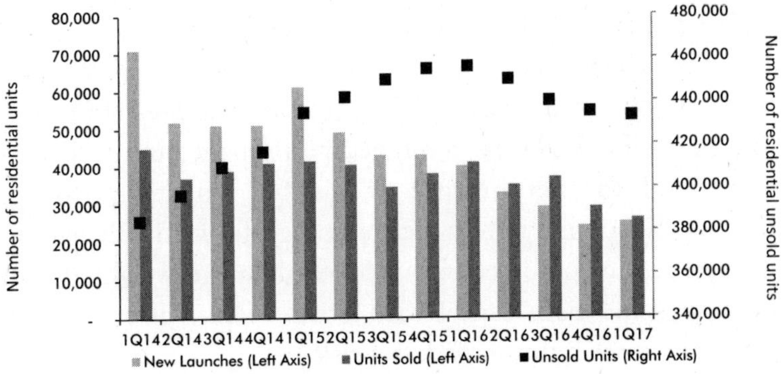

Source: JLL

Exhibit 42: The inventory pile-up in residential real estate

Cities	Quarters of unsold inventory (Q1 2017)	Years to clear existing inventory
Ahmedabad	34	8.5
Bengaluru	38	9.5
Chennai	45	11.3
Hyderabad	33	8.3
Kolkata	46	11.5
MMR	55	13.8
NCR	58	14.5
Pune	34	8.5
Average Total of 8 cities	**46**	**11.5**

Source: BusinessLine, Liases Foras

Portfolio allocation: Does it make sense to invest in real estate?

Having understood all this, you have to ask yourself: does real estate deserve a place in your portfolio? We have seen, in isolation, the answer is an emphatic NO. Let us look at the only other plausible reason: does it offer diversification?

It is established wisdom to have a diversified portfolio because it brings the volatility or risk of the portfolio down without compromising returns significantly. It is worth going into a bit of asset allocation theory at this point to understand how diversification works. When two asset classes are mixed in a portfolio, while the combined performance is a weighted average of the performance of the two underlying assets, the combined risk is not such a straightforward calculation. Typically, the combined risk is lower than the weighted sum because some risks cancel each other. Thus, diversification offers the same return with lesser risk.

However, as the eagle-eyed reader would have figured out, diversification only works if the asset classes are less than perfectly correlated with each other. If both asset classes behave in a very similar manner, then the diversification of risk simply does not happen. For example, adding bonds to your equity portfolio reduces your risk significantly without a proportionate reduction in returns. However, buying a stake in private equity funds does not reduce your risk in a meaningful way because the prices of both asset classes (equity and private equity) move in a similar way.

Given that backdrop, let us now study the correlation between equity and real estate. Given the lack of data in the Indian milieu, we again looked at data in the US. The long-term correlation between Dow Jones and US property (as measured by Robert J. Shiller's Real Home price index) was a staggering 78 per cent, implying that American stock markets and American real estate prices, more or less, move in sync. In comparison, according to consulting firm Aon Hewitt, the long-term correlation between US equity and bonds is around zero.

Advice for Mr Talwar and Mr Sanghvi

There is no denying that real estate had a great run until 2013. But one has to remember that part of it was to make up for decades of no price appreciation and part of it was a bubble building up. We have learnt from the global experiences that real estate has long cycles of boom and bust. Sitting in the comfort of Ambit House in August 2017, a correction in Indian residential real estate appears inevitable. Even if prices don't crash, it is quite unlikely that they will go up in a meaningful manner (a phenomenon that Indian investors politely call 'time correction').

Mr Talwar and Mr Sanghvi, meanwhile, will have to throw their preconceived notions regarding real estate out of the window if they want to have any hope of generating a healthy post-tax return that can give them a corpus to support their families. We shall delve into this in greater detail in the penultimate chapter.

The three key takeaways from this chapter:

1. In India and developed markets, real estate has given far lower returns compared to equity over long periods of time. Along with that, its high correlation with equity means that real estate offers little by way of diversification. A combination of these two factors means that this asset class does not really deserve a place in most investors' portfolios.

2. Real estate is the most illiquid asset with the highest transaction costs, which are now in excess of 10 per cent. Furthermore, unfavourable taxation compared to equities make it even less desirable for investment.
3. India has had a once-in-a-lifetime bull run in real estate between 2003 and 2013. However, this took the prices of residential real estate into bubble territory and—just as importantly—out of bounds for the vast majority of end-users. Even if there is no drastic fall in prices, a time correction is imminent, implying many years of poor price performance.

CHAPTER 5

Small Is Beautiful

'At the end of the day, small business success should just be a way station on your way to large business success.'

—Lloyd Blankfein, CEO, Goldman Sachs (June 2016)

How Indians fell in and out of love with stocks

It was between 1990 and 1995 that retail investors in India fell in love with stock market investing for the first time. This period started with the BSE Sensex quadrupling in less than twenty months—from 1000 points in July 1990 it crossed 4000 points[1] in March 1992, supported by the liberalization of economic policies triggered by the P.V. Narasimha Rao-led Congress government. Investors' love for the stock market was such that the number of retail investment folios that existed

1 As per the Index calculation methodology for Sensex, the level of index at any point of time reflects the Free-float market value of 30 component stocks relative to a base period. The base period of Sensex is 1978–79 and the base value is 100 index points.

in 1995 was more than the number today. The effect of this investor interest was also reflected in IPOs—during 1992–96, around 4000 companies went public (implying around four IPOs per day).

> In 1989–90, stocks were trading at price to earnings multiples of 1x, 2x and 3x. Some stocks were even trading below earnings! By 1994 I thought I knew stock market investing because of the multi-baggers that I had made between 1989 and 1994. Then 1994–96 turned out to be very testing years. Once you have had a thirty bagger [i.e. a stock which goes up 30-fold], inevitably, if you are an equity investor, you'll get drunk and make a set of mistakes. These mistakes pushed our portfolio into very bad shape by 1996. We lost a lot of money because I had not realized that what had happened between 1989 and 1994 was a one-time event . . . basically we had reaped in those years the fruits of liberalization and were lucky to be in the right place at the right time.
>
> —Sankaran Naren, CIO of ICICI Prudential Mutual Fund[2]

The 1990s' euphoria also coincided with a period when the stock market was one of the preferred avenues for deploying black money for thousands of households. Most IPOs in that decade were orchestrated by 'fly-by-night' operators working in cahoots with shady brokers (some of whom ended up behind bars). Although the SEBI had been set up in 1992, pricing controls had been removed. That, combined with the lack of

---

[2] Saurabh Mukherjea, Page 99, *Gurus of Chaos: Modern India's Money Masters* (2014).

proper regulations and infrastructure, facilitated fraudulent activities by operators. For example, offer documents used to be six to eight pages long in those days (versus over 500 pages now) since SEBI did not require too many disclosures. Defaulting promoters and those against whom regulators had passed orders were not barred from launching another IPO. Those days, almost all issues were aimed only at retail investors (versus 50 per cent reservation today for qualified institutional buyers), who more often than not became part-time venture capitalists taking huge risks.

The scandals of the early 1990s prompted the SEBI to initiate a clean-up of stock market practices from 1996. The most critical of these measures was the dematerialization of shares, i.e. a shift to electronic share certificates from physical share certificates. This development curbed a range of malpractices which hinged on duping investors with 'forged share certificates'.

Unfortunately, this positive regulatory change had a massive adverse impact on retail inflows into the stock market over the next twenty years (see exhibit 43 below). For two decades after this momentous change in 1996, Indian investors routed their black money savings away from the stock market and towards real estate and gold. By 2013, property prices in Mumbai started rivalling those in London and New York's suburbs and Indians became the world's biggest buyers of gold. Rental yields in India's residential property markets are now amongst the lowest in Asia (see Exhibit 39 in Chapter 4), thus pointing to significant overvaluation of this asset class mainly because it can absorb black money.

Exhibit 43: Domestic equity mutual fund flows in India have been weak post 1996*

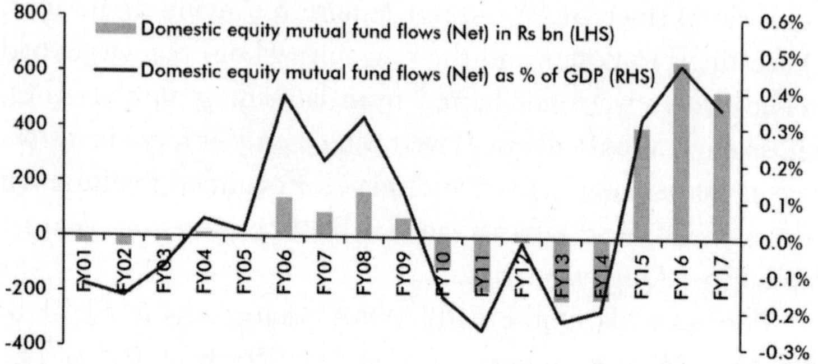

Source: Ambit Capital, Bloomberg

**This chart shows 'net' inflows, i.e. inflows net of outflows*

Whilst official figures are not available to quantify the size of the black economy, research conducted by analysts at Ambit Capital suggests that more than 30 per cent of India's real estate sector is funded by black money.

The retail investor returns to the stock market

However, there has been a trend reversal in investors' choice of asset classes since 2015, the year in which the NDA launched its multi-pronged attack on black money. As quoted in Ambit Capital's July 2015 report on the crumbling of the residential real estate sector: 'We are seeing a broad-based real estate pullback, with prices correcting in most Tier 1 and Tier 2 cities alongside sharp drops in transaction and new launch volumes. The drivers for this slowdown are a mix of supply-side factors and demand-side factors.'

The NDA's success in dramatically reducing the flow of black money seems to have been centred around:

Moving India's subsidy and benefits system to Direct Benefit Transfer: The Indian government disburses subsidies and benefits worth 4 per cent of the GDP, or Rs 6 lakh crore (US$ 100bn). In the past, at least half of this amount was stolen or pilfered by politicians and civil servants who would use this money—which had now become black since it was stolen money—to invest in land, real estate and jewellery. Within three months of being elected Prime Minister in May 2014, Narendra Modi promised to move India's subsidy and benefits system to Direct Benefit Transfer, i.e. the direct transfer of 4 per cent of the GDP from the government's bank accounts to the recipients' bank accounts. He then took steps to implement this policy announcement and thus significantly reduced the amount of stolen (black) money in the hands of civil servants and politicians.

Demonetization: On 8 November 2016, the government demonetized 86 per cent of the country's total currency in circulation. This resulted in the forced deposit of over Rs 15 lakh crore (US$ 230bn or 10 per cent of the GDP) into the banking system, of which a sizeable proportion is likely to have been black money.

The Real Estate Regulatory Act (RERA): This Act came into effect on 1 May 2017. Over the last two decades, gullible real estate customers have fallen victim to builders who haven't felt the need to ensure transparency, accountability and sound business practices. Their modus operandi was booking profits on the back of substandard construction materials, acquiring and building on plots which do not have clear title and/or development permissions and ignoring local development rules. These builders were also the ones who accepted unaccounted cash, thereby cheating the government of stamp duty and registration revenues. RERA imposes a range of rules and obligations on the builders, aimed at increasing transparency and accountability, which will make it harder for the builder to either short-change the buyer or to use black money. For example, developers have to put 70 per cent of the funds collected from buyers in a separate account to meet the construction cost of the project rather than the erstwhile practice of diverting these funds for other purposes such as land acquisition.

Goods and Services Tax (GST): The introduction of GST in July 2017 should increase tax compliance across the country as those who don't comply will find it difficult to get customers. Why? Because in the post-GST world, the buyer of any goods/service pays GST at the point of purchase and then gets an input tax credit when he (as a seller) reports his expenses. In such a world, if any buyer does not report his purchases, he fails to get the input tax credit and therefore ends up with a higher effective tax burden. Thus the GST creates a massive incentive for economic agents to avoid having any commercial dealings with tax evaders.

Consequently, since 2014, investors have become cautious of investing in residential real estate, leading to a stagnation or reduction in the prices of real estate across the top metropolitan cities.

Left with no better choices, affluent Indians are rediscovering the delights of the stock market. The annual run-rate of *gross* inflows from retail investors in India has risen from Rs 48,154 crore (US$ 7.5bn) in FY14 to Rs 2.5 lakh crore (US$ 39bn) in FY17, an annualized growth rate of 73 per cent. More generally, *net* inflows from retail investors to all types of mutual funds have risen from Rs 54,083 crore (US$ 8.5bn) in FY14 to Rs 3.4 lakh crore (US$ 53.7bn) in FY17, an annualized growth rate of 85 per cent.

Exhibit 44: There is an increase in mutual fund investor accounts from 3.95 crore in September 2014 to 5.82 crore in June 2017

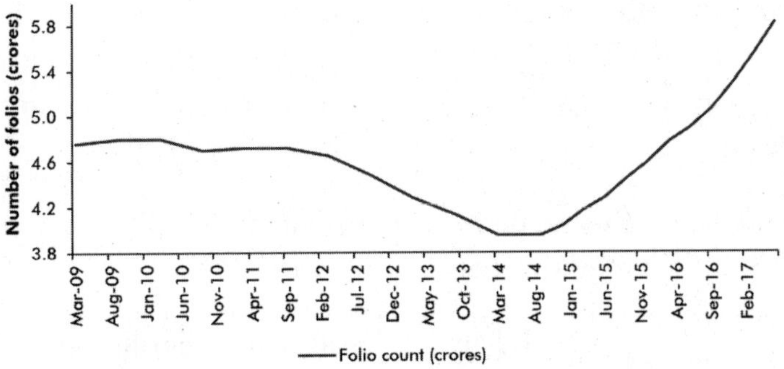

Source: AMFI

The active diversion of savings from the physical form towards the financial form has increased the corpus of bank deposits, bonds outstanding and market cap of the market. The exhibit below shows this trend. Given that bank deposits are the cheapest source of capital for any bank, a structural rise in bank deposits is likely to lead to a reduction in the rate at which banks lend money.

Exhibit 45: Household financial savings are surging in India

Head	FY12	FY13	FY14	FY15	FY16	FY17
Total household savings (in Rs trn)	20.6	22.3	22.9	25.5	26.2	28.3
Financial savings (as % of total household savings)	**45%**	**48%**	**52%**	**50%**	**58%**	**62%**
Households' financial savings (in Rs trn)	9.3	10.6	11.9	12.8	15.1	17.5

Source: CEIC, Ambit Capital

Small-caps outperform large-caps for different time periods, across the world[3]

As a generation of affluent Indians venture into the stock market, they are going down the market cap spectrum in the hunt for better returns (see the exhibit below). Hence, it is worth estimating the potential of smaller companies to outperform large-caps.

Exhibit 46: Small- and mid-cap mutual funds in India have seen significant gross inflows between 2014 and 2017

	Equity MF gross inflows (Rs cr)	Small- and mid-cap MF gross inflows (Rs cr)	Small- and mid-cap as a % of total equity MF inflows
30 June 2011 to 30 June 2014	51,287	6687	13%
30 June 2014 to 30 June 2017	1,56,255	38,805	25%

Source: Ambit Capital using data from Value Research

Across the world and across various time periods, small-caps have outperformed large-caps in most stock markets. For example, as seen in the exhibit below, the outperformance of small-caps over large-caps for rolling five-year compounded annualized return from 1998 to 2004 has been 5.9 per cent in the US, while the same has been 4.6 per cent in the Asia–Pacific region (excluding Japan). In particular, more often than not,

[3] Shares of companies with a market cap of Rs 10,000 crore or more are generally regarded as large-cap stocks. Shares of companies with a market cap between Rs 3000 crore and 10,000 crore are mid-cap stocks and those less than Rs 3000 crore market cap are small-cap stocks.

small-caps have outperformed large-caps in various countries over the past decade (see exhibits below).

Exhibit 47: Small-cap indices' outperform large-cap indices in rolling five-year CAGR (the x-axis indicates the start date of the five-year period)

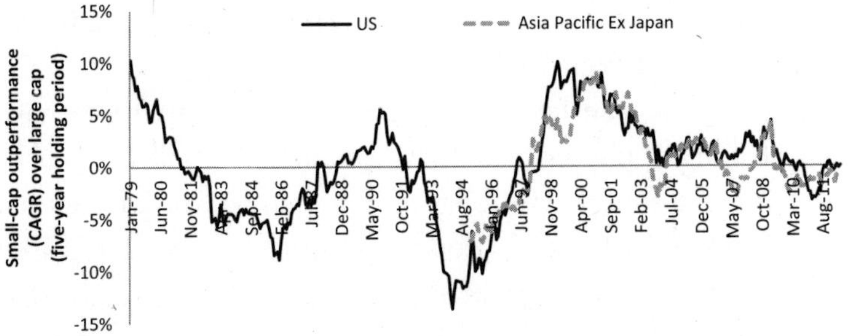

Source: Bloomberg, Ambit Capital. Small-cap indices used for the US and Asia–Pacific (ex-Japan) are Russell 2000, and Asia–Pacific (ex-Japan) Small-cap Index respectively. Large-cap indices used for the US and Asia–Pacific (ex-Japan) are Russell 1000 and Asia–Pacific (ex-Japan) Large-cap Index respectively

Exhibit 48: Annualized outperformance of small-caps over large-caps over 2000–13

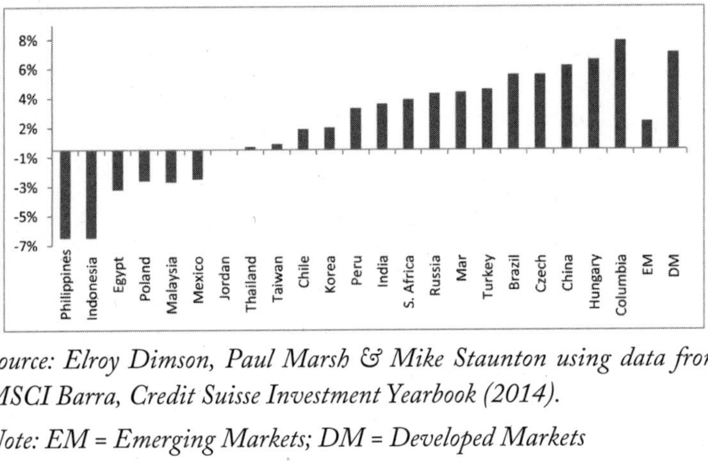

Source: Elroy Dimson, Paul Marsh & Mike Staunton using data from MSCI Barra, Credit Suisse Investment Yearbook (2014).

Note: EM = Emerging Markets; DM = Developed Markets

However, over a long holding period (thirty to forty years), neither the US nor the Asia Pacific ex-Japan indices have shown a meaningful outperformance of small-cap over large-cap. The outperformance of thirty-nine-year CAGR from 1978 to 2017 for the US small-cap Russell 2000 over US large-cap Russell 1000 has been only 0.8 per cent. In fact, Asia Pacific ex-Japan small-cap index has underperformed large-cap index by -0.6 per cent between 1995 and 2017.

In India, as can be seen in the exhibit below, there have been prolonged phases of outperformance of small-cap stocks over large-cap stocks. The longest such phase of the past decade lasted from 2013 to 2017. For this comparison, we have used the BSE 100 index as the benchmark for large-caps and BSE small-cap index as the benchmark for small-caps. (Note: the BSE Small-cap includes 768 stocks with a median market cap of Rs 1600 crore.) Over the past eight years (2009 to 2017), the BSE small-cap index has beaten the BSE 100 by 4.6 per cent per annum.

Exhibit 49: One-year rolling returns of the BSE small-cap index minus the BSE 100 (the x-axis indicates the start date of the one-year period)

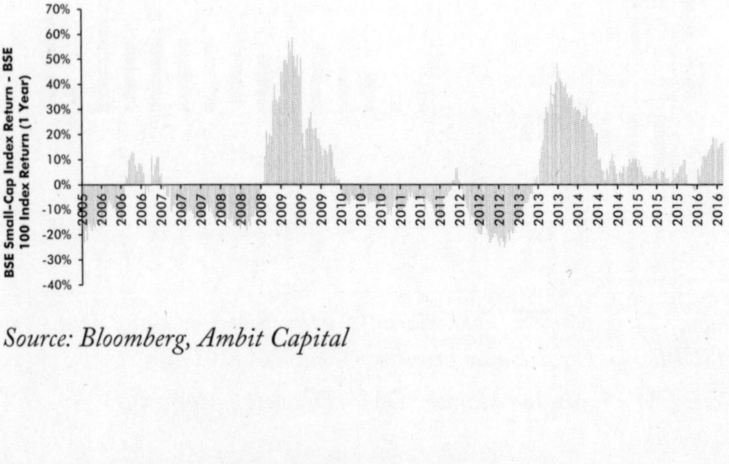

Source: Bloomberg, Ambit Capital

Why should a portfolio of 'great' small-caps outperform the broader large-cap universe?

This question can be answered in two ways: smaller companies have the potential to grow their profits much faster than large companies and, secondly, as small companies grow they are 'discovered' by the stock market. That is to say, successful small-caps gradually attract more research coverage from brokerage analysts and thereafter attract more interest from institutional investors with deep pockets. Let's look at each of these two effects given their relevance in contemporary India.

Small-cap companies grow faster: Fundamentally, smaller companies' profits grow faster than large-caps, particularly in periods when credit availability is plentiful, economic growth is accelerating, and there are ample undervalued competitors (listed or unlisted) that can be acquired. When M&A take place at reasonable valuations and with the aim of taking synergy benefits, they are share price accretive. High valuations and forays into totally different business lines destroy value. Conversely, small-caps tend to underperform when these conditions are reversed.

Small-caps' outperformance on fundamentals can also be supported by the presence of complacent large-cap incumbents in an industry undergoing disruption or ecological changes which redefine the framework of competitive advantages for that industry. Ralph Wanger, founder of Chicago's Wanger Asset Management, in his insightful book *A Zebra in Lion Country*[4] calls this phenomenon 'Darwinism in the Marketplace', which implies that in any environment some creatures are going to be more successful in adapting than others, and those adaptable

---

4 Everett Mattlin and Ralph Wanger, *A Zebra in Lion Country: Ralph Wanger's Investment Survival Guide*, Touchstone, 26 February 1999.

creatures are the ones that will thrive and prosper. Ambit Capital's research shows that in India the average probability of a sector leader (defined as companies that featured in the top quartile on Ambit Capital's 'greatness framework' in their respective sectors) remaining a sector leader five years later is only 15 per cent.[5] That implies that 85 per cent of BSE 500 companies slide towards mediocrity within five years of achieving greatness. In fact, the average probability of a 'great' company actually becoming a sector laggard five years later is 25 per cent.

In most cases, such a slide into mediocrity is caused by hubris and arrogance amongst the management and promoters of a large successful company. When a company is on top of its game with record operating profits and dizzy valuation multiples, success and adulation intoxicates the top brass. Arrogance sets in and the company loses sight of the factors which made it successful in the first place.

On the other hand, owners and managers of small companies (often they are the same person) are hungry to grow, hungry to achieve greatness and all the perks which come with it. They tend to be intensely driven and, unlike large companies, do NOT have to go through layers of management hierarchy in order to respond to changes in the business environment. This helps smaller companies consistently grow profits faster than larger companies.

Small-cap companies get 'discovered': More often than not, small-cap firms suffer from neglect because they are not in the news and are not covered by the major brokerage

---

5 Ambit's 'greatness framework' uses the last six years of financial statements to assess which BSE 500 companies have most consistently invested in growing their business, turned those investments into profits, operating cash flow and then reinvested that cash flow.

houses. Consequently, investors are simply not aware of what is happening in these companies. Brokerages which publish research on listed stocks are one of the biggest sources of company-specific information for investors. Small-caps have significantly less sell-side coverage than large-caps as shown in the exhibit below.

Exhibit 50: Median analyst coverage per stock: Sell-side analyst coverage dwindles with size

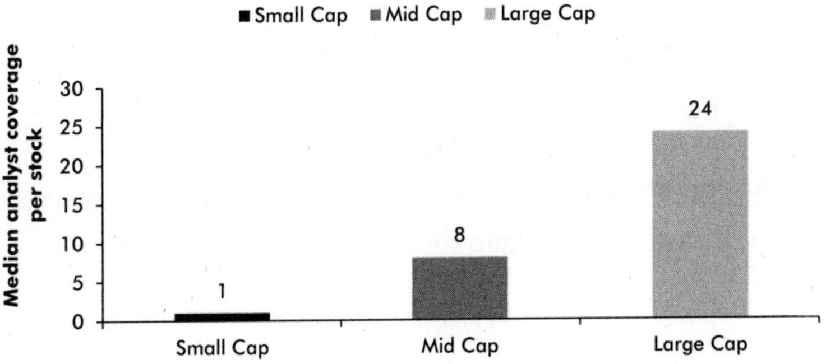

Source: Bloomberg, Ambit Capital. Data as of August 2017; Small-cap = Market-cap below Rs 3000 crore; Mid-cap = Market cap between Rs 3000 crore and Rs 10,000 crore; Large-cap = Market-cap above Rs 10,000 crore.

Besides coverage by brokerage analysts, institutional investors' investment policies around liquidity or size may prevent them from allocating money to small-cap stocks in a meaningful way. Thus, brokerages cannot generate enough revenues from institutional trading commissions on small-caps. Lack of such potential revenues diminishes their incentive to provide broad research coverage of small-caps, creating a lower level of market efficiency. For instance, within the apparel industry, a stock like Kewal Kiran Clothing with a market cap of Rs 2010 crore (in July 2017) and a 26 per cent free float will have far less information flow and market attention than a stock like Page Industries that has a market cap of Rs 18,825 crore and 49 per cent free float.[6] As per Bloomberg, only seven sell-side analysts cover Kewal Kiran Clothing's stock compared to fifteen analysts covering Page Industries. It is no surprise therefore that Page Industries' shareholding has 42 per cent institutional investors whilst Kewal Kiran has only 21 per cent. Globally, roughly 20 per cent of small-cap stocks do not have any sell-side coverage.

Finally, the greater number of small-cap stocks compared to the number of large-cap stocks makes it difficult for sell-side brokerages to cover the small-cap universe. As shown in the chart below, the total number of small-cap stocks listed in India is more than ten times that of mid-caps and large-caps.

Exhibit 51: The number of companies in the small-cap universe is significantly higher than those in the large-cap and mid-cap universe

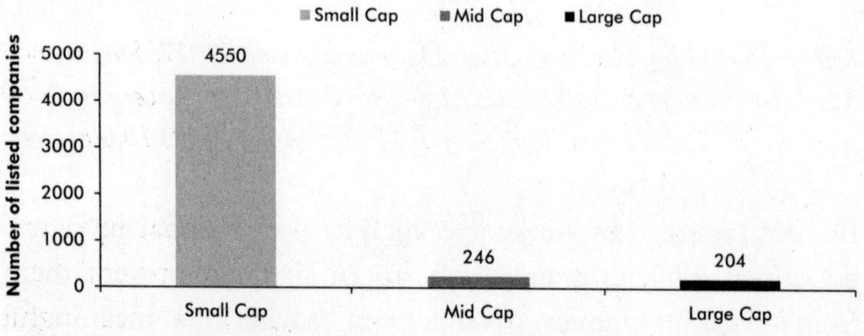

Source: Bloomberg, Ambit Capital. Data as of August 2017. Small-cap = Market cap below Rs 3000 crore; Mid-cap = Market cap between Rs 3000 crore and Rs 10,000 crore; Large-cap = Market cap above Rs 10,000 crore.

6 'Free float' refers to the regular shares that a company has issued to the public and that are available for investors to trade in the open market.

The drop in the cost of capital helps small-caps disproportionately

In contemporary India, as the cost of capital falls (thanks to the enhanced flow of household savings into the financial system), smaller businesses benefit disproportionately relative to the large, highly reputed household names that dominate the stock market. There are two key reasons for this. First, the cost of capital in India is higher than that of most other emerging markets.

Exhibit 52: Lending rates in India are structurally higher than those of peers

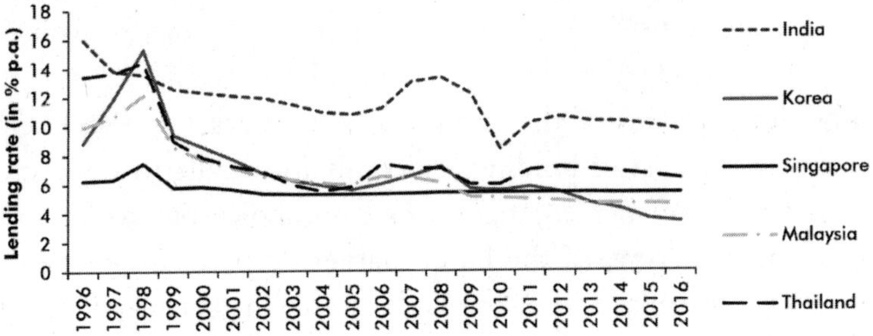

Source: CEIC, Ambit Capital

Note: Lending rate, as defined by the IMF, is the bank rate that usually meets the short- and medium-term financing needs of the private sector.

Secondly, for smaller businesses, the cost of capital is higher than the Indian norm regardless of whether they borrow from banks or from the bond market.

Exhibit 53: SMEs in India face higher borrowing costs from banks

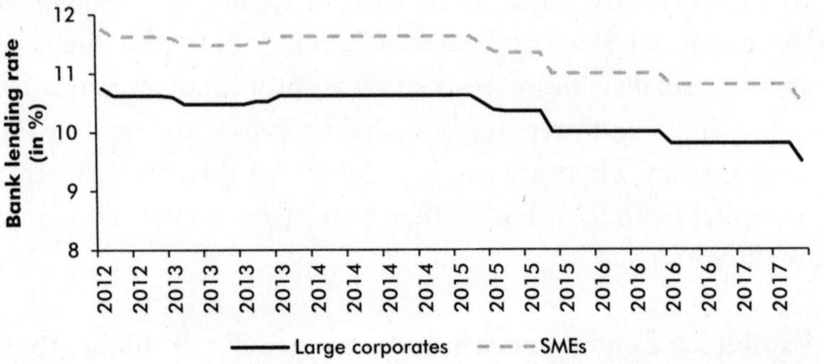

Source: RBI, Ambit Capital

Note: The lending rate used is the average of the rate offered by the five largest banks in India.

The development of the corporate bond market is also likely to lower the cost of funding, especially for smaller companies; historically, smaller companies had no choice but to borrow from banks. Now, as the bond market deepens, high-quality smaller companies will increasingly be able to get cheaper credit from the bond market than from the banks. For example, a small-cap company such as La Opala seems to be borrowing money from banks at 9.65 per cent per annum (as per its FY16 Annual Report). Were the same company to borrow money from the Commercial Paper market, it would be able to lower its cost of borrowing to around 7 per cent.

Investors need professional help in identifying high-quality small-caps

In general, small companies are riskier than the larger ones. There are both fundamental as well as non-fundamental reasons for this risk.

On the fundamental side, smaller companies often stumble in trying to become big. Significant investments in systems and processes across functions—such as Human Resources (HR), Information Technology (IT), data analytics, supply chain, manufacturing and advertising—are often not needed to run a small company. However, the lack of proactive investments in such systems and processes makes it harder for these firms to scale up without running into logistical or financial issues. We reproduce a quote from Captain Gopinath, founder of Air Deccan, which was eventually sold to Kingfisher Airlines in spite of being the pioneering low-cost carrier in India. In his book *Simply Fly*[7] (2012), Gopinath laments: 'Given a little more time, Deccan could have weathered the storm and overcome the cash crunch but time was running out. I might have pulled it off had my IT system not collapsed. We had to bear in mind the welfare of 4000 employees; the public insurance funds and retail investors we had to answer to.'

These problems are inflated in India because often promoters are not willing to empower professionals in senior managerial roles. Instead, the promoters stuff the Board of Directors and the senior ranks of the management team with friends and family members. The lack of a high-quality professional management team means that as and when problems arise (as they inevitably do in most companies), many smaller companies often do not have the management bandwidth to deal with them. One such example is that of TTK Prestige between 1999 and 2003, when the firm went from a position of strength to the brink of bankruptcy in just four years (see exhibit below). This downfall was due to a combination of labour issues in its manufacturing plant in Bangalore, a recessionary environment in India, stiff competition in its export markets (US), increase in excise

[7] G.R. Gopinath, *Simply Fly: A Deccan Odyssey*, Collins, 2011.

duty on pressure cookers from 8 per cent to 16 per cent and the failed launch of a new product leading to inventory write-offs. Recollecting this troublesome period, K. Shankaran, Director at TTK Prestige, said in May 2013, 'The biggest issue we faced was that although we had grown to a decent size, we were still running TTK Prestige as a small company. There was no segregation of responsibilities amongst senior managers and hence every senior manager was working like a jack of all trades. We had to change that.'

Exhibit 54: TTK Prestige's deteriorating financials from FY2000 to FY2003

(Rs mn)	FY2000	FY2001	FY2002	FY2003
Revenues	1303	1242	1272	1048
Revenue growth	-4%	0%	2%	-18%
EBITDA	100	84	96	(59)
EBITDA margin	8%	7%	8%	-6%
Net Profit	36	16	7	(115)
Net Profit growth	-61%	-57%	-55%	-1737%
Net Profit margin	3%	1%	1%	-11%
Total Debt	339	498	666	809
Capital Employed	1141	1293	1439	1266
RoE	**5%**	**2%**	**1%**	**-19%**
RoCE	8%	6%	4%	-4%
Debt/Equity(x)	0.42	0.63	0.86	1.77

Source: Company, Ambit Capital

Moreover, smaller firms often grow at a rapid rate riding on the back of the success of a single product. When demand for their core product dips due to fads, fashion or the economic cycle the smaller firms find their revenues plunging far more sharply than bigger and more diversified businesses. For example, Eicher Motors almost stopped producing its famous Enfield Bullet motorcycles as the firm went into deep financial distress with the motorcycles division incurring losses in the year 2000. Enfield's sales had dropped to 2000 units a month against a manufacturing capacity of 6000 a month. Though the bikes had diehard fans, there were also frequent complaints of engine seizures, snapping of the accelerator or clutch cables, electrical failures and oil leaks. Many found them too heavy, difficult to maintain, with the gear lever inconveniently positioned and a daunting kick-start. It wasn't until there was an inter-generational change in management when Siddhartha Lal took charge of the motorcycle division in 2000, and of the entire firm in 2006, brought in Volvo as a JV partner in 2007, and diversified and professionalized the business that the firm began its glorious run. Over the last ten years (FY07–FY17), Eicher's profits and share price have compounded at 40 per cent and 56 per cent per annum respectively.

Whilst large companies have their share of major accounting issues (Satyam, Enron, Worldcom, Global Trust Bank—the list of prominent companies which cooked their books is long), such issues show up more often in smaller companies where a combination of fly-by-night auditors, unscrupulous promoters and weak/non-existent sell-side research coverage create greater scope for accounting skullduggery. As per Ambit Capital's proprietary forensic accounting model, the probability of a company having significant accounting issues increases as the market cap of the company decreases (see Exhibit 55).

Exhibit 55: Larger capitalization firms have better accounting scores on average

Number of firms in the bucket	Market cap range (Rs bn)	Market cap range (US$ bn)	Average accounting score	Average share price performance	% stocks in 'Zone of Darkness'*
Top 50	Rs 360bn–Rs 4187bn	US$5.3bn-US$62bn	216	13.2%	28%
Next 100	Rs 82bn–Rs 348bn	US$1.2bn-US$5.1bn	221	18.8%	21%
Next 100	Rs 37bn–Rs 82bn	US$ 0.55bn-US$1.2bn	212	15.5%	26%
Bottom 161	Rs 3.7bn–Rs 36.9bn	US$ 0.05bn-US$0.55bn	204	11.7%	39%

Source: Ace Equity, Capitaline, Bloomberg, Ambit Capital

Note: Accounting score is based on Ambit Capital's proprietary account framework using annual financial statements over FY11–16; stock price performance is from November 2010 to November 2016 (on a CAGR basis). Universe for this exhibit is BSE500.

**'Zone of Darkness' is defined as the bottom 30 per cent of the companies in the entire universe.*

As a result, whilst the scope for generating superior long-term investment returns is significantly greater with small-caps (relative to large-caps), the need for professional help is disproportionately greater than is the case with large-caps. The good news is that the Indian fund management community now offers several high-quality small-cap and mid-cap funds (both in the mutual fund format and in the PMS format). More specifically, whilst the BSE 100 has compounded at 16.7 per cent per annum over the past eight years, the BSE Small-cap index has compounded at 21.4 per cent per annum over the same period. Therefore, investing in small-caps alongside such a fund manager can materially boost investors' long-term returns. We shall return to this point in the final chapter of the book.

The three key takeaways from this chapter

1. Over the past two decades, small-caps have outperformed large-caps in most large stock markets. There are two key drivers of this outperformance: smaller companies have the potential to grow their profits much faster than large companies and, secondly, as small companies grow in size they are 'discovered' by the stock market. That is to say, successful small-caps gradually attract more research coverage from brokerage analysts and thereafter attract more interest from institutional investors with deep pockets.
2. Ever since the NDA-led government launched its multi-pronged attack on black money in India (2015), affluent Indians have diverted savings away from real estate and towards the financial system. This deepening of the financial markets is helping reduce the cost of capital in India, which in turn benefits smaller businesses disproportionately (relative to large household names that dominate the stock market).
3. Whilst the scope for generating superior long-term investment returns is greater with small-caps, the need for professional help is disproportionately greater. This is

because small companies are riskier than the larger ones due to both fundamental as well as non-fundamental reasons. The good news is that the Indian fund management community now offers several high-quality small-cap and mid-cap funds.

CHAPTER 6

How Patience and Quality Intertwine

'I have seen many storms in my life. Most storms have caught me by surprise, so I had to learn very quickly to look further and understand that I am not capable of controlling the weather, to exercise the art of patience and to respect the fury of nature.'

—Paulo Coelho

Over the past twenty-six years, the BSE Sensex, a commonly used benchmark for stock market returns, has delivered compounded annual returns of 13.7 per cent. This return is 5.7 percentage points higher than the risk-free rate of around 8 per cent prevalent during this period and 6 percentage points higher than the Consumer Price Index inflation of 7.6 per cent per annum over the same period. By all accounts, the Sensex has given a satisfactory return over the past twenty-six years. Despite this, the common perception amongst investors in India is that 'more often than not, people lose money in equity markets'. What explains this investor pessimism with respect to equities, given that the asset class has given healthy returns?

The answer to this can be best understood through Shlomo Benartzi and Richard Thaler's paper published in 1995, which termed it 'myopic loss aversion'.

They defined 'loss aversion' as: 'We regret losses two to two-and-a-half times more than similar-sized gains.' Let us assume we buy two stocks—A and B—for Rs 100 each and sell them for Rs 95 and Rs 110 respectively. We thus book a gain of Rs 5 in total (gain of Rs 10 on stock B minus the loss of Rs 5 on stock A). In this situation, applying the logic of Benartzi and Thaler, we will regret the Rs 5 loss on stock A at least as significantly (if not more) as we would rejoice in the gain of Rs 10. Hence, by this logic, for an investor to stop regretting investments in equity markets, his probability of generating profits needs to be at least twice as much as the probability of generating losses.

As shown in Exhibit 15 in Chapter 2 (replicated again below), the probability of a positive return from BSE Sensex over the past thirty years (1987–2017) has risen exponentially as we increase the holding period from one month to ten years. Given Benartzi and Thaler's framework, to understand at what point investors lose their regret about investing in equities, we simply need to look for where in the chart below is the probability of generating profits twice as much as the probability of generating losses. This inflection point for BSE Sensex is the one-year holding period, when the probability of generating gains was 68 per cent and the probability of generating losses was 32 per cent.

Exhibit 56: The probability of generating positive returns increases with the holding period for BSE Sensex

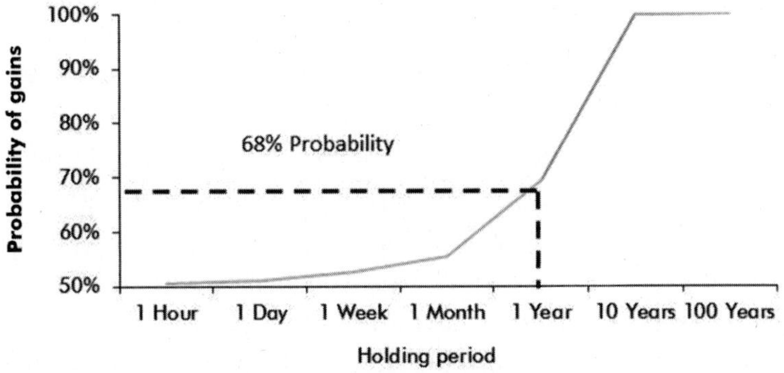

Source: Bloomberg, Ambit Capital

Note: Period under consideration is March 1987–March 2017. The investment horizons are calculated on a rolling basis and we are assuming that equity returns are normally distributed. During 1987–2017, the Sensex delivered a mean annual return of 14.5 per cent with a standard deviation of 28.6 per cent.

There are two ways to interpret this conclusion. Firstly, investors who do not have even a year of patience are likely to believe that 'more often than not, people lose money in equity markets'. And secondly, as Benartzi and Thaler suggest, 'myopia' implies that the more frequently we evaluate our portfolios (and hence the shorter our investment horizon is), the more likely we are to see losses and hence suffer from loss aversion. Inversely, the less frequently investors evaluate their portfolios, the more likely they are to see gains.

Let us now understand how an increase in patience, i.e. holding period, beyond a year benefits investment returns disproportionately.

How patience affects returns for holding periods longer than one year

Let us introduce a term called the 'patience premium'. This is the difference between annualized returns generated by a stock or an index over any holding period compared to the return generated by the same stock or index over a one-year holding period. A positive value of 'patience premium' implies that the longer the holding period of a stock, the higher is the return generated from it for an investor. For example, if holding stocks for five years gives you 10 per cent annualized returns whereas holding stocks for one year gives you 7 per cent returns, then the patience premium is 3 per cent (10 per cent minus 7 per cent). Our analysis shows that, in general, there is a significant patience premium and that this premium grows as you increase the holding period from three years to ten years (see next chart).

Exhibit 57: Median equity returns for the Sensex are the highest over the ten-year investment horizon

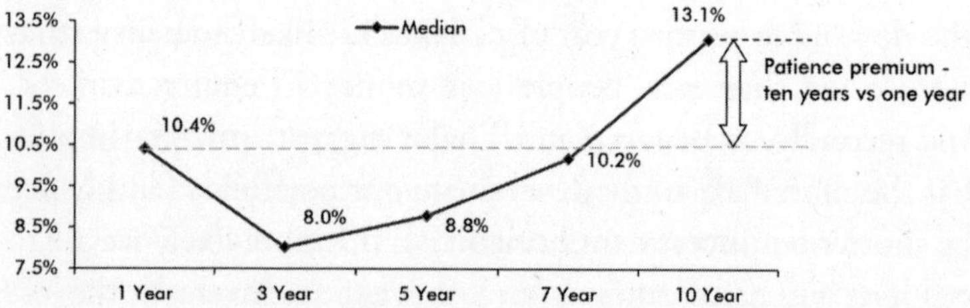

Source: Bloomberg, Ambit Capital

Note: Period under consideration is January 1991–February 2017. The investment horizons are calculated on a weekly rolling basis. For instance the median one-year return is the median returns generated by considering 1311 one-year periods including 01/01/1991 to 01/01/1992, 08/01/1991 to 08/01/1992 and so on.

As the exhibit shows, over the past twenty-six years for the Sensex, the 'patience premium' did NOT exist for the three-year and five-year investment horizons compared to a one-year investment horizon, i.e. investors were not incrementally rewarded for being patient for five years versus one year.

So does this mean that as long as a Sensex investor's investment horizon is less than five years, there is no benefit in being patient? No, it does not. As the holding period increases from one year towards three and five years, volatility (and hence risk) of returns for a Sensex investor reduces significantly as highlighted in the following points:

- The one-year investment horizon has the widest range of equity returns, from a peak of 256 per cent delivered over April 1991 to April 1992 to a trough of -56 per cent delivered over December 2007 to December 2008. The one-year investment horizon can be an intense roller-coaster ride.
- The range of equity returns narrows over the three-year investment horizon from a peak of 62 per cent (CAGR) delivered over January 1991 to January 1994 to a trough of -18 per cent (CAGR) over April 2000 to April 2003.
- The range narrows considerably over the five-year investment horizon. The early '90s saw some of the highest returns, with a peak of 47 per cent (CAGR) recorded in the period spanning October 2002 to October 2007 and a trough of -8 per cent (CAGR) recorded over August 1997 to August 2002.
- The range of returns narrows further in the seven-year rolling period. The highest return of 29 per cent (CAGR) was delivered over October 2002 to October 2009 and the lowest of -7 per cent (CAGR) was recorded over September 1994 to September 2001.
- The ten-year rolling period offers the tightest range of returns with least returns at -3 per cent (CAGR) over April 1992 to April 2002. The peak return of 21 per cent

(CAGR) was earned in the period spanning May 2003 to April 2013. The ten-year rolling period is also the period with the highest median return of 13.1 per cent.

The more volatile the return over time, the riskier it is. For instance, a government bond which delivers an 8 per cent annualized return over ten years is less risky than a listed company's stock price which delivers 8 per cent annualized returns over ten years. This is because the government bond delivers more or less 8 per cent return each year with very low volatility, whereas the company's stock delivers the same 8 per cent CAGR in a volatile manner. What statisticians call 'standard deviation' can measure this volatility, and hence risk, in an asset's return profile. As shown in the exhibit below, over the past twenty-six years, for the Sensex, the degree of risk involved in a one-year holding period has been three to four times higher than the risk involved in a five-year holding period and six times higher than the risk involved in a ten-year holding period.

Exhibit 58: BSE Sensex's one-year investment horizon is the riskiest with risk levels being six times that of the ten-year horizon

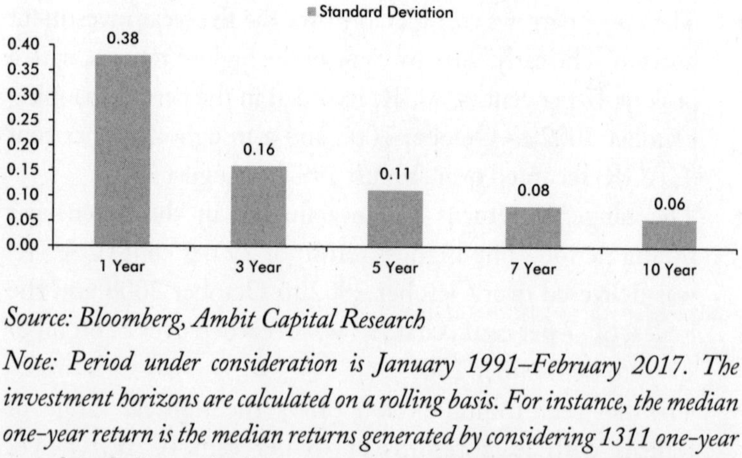

Source: Bloomberg, Ambit Capital Research

Note: Period under consideration is January 1991–February 2017. The investment horizons are calculated on a rolling basis. For instance, the median one-year return is the median returns generated by considering 1311 one-year periods including 01/01/1991 to 01/01/1992, 08/01/1991 to 08/01/1992 and so on.

So what does all of this mean for investors looking to optimize their returns from equity investing whilst reducing risk? The exhibit below puts all of the analysis discussed in this chapter so far into one graphic. The best way to grow one's wealth is to be in the bottom-right corner of this exhibit, i.e. high return with low risk. Conversely, the worst way to grow wealth is to be in the top-left corner of this exhibit, i.e. low return with high risk. The Sensex's return over the past twenty-six years suggests that as the investment holding period increases from one year to ten years, the investor's position on the exhibit moves from top left to bottom right.

Exhibit 59: The Risk vs Return trade-off for the Sensex improves as the holding period rises (The size of the bubble denotes the holding period; the dotted-bordered bubble relates to the one-year holding period of the ten-year government bond; the plain shaded bubbles relate to the Sensex.)

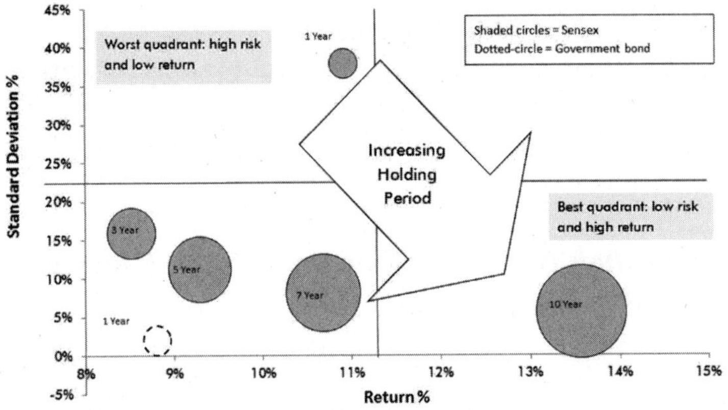

Source: Bloomberg, Ambit Capital

Note: Period under consideration is January 1991–February 2017. The investment horizons are calculated on a rolling basis. For instance, the median one-year return is the median returns generated by considering 1311 one-year periods including 01/01/1991 to 01/01/1992, 08/01/1991 to 08/01/1992 and so on.

Adding the quality premium to the patience premium

Let us assume that the 'quality' of a stock is defined as the quality of its returns profile—healthy and sustainable, i.e. consistently good, being better than weak and unsustainable. In order to understand how improving the quality of a stock portfolio affects its performance for various holding periods, we re-run the analysis highlighted above whilst replacing Sensex returns with the seventeen iterations of Coffee Can Portfolios of 2000 to 2016.[1]

We introduce a new term here, the 'quality premium', which we define as the difference between the annualized returns generated by a stock or a portfolio and the benchmark index (say, the Sensex) over a particular holding period. A positive value of the 'quality premium' implies that increasing the quality of the stock portfolio generates better returns for the same investment horizon. So, for example, if Rakshit's portfolio generates a return of 17 per cent over a ten-year period whilst the Sensex generates 13 per cent over the same ten-year period, the quality premium for Rakshit's portfolio is 4 per cent (17 per cent minus 13 per cent).

Our research on the Sensex's returns over the past twenty-six years and the returns generated by the Coffee Can Portfolios since 2000 has produced some very interesting conclusions, which we summarize below.

Observation No. 1: The shorter the holding period, the higher the quality premium

This observation is counter-intuitive. Interestingly, it is strikingly similar to the comparison between the batting averages of two cricket legends—Rahul Dravid and Virender Sehwag—for

---

[1] We have not included the 2017 Coffee Can Portfolio in this analysis as it was only three months old when the manuscript for this book was finalized.

various formats of the game. Dravid was a great defensive batsman with an effortful (rather than effortless) batting style which lacked flamboyance—characteristics that sound perfect for the test match format, i.e. five-day matches. Sehwag, on the other hand, was an aggressive batsman, ready to flirt with unimaginable risks and looking to hit almost every ball over the boundary—characteristics that sound perfect for one-day internationals (50-over matches) and T20 international matches (20-over matches). While Dravid is perceived to be the accumulator of runs, Sehwag is perceived to be the prolific scorer of runs. However, the table below shows an interesting comparison. Not only does Dravid outperform Sehwag in every version of cricket, Dravid's outperformance (as measured by his batting average) is the widest in T20 and the narrowest in Test cricket.

Exhibit 60: Rahul Dravid has a higher batting average than Virender Sehwag in all formats of cricket

	T20	ODI	Test
Rahul Dravid	31	39	52
Virender Sehwag	22	35	49
Dravid's outperformance vs Sehwag	**41%**	**11%**	**6%**

Source: Cricbuzz.com

The late Peter Roebuck, one of the world's greatest cricket writers, wrote, 'Dravid has a simple game founded upon straight lines. Reasoning that runs cannot be scored in the pavilion, he sets out to protect his wicket. Curiously, this thought does not seem to occur to many batsmen, a point many a long-suffering coach could confirm.' Michael Lewis's celebrated book, *Moneyball: The Art of Winning an Unfair Game*, which went on to become a movie starring Brad Pitt, highlights the Rahul Dravids of Major League Baseball in US.

When it comes to stock markets, intuition suggests that shorter investment horizons are akin to speculative investing, where investors do not need to focus too much on the quality of the company to generate good returns. Over longer investment horizons, one would intuitively imagine, investors would need to rely on high-quality companies for superior returns. However, the chart below shows that whilst the quality premium exists across all holding periods for the CCP, *the quantum of the quality premium is higher for shorter holding periods* (three years and five years) compared to longer holding periods (seven years and ten years). Hence, the extent of outperformance that an investor can generate by upgrading the quality of his/her portfolio is greater for shorter holding periods (compared to longer holding periods).

Exhibit 61: The 'Quality Premium' (Coffee Can Portfolio median returns minus Sensex median returns) exists for all investment horizons

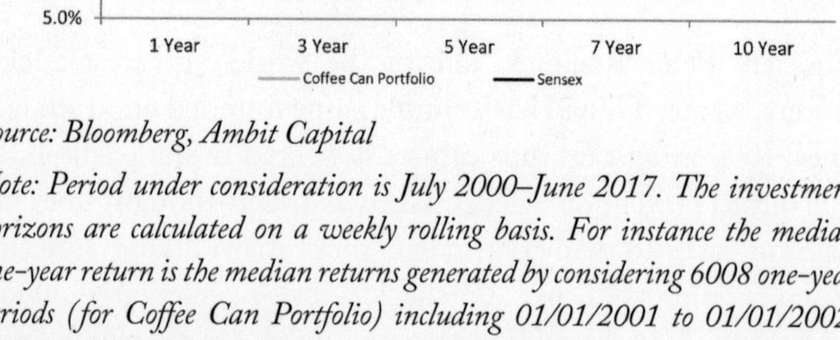

Source: Bloomberg, Ambit Capital

Note: Period under consideration is July 2000–June 2017. The investment horizons are calculated on a weekly rolling basis. For instance the median one-year return is the median returns generated by considering 6008 one-year periods (for Coffee Can Portfolio) including 01/01/2001 to 01/01/2002, 08/01/2001 to 08/01/2002 and so on. Sensex returns are slightly different from those shown in the second exhibit of this chapter because of the different time periods in consideration.

Why does this happen? Why do the Coffee Can Portfolios (CCPs) outperform the Sensex so handsomely over the three-year and five-year horizons? Remember, over shorter holding periods the Sensex's returns are more volatile whilst over longer holding periods the volatility in the Sensex's returns reduces very sharply. The CCPs are full of companies that are the Rahul Dravids of the business world—rare, determined and constantly seeking to improve the edge or the advantage they enjoy vis-à-vis their competitors. As a result, the CCPs are able to deliver healthy returns with low volatility even over three-year and five-year horizons. Basically, the inherent consistency in the performance of the CCP companies gives the CCPs an even bigger advantage over the Sensex over the three-year and five-year horizons. As with Rahul Dravid, and the CCP companies: 'when the going gets tough, the tough get going'.

Observation No. 2: A high-quality portfolio with a very long holding period delivers the highest return with the lowest risk

The principle of 'risk-return trade-off' says that 'potential return rises with an increase in risk', i.e. low levels of uncertainty or risk are associated with low potential returns, whereas high levels of uncertainty or risk are associated with high potential returns. While this principle holds true as an investor chooses between equities as an asset class over, say, government bonds, it is not necessarily true when an investor is seeking to optimize performance *within* an asset class such as equities. To be specific, it is possible—and desirable—to increase the return from an equity portfolio whilst reducing the risk associated with such a portfolio.

The exhibit below compares the volatility of returns for each holding period of the CCP (as measured by standard deviation) and shows that the longer one holds a Coffee Can Portfolio, the lower the volatility of returns.

Exhibit 62: The volatility associated with Coffee Can Portfolios reduces as the holding period lengthens

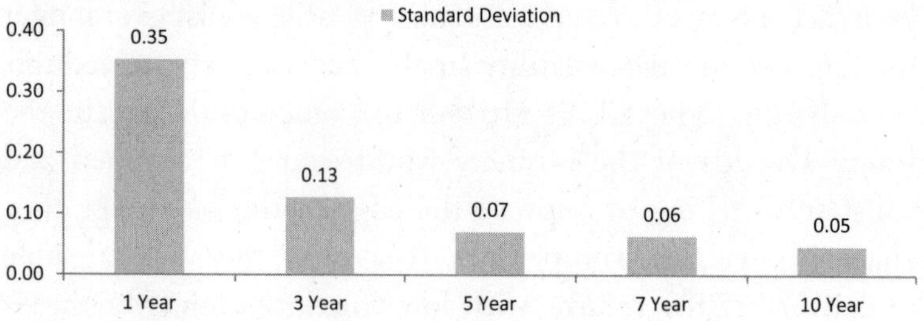

Source: Bloomberg, Ambit Capital

Note: Period under consideration is July 2000–June 2017. The investment horizons are calculated on a weekly rolling basis. For instance, the standard deviation of one-year return is the standard deviation of returns generated by considering 6008 one-year periods (for all the CCP iterations) including 01/07/2000 to 01/07/2001, 08/07/2000 to 08/07/2001 and so on.

To appreciate the power of this, we have created another exhibit which shows how the risk-return trade-off changes with time. This time, in addition to showing the returns from the Sensex and the ten-year government bond, we have also shown the returns from the Coffee Can Portfolio on this chart.

Exhibit 63: Coffee Can portfolios have a better risk-return trade-off than the Sensex for all investment horizons (The size of the bubble denotes the holding period; the dotted-bordered bubble relates to the one-year holding period of the ten-year government bond; non-shaded bubbles relate to Coffee Can Portfolios and the plain shaded bubbles relate to the Sensex)

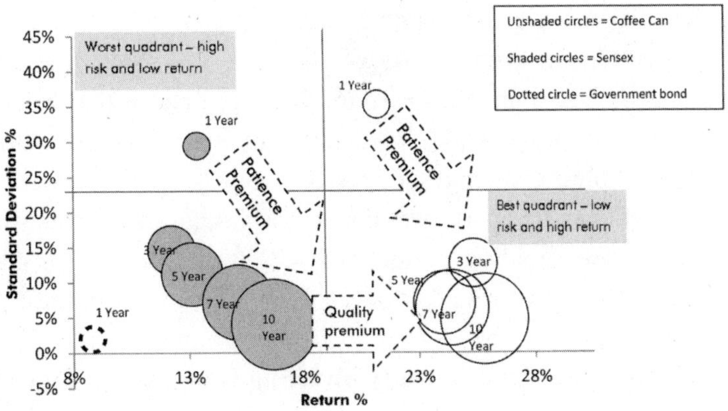

Source: Bloomberg, Ambit Capital

Note: Period under consideration is July 2000–June 2017. The investment horizons are calculated on a weekly rolling basis. For instance the median one-year return is the median returns generated by considering 6008 one-year periods (for all the CCP iterations) including 01/07/2000 to 01/07/2001, 08/07/2000 to 08/07/2001 and so on.

The key message of this chart is that whilst both portfolios—the Sensex and the CCP—produce better returns (alongside lower volatility) if held longer, the CCP beats the Sensex by a wide margin when it comes to producing superior returns (with its volatility being even lower than that of the Sensex). An investor who is able to combine patience with high-quality portfolio construction thus pulls off the holy grail of investing—

outstanding returns with low levels of volatility. That is the essence of the Coffee Can Portfolio.

The three key takeaways from this chapter:

1. **Patience premium in equity investing**: Given the behavioural concept of 'Myopic loss aversion' defined by Shlomo Benartzi and Richard Thaler, investors who do not have even a year of patience, i.e. stock holding periods less than one year, are likely to believe that 'more often than not, people lose money in equity markets'. For stock holding periods greater than one year, the Sensex's return over the past twenty-six years suggests that as the investment holding period increases from one year to ten years, the investor's position on a risk-reward matrix moves from 'high-risk low-return' to 'low-risk high-return'.
2. **Quality premium in equity investing is higher for shorter time periods**: Let us assume that the 'quality' of a stock is defined as the quality of its returns profile—healthy and sustainable being better than weak and unsustainable. Intuition suggests that shorter investment horizons are akin to speculative investing, where investors do not need to focus too much on the quality of the company to generate good returns. Over longer investment horizons, one would intuitively imagine, investors would need to rely on high-quality companies for superior returns. However, our analysis shows that whilst the quality premium exists across all holding periods for the Coffee Can Portfolio (CCP), *the quantum of the quality premium is higher for shorter holding periods* (three years and five years) compared to longer holding periods (seven years and ten years). Hence, the extent of outperformance that an investor can generate by upgrading the quality of her/his portfolio is greater

for shorter holding periods (compared to longer holding periods).

3. **Combining quality premium with patience premium:** Whilst both the Sensex and the Coffee Can Portfolio (CCP) produce better returns (alongside lower volatility) if held longer, the CCP beats the Sensex by a wide margin when it comes to producing superior returns (with its volatility being even lower than that of the Sensex). An investor who is able to combine patience with high-quality portfolio construction thus pulls off the holy grail of investing—outstanding returns with low levels of volatility.

CHAPTER 7

Pulling It All Together

'A man who has committed a mistake and doesn't correct it is committing another mistake.'

—Confucius (551 BC–479 BC)

'Never forget that risk, return, and cost are the three sides of the eternal triangle of investing.'[1]

—John C. Bogle, founder of Vanguard, the world's largest index fund manager

Let us return to our protagonists, Mr Talwar and Mr Sanghvi, and see how the knowledge from the preceding chapters of this book helps them. Essentially, what this book has highlighted is that:

[1] John C. Bogle, *Bogle on Mutual Funds: New Perspectives for the Intelligent Investor*, John Wiley & Sons, 2015.

Investing for long periods of time in high-quality portfolios . . .

↓

. . . with a higher weightage to high-quality small-cap companies . . .

↓

. . . while ensuring that you don't pay too much by way of fees . . .

↓

. . . and avoiding investment traps like real estate and gold . . .

↓

. . . should lead to significant and sustainable wealth creation.

Mr Talwar: Piecing it together for a secured life

On a Saturday afternoon, when Nikhil sat down with Mr Talwar to assess his financial position, they ended up spending more than three hours. Several cups of tea were downed and a plateful of pakoras was consumed. As the discussion progressed, Mr Talwar realized that he had never conducted an exercise like this before. Though he broadly knew his goals, which were primarily his responsibilities, it was only after he put them down on a sheet of paper that he realized that even the smallest of his goals (or ambitions) had a monetary cost which would not be fulfilled automatically. In short, every goal needed a plan.

There are several elements in financial planning, but the critical element is the 'time value of money'. If you have to buy a car five years later, which costs Rs 10 lakh today, you will end up paying more than Rs 16 lakh if we assume a 10 per cent annual increase in the cost of the car. So, if you had earmarked Rs 10 lakh to buy a car and earned a 5 per cent post-tax interest on that money (say, from a fixed deposit), your money pot would have grown to Rs 12.8 lakh, i.e. Rs 3.2 lakh short of the amount you need to buy the car five years later. This predicament would have arisen even though today you had exactly the amount you need to buy the car.

The root cause of the problem here is inflation. Unless we plan carefully, thanks to inflation, the prices of the things we want to buy in the years to come will grow faster than our ability to compound our savings. Chemistry teaches us how two elements come together to make a compound, which can be something entirely different and altogether more formidable than the original underlying elements. For example, in isolation, carbon and oxygen are harmless. But when these two elements combine to form carbon monoxide, we end up with a gas so toxic that it was used as a method of execution by the ancient Greeks. Similarly, when time and inflation combine, they form a very powerful adversary which demands an equally powerful reactive strategy.

Here is what Mr Talwar's current portfolio looked like:

Exhibit 64: Mr Talwar's current portfolio

	Assets	**Value in Rs lakhs**	**% Allocation**
1	House #1	250	42.2%
2	House #2	150	25.3%
3	Loan to developers	85	14.4%
4	Gold	60	10.1%
5	Fixed deposits	25	4.2%
6	Insurance sum assured	12	2.0%
7	Cash	5	0.8%
8	Stocks	5	0.8%
	Total Assets	**592**	**100%**

Source: Ambit Capital

Mr Talwar's portfolio is mainly invested in real estate as he has two houses—one in which he stays and the other which is still under construction but where the developer has run out of money. Mr Talwar has only 7 per cent of his investments in financial instruments and 10 per cent in gold. This pattern of investment is unfortunately all too common in India. As per the Housing Finance Committee's 2017 report, Indians hold 77 per cent of their assets in real estate and 11 per cent in gold. Only 5 per cent of household assets are in the form of financial instruments.

Goals

We all have goals, some of which are personal and some of which are for our family. Almost all of these goals carry a financial cost. Our ability to meet those costs becomes the bedrock of our peace of mind and happiness.

Our goals can be bucketed into three categories: [2]

1. **Security**: These goals are extremely important to us and provide protection from anxiety.
2. **Stability**: These goals are not as important as the security-related goals; however they ensure that we maintain a desired standard of living.
3. **Ambitions**: These goals may not be necessities but they help us achieve upward wealth mobility and give us a certain status in our social circle.

Nikhil used the above categorization and helped Mr Talwar organize his goals. This categorization is shown in Exhibit 65.

---

[2] Our construct here has been influenced Ashvin B. Chhabra's superb book, *The Aspirational Investor: Investing in the Pursuit of Wealth and Happiness* (2015). The idea here is to illustrate how the category in which any individual's goal is classified depends on the individual's wealth and income level.

Exhibit 65: Mr Talwar's goals in three categories

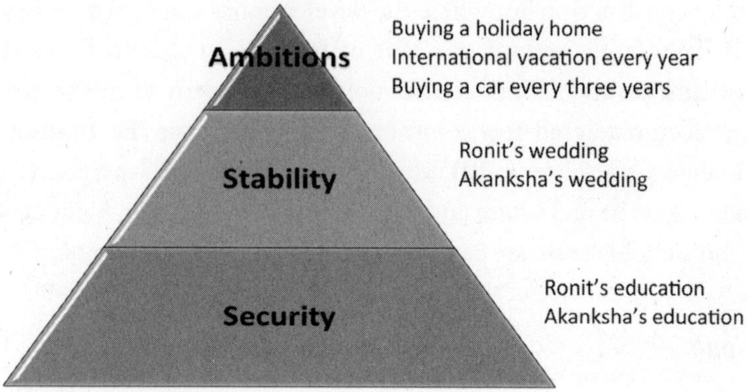

Source: Ambit Capital

Mr Talwar's most important needs are his children's education (security), followed by their weddings (stability). However, in addition, Mr Talwar has aspirational goals too that seem aggressive (ambitions). Specifically, he wants to buy a holiday home in Mussoorie before he retires, take his family for an international vacation every year and buy a car every three years. These goals cannot be met realistically by the cash flow he is expected to generate over the course of his life.

Mr Talwar is fifty years old at present and, barring a lottery win, has only one source of money—his income. Apart from a couple of promotions and a few good years of bonuses in the remaining decade of his career, he does not have anything else to bank on. Given this more or less fixed inflow, the only variable in his financial planning is the rate of return his investments can generate.

As explained in Chapter 1, the required rate of return that his investments need to generate to be able to meet all his goals is a staggering 21 per cent per annum. This was calculated by the financial planning software after taking into account the actual cost of these goals today as well as the impact of inflation on that cost. For example, Akanksha's wedding, which Mr Talwar reckons can be managed in Rs 70 lakh today, will require an outlay of Rs 1.2 crore in 2024 when it is actually expected.

The 'asking run rate' of 21 per cent for Mr Talwar seems steep, especially compared to the kind of returns he has generated in the past. After accounting for the losses on his real estate investments, his portfolio has only given him an annualized return of 4 per cent since 1990, the year he started working.

There was no way he could hope to achieve a 21 per cent per annum return every year. This meant Mr Talwar would have to amend his 'ambitious' goals.

Ultimately, he lets go of his objective to buy a holiday home and reduces the frequency of overseas vacations and purchase of a new car to three and five years respectively. With these changes, Mr Talwar's required rate of return drops to a more achievable number of 16 per cent per annum.

This is what Mr Talwar's revised goals look like:

Exhibit 66: Mr Talwar's goals after pruning some of them down

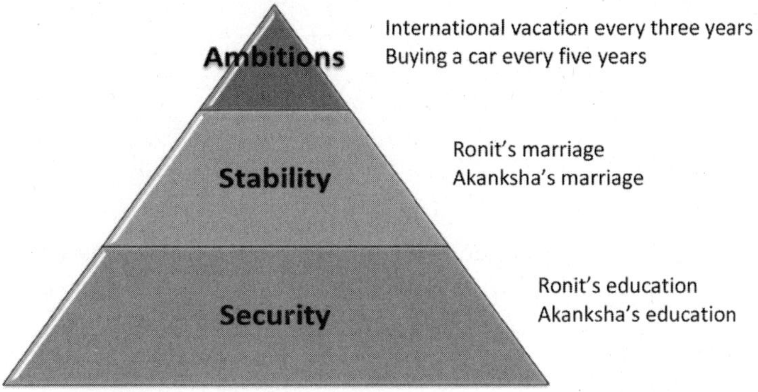

Source: Ambit Capital. Our construct here has been influenced by Ashvin B. Chhabra's book, The Aspirational Investor: Investing in the Pursuit of Wealth and Happiness *(2015).*

Nikhil also helps Mr Talwar plot his cash flow after considering his future income, expenses and goals. The cash flows showed a sharp dip after Mr Talwar's retirement in 2027 since his income stops but the monthly expenses continue as he expects to maintain the lifestyle he enjoys at present. And why not! After all the years of toil, this is the least that Mr Talwar expects. Therefore, in addition to generating 16 per cent compounding on his investments, Mr Talwar needs to invest in a manner which throws off adequate cash flows from the time he retires.

Exhibit 67: Mr Talwar's net worth going forward

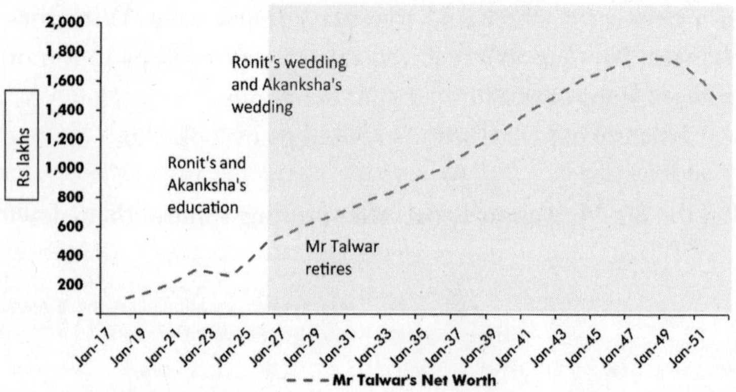

Source: Ambit Capital

To achieve a 16 per cent per annum return, Nikhil makes the following asset allocation for Mr Talwar:

Equity: 80 per cent
Debt: 20 per cent
This break-up assumes pre-tax 18.8 per cent per annum return from equity and 8 per cent per annum return from debt. The

blended return from these asset classes comes to 16.6 per cent per annum. With the asset allocation nailed, Nikhil proceeds to help Mr Talwar figure out what to do inside each asset class.

Equity allocation

Nikhil was clear about how Mr Talwar should participate in equity. He divided Mr Talwar's equity investments down to three buckets—large-caps, multi-caps and small-midcaps.

The large-cap portfolio

Large-cap stocks are the anchor for any investment portfolio as these are time-tested companies with a long and consistent track record of generating returns for shareholders. Typically these are companies that have been around for several decades and are profitable businesses which have been through multiple economic cycles. The robustness of these companies means that their share prices are less vulnerable in case of a sharp market pullback (in comparison to small-cap stocks). This in turn helps reduce the volatility in the overall value of the portfolio.

Whilst the definition of large-cap stocks is not cast in stone, we view any company with a market capitalization of more than Rs 20,000 crore as a large-cap company. In July 2017, there were 123 such companies listed in the Indian stock market.

For investment in large-cap stocks, Nikhil chose an ETF.

ETFs, or Exchange Traded Funds, are typically passive funds based on a particular index. For example, a Nifty ETF fund has a portfolio which mimics the Nifty and has the same fifty stocks in the same proportion. There is no highly paid fund manager looking after an ETF; it is managed by traders who just have to buy and sell stocks to ensure similarity to the underlying index. Thus, the ETF's performance also mimics that of the Nifty. We learnt in Chapter 3 that the outperformance of large-cap mutual funds (vis-á-vis the index) has more or less vanished over the last decade. ETFs have, therefore, become the best way to invest in large-cap stocks. These ETFs typically have an annual expense ratio of 0.2 per cent compared to the 2–2.5 per cent that the actively managed funds charge.

The multi-cap portion of the portfolio, Nikhil was clear, had to go into the Coffee Can Portfolio. Mr Talwar was looking for healthy returns over the next ten years. As explained in Chapter 2, and in the preceding chapter, a basket of good-quality companies which has a consistent track record on revenue growth and return on capital employed almost always beats the index by a comfortable margin.

The Coffee Can Portfolio (managed inside a PMS) can be expected to return 20 per cent annually while a Nifty ETF should deliver a 15 per cent annualized return over the next ten to fifteen years. With 20 per cent allocation to each of these strategies, these two investments act as a solid anchor to Mr Talwar's portfolio. Though the Coffee Can Portfolio is expected to give higher returns, the importance of diversification cannot be overstated. Thus, an equivalent allocation to a Nifty ETF will bring down the dependence on a single strategy, however dependable that strategy might be.

The small-midcap portfolio

We define a small-cap company as one with a market capitalization of less than Rs 3000 crore. (Some people use the benchmark as the market capitalization of the 401st company in BSE 500 which is almost the same number). Given that we define a large-cap company as one with a market capitalization of more than Rs 20,000 crore, by default mid-caps are companies with a market cap larger than Rs 3000 crore but smaller than Rs 20,000 crore.

As discussed in Chapter 5, smaller companies have outperformed larger-cap companies albeit with higher volatility. This is because there is far greater upside possible in a small company than in a large-cap company. The higher growth in smaller companies, however, comes with lower probability of delivering upon this growth. Thus, in a small-cap portfolio, an investor is advised to pick up a larger number of stocks. This does not mean that he/she should pick up low-quality stocks; it just means that there will be some stocks which will be multi-baggers and yet some which will fail to deliver on their promise. As is the nature of portfolio returns, the winners will end up more than compensating for the losers provided the investor buys and leaves the portfolio untouched for a long period of time.

Nikhil reminded Mr Talwar that small-cap companies have higher volatility and would almost certainly fall more than the broader market in a market correction. However, given Mr Talwar's ten-year investment horizon, a good small-cap portfolio held through an entire market cycle should boost the return of his overall equity portfolio. Nikhil told Mr Talwar that he could expect a return of more than 20 per cent per annum from his small-cap portfolio (whilst the Nifty tracker and the CCP are expected to deliver 15 per cent and 20 per cent per annum respectively).

Like in the case of the large-cap basket, here too Nikhil offered two buckets—mutual funds (through the 'Direct Scheme' route) and the 'Good and Clean' investing approach for small-midcaps.

Unlike large-cap mutual funds which have lost the edge they enjoyed over indices, small-cap mutual funds continue to outperform their benchmark, the BSE Small-Cap Index. The reasons for this outperformance were detailed in Chapter 5. To summarize, there is still considerable information asymmetry in small-cap stocks as these companies are neither well-researched by brokerages nor are they in the media limelight. As a result, fund houses can benefit from their large research teams pouring through reams of data (annual reports, management conference call transcripts, newspaper clippings, etc.). Remember there are around 5000 stocks listed in India and 4500 of these are small-caps! So, almost by definition, there are a number of hidden gems waiting to be discovered in this ocean of stocks.

To Nikhil, it was obvious that investments in good mutual funds should be via the 'Direct Scheme' route. Nikhil and his firm had seen the writing on the wall two years ago and had built their business model around getting paid by investors like Mr Talwar for 'advice' rather than being paid by mutual fund houses (for 'distributing' funds). Nikhil told Mr Talwar that he would charge him 1 per cent of his portfolio as an advisory fee every year. At Rs 6 lakh annually (on a Rs 5.9 crore portfolio), Mr Talwar found this to be reasonable, considering that Nikhil's interests were totally aligned with Mr Talwar. (In contrast, had Nikhil been paid by the mutual fund houses through 'distribution fees', his incentives would drive him to sell the most expensive funds to Mr Talwar irrespective of whether that was good or not for Mr Talwar's financial health.)

Direct schemes have triggered a revolution. From almost zero in 2012, direct schemes now (in July 2017) command close to 40 per cent of the mutual fund industry's assets under management. At this rate, it is but inevitable that in the foreseeable future they will account for the majority of mutual fund inflows in India.

Exhibit 68: Direct schemes are pulling away assets under management from distributors

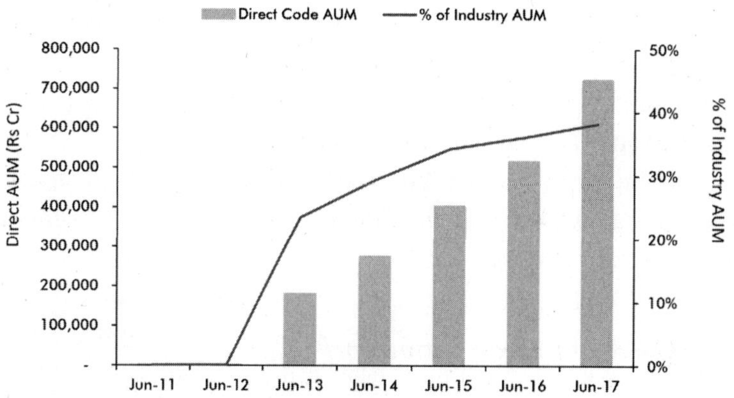

Source: MFI, ICRA, Ambit Capital

Nikhil chose three small-cap mutual fund schemes for Mr Talwar, all with 'growth' options. Growth schemes do not offer any dividends to the investor. As a result, the fund returns even more money when it is eventually encashed as the dividends are reinvested. For Mr Talwar, who was comfortably placed with respect to cash flows from his salary, growth schemes made sense; he could always redeem a portion if he needed any capital. Nikhil reminded Mr Talwar that long-term capital gains tax on all equity investments was zero.

Next up was the 'good and clean' investing approach for small-midcaps.[3] Since there are over 4500 small-cap stocks in India and very few of these companies are well-researched,

---

[3] Ambit has applied for trademarks on 'Good & Clean' and 'G&C' which are pending approval/registration.

smaller companies' promoters are notorious for their propensity to fabricate financial statements. Leaving aside their 'cleanliness' with regard to accounting and corporate governance, most Indian companies struggle to invest their capital sensibly because promoters rarely follow a specific strategy for extended periods of time and because the ability to execute day in, day out, month after month, year after year is a discipline that very few Indian management teams have mastered.

Nikhil explained to Mr Talwar how Ambit's good and clean construct helps identify high-quality companies using a set of highly effective filters.

The Good and Clean framework

There are two filters that are run on the whole universe of stocks:

'Good': helps in identifying stocks that have done a great job in creating shareholder value—right from judicious capital expenditure to profitability and to return of surplus cash to shareholders.

'Clean': helps in identifying how good the company's corporate governance is and what the quality of their published accounts is. It is a measure of the long-term sustainability of a company and its performance.

The focus on 'good' helps generate the upside while not compromising on 'clean' reduces the downside risk. One cannot overemphasize the value of limiting the downside. Exhibit 69 shows the extra amount of upside that a manager needs just to make up for the downside faced. For example, after a 50 per cent downside, a portfolio manager has to give a 100 per cent performance just to get back where he began. And that is why Warren Buffett's famous two rules on investing are: *Rule No. 1 – Never lose money. Rule No. 2 – Don't forget rule number 1.*

Exhibit 69: You need more upside to make up for the downside

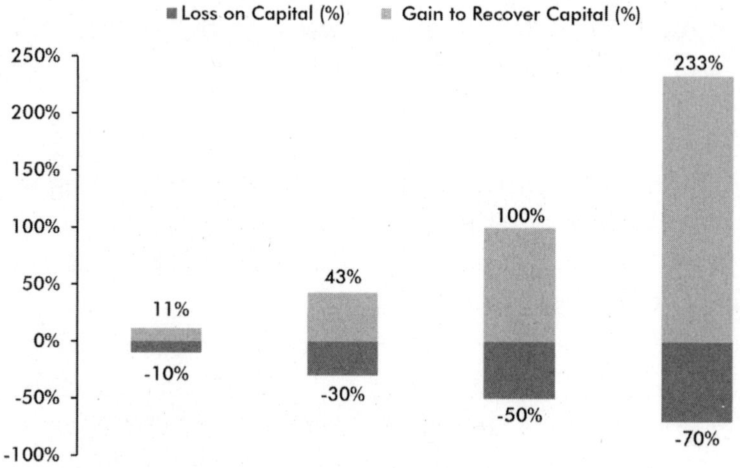

Source: Ambit Capital

Exhibit 70: Good: The greatness framework

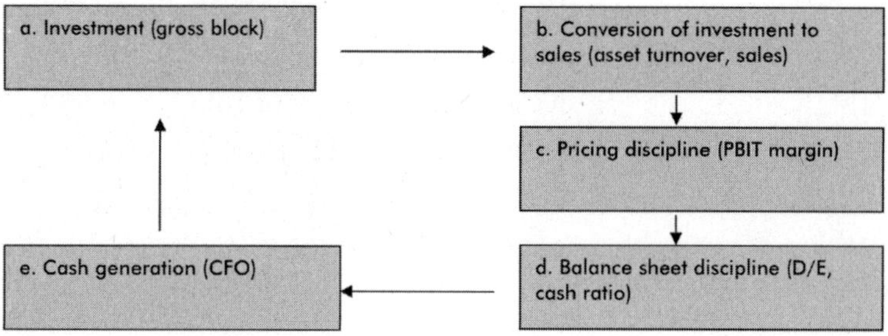

Source: Ambit Capital

As shown in the preceding exhibit, the 'good' framework essentially hinges on using publicly available historical data to assess which firms have, over a sustained period of time, been able to relentlessly and consistently:

(a) Invest capital,
(b) Turn investment into sales,
(c) Turn sales into profit,
(d) Turn profit into balance sheet strength,
(e) Turn all of that into free cash flow,
(f) Invest free cash flows again.

All of these parameters are calculated quantitatively using the factors listed in the exhibit below:

Exhibit 71: The Greatness Factors

Category	Criteria
1. Investments	a. Above median gross block increase
	b. Above median gross block increase to standard deviation
2. Conversion to sales	a. Improvement in asset turnover
	b. Positive improvement in asset turnover adjusted for standard deviation
	c. Above median sales increase
	d. Above median sales increase to standard deviation
3. Pricing discipline	a. Above median PBIT margin increase
	b. Above median PBIT margin increase to standard deviation

	Category	Criteria
4.	Balance sheet discipline	a. Below median debt-equity decline b. Below median debt-equity decline to standard deviation c. Above median cash ratio increase d. Above median cash ratio increase to standard deviation
5.	Cash generation and PAT improvement	a. Above median CFO increase b. Above median CFO increase to standard deviation c. Above median adjusted PAT increase d. Above median adjusted PAT increase to standard deviation
6.	Return ratio improvement	a. Improvement in ROE b. Positive improvement in ROE adjusted for standard deviation c. Improvement in ROCE d. Positive improvement in ROCE adjusted for standard deviation

Source: Ambit Capital

'Clean': The accounting framework

The framework checks for the quality of a company's accounting using eleven ratios.

Exhibit 72: Accounting Checks

Category	Ratios
P&L mis-statement checks	Cumulative CFO/Cumulative EBIDTA Volatility in depreciation rate Volatility in non-operating income (NoI) (as a percentage of net revenues) Provisioning for doubtful debts as a proportion of debtors more than six months
Balance sheet mis-statement check	Cash yield Change in reserves (excluding share premium) to net income excluding dividends Contingent liability as a proportion of net worth
Pilferage checks	Miscellaneous expenses as a proportion of total revenue CWIP to Gross block Cumulative CFO plus CFI to median revenues
Audit quality checks	CAGR in auditors remuneration to CAGR in consolidated revenues

Source: Ambit Capital

Exhibit 73 highlights the importance of the 'cleanness' check. If we rate the BSE 500 companies on the basis of 'cleanness' and divide them into ten groups (or deciles), data shows that the companies with the worst scores, i.e. the least clean companies, gave the worst returns to shareholders.

Exhibit 73: The three zones on accounting quality

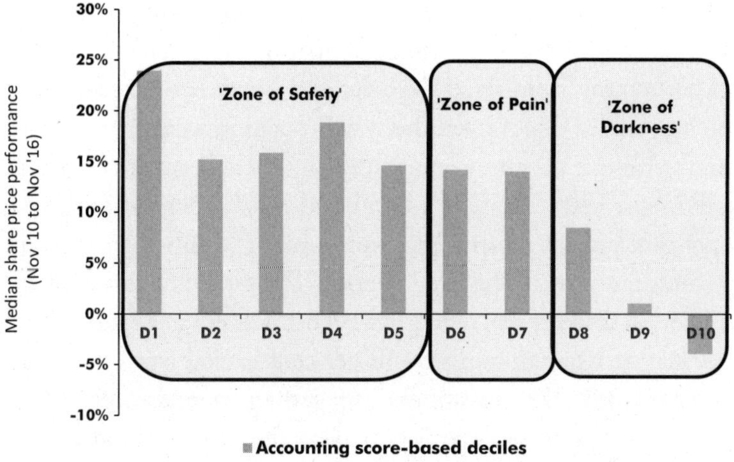

Source: Ace Equity, Capitaline, Bloomberg, Ambit Capital

Note: Accounting score is based on annual financials over FY11–16; stock price performance is from November 2010 to November 2016.

The Debt Allocation

With the equity allocation nailed down (20 per cent in a Nifty tracker, 20 per cent in Coffee Can PMS, 20 per cent in small-cap mutual funds and 20 per cent in the Good & Clean PMS), Nikhil and Mr Talwar now move on to discussing the allocation of his debt portfolio. Here Nikhil cautioned Mr Talwar to not expect very high returns. He explained to Mr Talwar that debt was like the non-striker in a batting partnership, somebody who will hold the other end whilst the big hitting and runs will be scored by the striker, which is equity in this case.

According to Nikhil, it was a no-brainer to invest in mutual funds for one's debt allocation. Mr Talwar, who had never looked beyond fixed deposits, wondered why. Nikhil explained the taxation benefit that debt mutual funds, i.e. mutual funds that invest in bonds issued by the government and by corporates, enjoy over all other bonds and fixed deposits.

While debt mutual funds are subject to long-term capital gains taxation of 20 per cent with indexation (long term is taken as three years), returns from fixed deposits and bonds are taxed fully at the income tax rate. Given the way indexation works, the mutual fund's effective tax rate works out to anywhere between 5 per cent and 15 per cent. Thus, if a bond and a fixed deposit both give 9 per cent pre-tax returns, an investor may get only a 6.3 per cent post-tax return with the fixed deposit. The same investor with the same 9 per cent pre-tax return can get 8.1 per cent in a mutual fund (because of what amounts to 10 per cent capital gains taxation). In other words, the investor ends up getting approximately 30 per cent more on a post-tax basis if he takes the debt fund route.

That said, Nikhil mentioned that investors need high-quality advice in order to be able to choose the right debt funds. Given the role of debt in a portfolio, the safety of capital should not be compromised for a few basis points of extra returns. Mr Talwar had heard from his friends about some debt funds which gave industry-beating returns. Nikhil then explained to him the fallacy in rewarding 'performance' in a debt fund.

A debt mutual fund's return is a function of:

1. Yield to Maturity (YTM),
2. Mark to Market (MTM),
3. Expense Ratio.

In its most simplistic form,
Debt Mutual Fund's Return = YTM + MTM - Expense

Mark to Market (MTM) is the return that a fund manager generates as a result of appreciation in bond prices (remember that a debt mutual fund is a collection of government and corporate bonds). This change in bond prices is in turn a function of the movement in interest rates[4] (yields to be more precise). Mutual funds in India manage more than Rs 11 lakh crore of debt assets (as on July 2017) and each of these funds has access to similar information sets. Hence, it is almost impossible for any one debt fund manager to consistently outperform the peer group. MTM returns, over a period of several years, are therefore similar for all debt funds (in a given class of debt funds; e.g. short-term bond funds, liquid funds). That leaves us with YTM and the expense ratio.

By now, you are familiar with the expense ratio. It is the fees you knowingly or unknowingly pay to the fund management house. So, let us focus on YTM.

The **Yield to Market (YTM)** of a mutual fund is a weighted average yield of all its investments. The yield of a mutual fund depends on the credit quality of its portfolio. If you are interested in investing in debt funds, you need to understand this relationship between credit quality and YTM.

All corporate debt is 'rated' basis the quality of the corporate's financial statement. These ratings are provided by rating agencies in India, including CRISIL, CARE, ICRA, India Ratings and Brickworks. Each issuer of debt gets a credit rating on the basis of its balance sheet strength. For example, government securities, with the highest credit strength, get a rating of 'AAA'. Similarly, a struggling company with poor debt management may get a rating of 'B'. A rating of 'D' means that a company has defaulted on its debt.

Based on these ratings, we assign a unique score to each rating category. For example, government securities get a score

---

[4] Bond price and interest rates are inversely related, i.e. when bond prices rise, interest rates fall, and vice versa.

of 10, AAA papers get a score of 9, AA+ papers get a score of 8.5, and so on. We then multiply the weights of these different papers in a given debt fund with their respective scores to arrive at the credit score for each debt fund.

Once the credit scores for each fund are calculated, we plot the YTM versus credit scores for all the short-term debt funds available in the mutual fund universe (see the exhibit below).

Exhibit 74: High inverse correlation between credit score and yield to maturity of debt funds

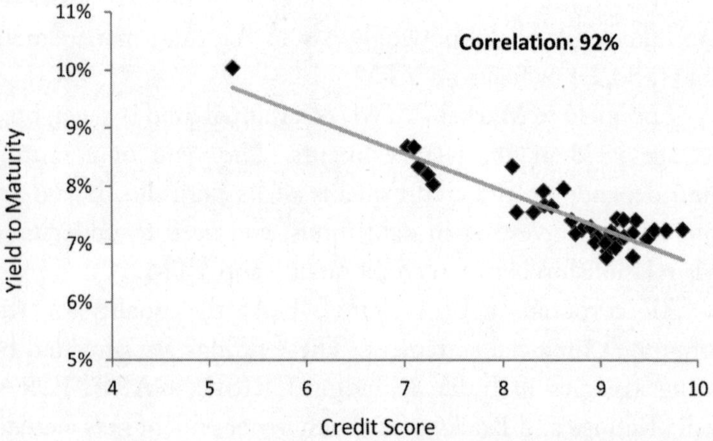

Source: MFI Explorer, Ambit Capital Research. Data as on 31 July 2017 for the short-term debt fund universe in India of forty-five funds.

The inverse correlation of 92 per cent shows the strength of the connection between credit score and YTM, implying that the higher returns given by higher performing debt funds are largely a function of the extra credit risk that the debt fund manager is taking. In other words, the single factor that drives higher YTM appears to be higher credit risk.

Thanks to this knowledge, Mr Talwar has understood why he should choose debt mutual funds on the basis of the quality of the portfolio rather than the historic returns given by these funds.

Mr Talwar's final portfolio

With all the bits of the portfolio now in place, Nikhil laid out the final investment plan for Mr Talwar (see the exhibit below). While it was a long-term plan, it needed periodic monitoring, which Nikhil would do along with Mr Talwar.

Exhibit 75: Proposed Portfolio Allocation for Mr Talwar

Asset Class	Category	Sub-category	% Allocation	Pre-tax Returns	Post-tax Returns
Equity	**Large-cap**	Large-cap ETFs	20.0%	15.0%	15.0%
	Multi-cap	**Coffee Can Portfolio**	**20.0%**	**20.0%**	**20.0%**
	Mid-cap	Small-midcap mutual funds	20.0%	18.0%	18.0%
		Good & Clean portfolio	**20.0%**	**22.0%**	**22.0%**
Debt	**Short-term**	Short-term mutual funds	20.0%	8.0%	7.4*%
Grand Total			**100.0%**	**16.6%**	**16.5%**
Total Assets		592			

Source: Ambit Capital

**Assumed 8 per cent effective tax for debt funds after considering Indexation.*

At this point, Nikhil reiterated the importance of low-cost funds—ETFs and direct schemes. As a comparison, he calculated that Mr Talwar's pretax returns would have fallen to an annualized 15.6 per cent from the 16.6 per cent shown in the exhibit above had he invested in regular schemes with higher expenses.[5]

Dusk was enveloping Noida and Mr Talwar's relief at being able to rationally plan his financial future was such that he brought out a twenty-year-old single malt he had saved for a special occasion. After Nikhil and he raised a toast to his long-term financial security, Mr Talwar turned on some music (Kishore Kumar: Greatest Hits from the 1970s) and stretched out on his favourite couch to relax.

Mr Sanghvi: The need for cash flows

The financial planning exercise was a good way for Mr Sanghvi to realize that his family was going overboard with expenses. The last time anybody had told Mr Sanghvi to watch how much money he spent was his father thirty years ago. Now it was Nikhil, a young man half his age, who was admonishing him. But Nikhil had the numbers in front of him to put Mr Sanghvi on the defensive.

Nikhil encouraged Mr Sanghvi to jot down all his goals (see Exhibit 76). They also plotted his cash flows alongside.

---

[5] As you may remember from Chapter 3, most equity mutual funds charge between 2.2 per cent and 2.5 per cent per annum. This compares with 0.05–0.2 per cent charged in ETF.

Exhibit 76: Mr Sanghvi's goals divided into three categories

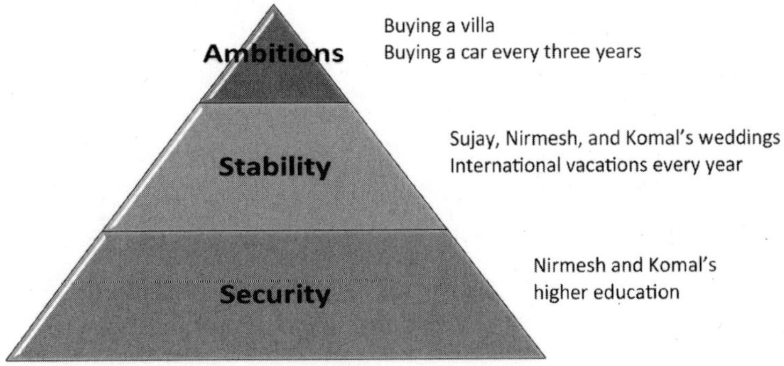

Source: Ambit Capital. Our construct here has been influenced by Ashvin B. Chhabra's book, The Aspirational Investor: Investing in the Pursuit of Wealth and Happiness (2015).

With Nikhil's help, Mr Sanghvi plotted his goals, which included Nirmesh and Komal's higher education abroad, lavish weddings for his three kids and buying a villa in the next four years. Apart from these, there were recurring goals like two to three international vacations every year and buying an expensive car every three years.

While Nikhil mentioned to Mr Sanghvi that his goals were steep and would need an aggressive asset allocation, Mr Sanghvi did not budge. He felt that with all the hard work he had put in all these years, this was the least he should be able to do.

Keeping the above goals in mind, Nikhil plotted Mr Sanghvi's net worth.

Exhibit 77: Mr. Sanghvi's net worth going forward

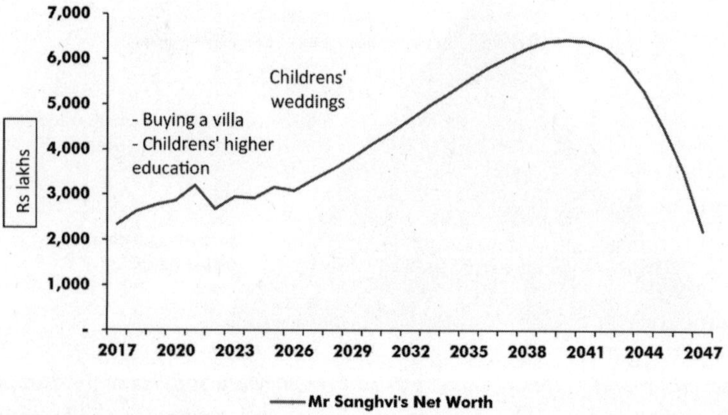

Source: Ambit Capital

Solutions for Mr Sanghvi

Mr Sanghvi's requirements are quite different from Mr Talwar's. While he also has the responsibilities of his children's education and weddings, they don't account for such a large proportion of his overall wealth. The biggest outflows for him are actually the annual/recurring expenditures underpinning his extravagant lifestyle. While he is willing to try and tighten his belt a bit, it will still require a 17.5 per cent annual return from his portfolio to match his cash flows.

Another big difference between Mr Sanghvi and Mr Talwar is that while the latter is still earning a salary and does not need to draw upon his portfolio for regular expenses, Mr Sanghvi is entirely dependent on his portfolio to meet expenses.

To address that, Nikhil does not have to change the nature of investments significantly. Instead, he makes Mr Sanghvi invest in 'dividend' (rather than 'growth') options in his mutual fund allocation. Also, the fact that capital gains were tax-free after a year meant that Mr Sanghvi could regularly redeem his investments in his PMS without impacting returns.

The plan for Mr Sanghvi

Nikhil first had to decide the capital allocation for Mr Sanghvi between equity and debt. Since the required rate of return was higher than in Mr Talwar's case, Nikhil decided to allocate a higher proportion of the portfolio to equity. The capital allocation for Mr Sanghvi was as follows:

Equity – 85 per cent,
Debt – 15 per cent

This breakup assumes 18.9 per cent per annum return from equity and 8 per cent per annum return from debt. The blended return of these two asset classes is 17.3 per cent per annum. With the asset allocation settled, Nikhil proceeds to help Mr Sanghvi figure out what to do with each asset class.

Equity strategy

For Mr Sanghvi, the return expectation from the portfolio was much higher than that for Mr Talwar. He also wanted regular cash flows. To meet the higher return expectation, Nikhil decided to give a higher allocation to small-midcaps compared to large-cap. His investments in mutual funds were made in the dividend paying options. Nikhil reminded Mr Sanghvi that dividends in equity mutual funds were tax-free. That would take care of one part of his annual cash flow requirements. The other part could be taken care through periodic redemptions of his portfolio whilst ensuring that the period of holding was more than a year (so that capital gains tax does not come into the equation).

Debt strategy

Nikhil kept the debt strategy for Mr Sanghvi the same as that for Mr Talwar—keep things straight and simple. There is no point in taking extra risk with debt as it defeats the purpose of the exercise. All the debt investment was to go to short-term debt funds.

Exhibit 78: Proposed Portfolio Allocation for Mr Sanghvi

Asset Class	Category	Sub Category	% Allocation	Pre-tax Returns	Post-tax Returns
Equity	**Large-cap**	Large-cap ETFs	20%	15%	15%
	Multi-cap	**Coffee Can Portfolio**	**20%**	**20%**	**20%**
	Mid-cap	Small-midcap mutual funds	20%	18%	18%
		Good & Clean portfolio	**25%**	**22%**	**22%**
Debt	**Short-term**	Short-term mutual funds	15%	8%	7.4*%
Grand Total			**100%**	**17.3%**	**17.2%**

Source: Ambit Capital

**Assumed 8 per cent taxation for debt funds after considering Indexation.*

Again, as in Mr Talwar's case, Nikhil calculated the drop in returns if Mr Sanghvi did not choose the low cost ETFs and direct option. The returns would drop from 17.3 per cent per annum to 16.5 per cent per annum.

What about your plan?

Throughout this book, we have attempted to introduce the simplest and most effective way of long-term wealth creation. Be it allocation between debt and equity, choosing between large-cap and mid/small-cap or selecting the underlying instruments, each decision goes a long way in how your capital grows in the long term. Almost as important as portfolio allocation are fees and fund expenses—high fees erode portfolio returns very significantly and hence thought and effort need to be given to expense minimization.

The investment world in India is vastly different today from what it was even a decade ago. On one hand, the relative outperformance of actively managed funds has come down but on the other the increased transparency and lower costs along with the advisory model (where you pay the adviser to look after your interests) promise a far more effective platform for investors to build long-term wealth.

The central theme in all our chapters is the power of compounding, which needs time to show its effectiveness. Many investors have developed cold feet at the first signs of volatility and exited. Only when you stay invested through multiple cycles will compounding be able to work its magic for you. It is thus important to curb the propensity to keep checking your portfolios regularly. We have shown how a 'Coffee Can' of good-quality stocks outperforms indices on a consistent basis.

Expensive funds have no place in a modern-day portfolio where it has become very hard for a specific fund manager to consistently outperform his peers. The impact of expenses is deceptively high on the portfolio because expenses compound too. All over the world actively managed funds are ceding ground to passive funds which charge a fraction of the former's fees. The SEBI has taken the lead in India and through direct schemes has removed the middlemen, i.e. distributors and brokers. The regulator is fighting a battle against the flawed distribution model where the investor's interests don't align with those of distributors. Already, the SEBI's push is resulting in many Indian families choosing the 'advisory' model.

India today presents a colossal opportunity for those who want to patiently and systematically generate wealth over the next two decades. While large-cap stocks will be the anchor for most investors, mid- and small-cap stocks have the potential to give super-normal returns to the investor. Think of Eicher Motor's eighty-four times return (55 per cent annualized) over the past ten years. However, it is important to invest in companies which are 'good & clean'. Retail investors have burnt their hands time and again by investing in unscrupulous companies. It is one of the reasons why India, even with a market capitalization of US$ 2 trillion, has one of the lowest rates of stock market participation. Less than 1 per cent of Indians have exposure to the stock market.

There is a Mr Talwar and a Mr Sanghvi in all of us, both in the state of our financial planning and in terms of the financial mistakes we make. For many of us, our portfolios haven't given the returns that we need. Ultimately, investment is as much about discipline as it is about being smart. We hope this book will help you remove the cobwebs of complexity and inefficiency in your investments and help you achieve financial security.

The three key takeaways from Coffee Can Investing: The Low-Risk Road to Stupendous Wealth

1. Create a financial plan which helps you deliver on your life goals. Unless you do so, you will be shooting in the dark. A financial plan helps you quantify and rationalize

your life goals. It also helps you set up a return expectation from your investment portfolio so that you can build an appropriate portfolio with just the right amount of required risk—no more, no less.

2. Understand the power of expenses. We have seen time and again the enormously damaging impact of compounding expenses over long periods of time. For each investment decision, the investor should choose the most inexpensive investment product.
3. Understand the power of high-quality investing and patience. There is an inherent volatility in the equity markets. To exit at the first sign of volatility or trying to time the market will rob you of an opportunity to derive handsome long-term gains. Also, given the long-term tenures of such investments, it is critical to choose only the highest quality investments.

CHAPTER 8

Designing Your Own Financial Plan

'Some people want it to happen, some wish it would happen, others make it happen.'

—Michael Jordan, basketball legend[1]

Throughout this book, we have sought to spell out relatively low-risk, high-return investment methods and highlighted the traps you need to avoid both with respect to your life goals and with regard to your financial objectives. It is important to link your investment style with your financial objectives; otherwise you will end up either taking unnecessary risks or undershooting your financial goals. The essential link between your investment style and your financial objective is made through financial planning.

In this chapter, we have focused entirely on how to carry out a financial plan effectively for yourself. While it is always beneficial to conduct this exercise with a sound financial adviser

1 Business Insider, http://www.businessinsider.in/105-inspirational-quotes-from-some-of-the-worlds-most-successful-people/On-taking-risks/slideshow/51283530.cms.

(like Nikhil Banerjee did for Mr Talwar and Mr Sanghvi), our endeavour is to leave you with enough expertise and tools to create a plan for yourself. Our approach has been inspired, in part, by the work done in this area by Ashvin B. Chhabra in his book, *The Aspirational Investor*.

We have made the Ambit Financial Planning Tool freely available at www.ambit.co/fp/ambitfp.xlsm. This tool helps you build your own financial plan with the help of basic information like your **annual cash flows** (primarily your income and expenses), your **liabilities** (primarily the loans you have taken), your **assets** (including your house, shares, mutual fund portfolio and any other investments you have made) and most importantly your **goals** (which include your financial as well as personal goals). The aim of this tool is to compute the required rate of return that your portfolio (or your assets) needs to generate so that your capital at all times is enough to meet your goals. Let us now look at each of the three factors one by one while we take you through an illustrative financial planning exercise for Mr Kumar, a thirty-year-old married man with two children. This exercise has been carried out using the Ambit Financial Planning tool highlighted above, but if you want, you can do it on an Excel sheet on your own.

Exhibit 79: Mr Kumar's biological details:

	Age	Year
Current Age	30	2017
Expected Age of Retirement	60	2047
Life Expectancy	85	2072

Source: Ambit Financial Planning Tool

The expected age of retirement and life expectancy helps the tool predict the cash flows, i.e. the income and expenses for

Mr Kumar for the rest of his life. Our income usually stops at retirement whereas expenses continue till we die.

Step 1: Key in your cash flows

The tool asks some basic questions about your annual cash flows. The model first considers the input for income earned during the year. It is important to provide the post-tax income rather than the 'cost to company' or the pre-tax income. An equally important input is the expected growth for the various items under your income. This ensures that the model accommodates the future earning power of an individual.

For Mr Kumar, who earns Rs 36 lakh per annum (post-tax), the cash flows associated with his income are as follows:

Exhibit 80: Mr Kumar's cash flow details

Income (in Rupees)	Monthly	Yearly	Income Ends in	Expected Growth
Salary + Bonus (post-tax)	3,00,000	36,00,000	2047	8%
Rent	NA	NA	NA	
Business Income	NA	NA	NA	
Other Income	15,000	1,80,000	2050	5%

Source: Ambit Financial Planning Tool

The tool then asks for expenses. As mentioned earlier, even though our primary income (salary) usually stops at retirement, expenses continue. Hence it is important to thoughtfully list them down along with the expected inflation in each expense category. As discussed in Chapter 1, inflation is a key input in determining future cash flows.

For Mr Kumar, his current monthly expense is Rs 1.82 lakh (which includes living expenses, home and car loan instalments).

Exhibit 81: Mr Kumar's monthly expenses (excluding EMIs)

Expenses (in Rupees)	Monthly	Yearly	Expenses End in	Expected Inflation
Regular Monthly Expenses	40,000	4,80,000	2072	10%
Utilities	8000	96,000	2072	5%
Grocery	25,000	3,00,000	2072	8%
Monthly Leisure	25,000	3,00,000	2072	12%
Medical Expenses	3000	36,000	2072	8%
Domestic Staff	8000	96,000	2072	5%

Source: Ambit Financial Planning Tool

Finally, in the cash outflow, the tool asks for ongoing loan repayments and their tenure. The tool considers Equal Monthly Instalments (EMIs) for loans under 'expenses' as they are cash outflows on a monthly basis rather than a lump sum loan to be repaid.

Exhibit 82: Mr Kumar's EMI details:

EMIs (in Rupees)	Monthly	Yearly	EMI Ends in
Home Loan	60,000	7,20,000	2035
Car Loan	13,000	1,56,000	2023
Education Loan	-	-	
Other EMI	-	-	

Source: Ambit Financial Planning Tool

On the basis of the cash flow estimates given and the expected rate of inflation, the tool then calculates the future cash flows along with the ending date. That takes care of the first part of financial planning.

Step 2: Key in your current portfolio and assets

The tool then asks you to list your assets or the current portfolio. Please note that the model classifies these assets as personal, market and aspirational based on the nature of the asset. Personal assets are those meant for consumption and one does not intend to trade or sell them. In Mr Kumar's case it is the house he lives in and the gold that belongs to his wife. Market assets are investments which carry the usual market risk, e.g. stocks, bonds and mutual funds. Aspirational assets are those which carry high risk, e.g. private equity funds, high-yield debentures, etc. For Mr Kumar, the breakup of assets, along with their respective classification is as below:

Exhibit 83: Mr Kumar's investment portfolio

Current Portfolio			
Asset (in Rupees)	Asset Type	Market Value	% Allocation
House	Personal	2,00,00,000	83.3%
Equity Shares	Market	15,00,000	6.3%
Mutual Funds	Market	8,00,000	3.3%
Gold	Personal	17,00,000	7.1%
Total		**2,40,00,000**	**100%**

Source: Ambit Financial Planning Tool

Step 3: Key in your goals

Your goals are at the heart of this whole financial planning exercise because ultimately you are doing this to ensure that you are able to meet those goals. Your goals could be one-time (e.g. children's higher education, their weddings) or they could be ones that you wish to achieve more frequently (e.g. buying a car, going on vacations).

Just like it does for your assets, the model has three classifications for goals as well: security, stability and ambition.

Security: These are goals you would absolutely not like to compromise with. These are 'must achieve' amongst all your life goals (e.g. children's higher education).

Stability: These are goals that are linked to the way you live on a day-to-day basis and help achieve a certain lifestyle or level of comfort (e.g. buying a car, going for a vacation).

Ambition: These are goals you wish to achieve. However, there may not be a major lifestyle impact if you don't achieve these goals, e.g. buying a holiday villa. Usually, these are goals one is willing to prune down in case of inadequate cash flow.

Exhibit 84: Mr Kumar's goals divided into three categories

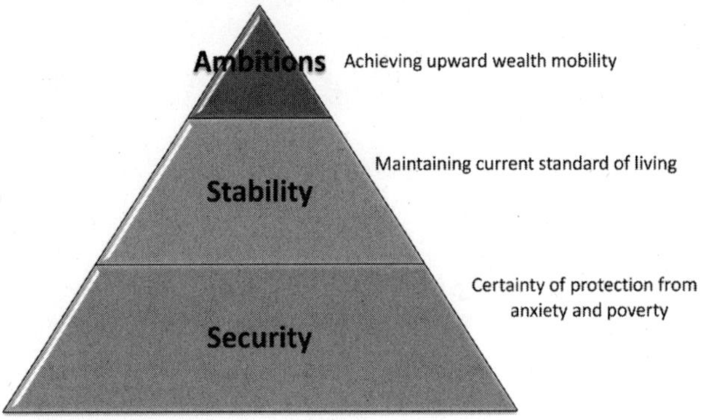

Source: Ambit Capital. Our construct here has been influenced by Ashvin B. Chhabra's book, The Aspirational Investor: Investing in the Pursuit of Wealth and Happiness (2015).

Although categorization of your goals may not have any real impact on the required rate of return you need, it helps you know which goals you can alter in case the required rate of return is too aggressive. For example, in the previous chapter, we saw that the initial required rate of return for Mr Talwar was a staggering 21 per cent. This made Mr Talwar alter the goals that were right at the top of the pyramid (ambitions)—buying a holiday home, going for international vacations, etc.

Exhibit 85: Mr Kumar's goals and supplementary income from goals:

Goal (one-time)	Priority	Type	Goal year	Current cost	Term (years)	Inflation	Future cost (Rs)	Loan to achieve goal (% of Future Cost)	Future Cost (Rs) ex-loan amount	Loan amount
Buying a second house	Aspiration	Physical asset	2030	3,00,00,000	13	4%	4,99,52,205	50%	2,75,19,974[2]	2,49,76,103
Kid's higher education (first child)	Safety	Expense	2035	50,00,000	18	8%	1,99,80,097	NA	1,99,80,097	NA
Kid's higher education (second Child)	Safety	Expense	2038	50,00,000	21	8%	2,51,69,169	NA	2,51,69,169	NA
Kid's wedding (first child)	Stability	Expense	2038	60,00,000	21	8%	3,02,03,002	NA	3,02,03,002	NA
Kid's wedding (second child)	Stability	Expense	2041	60,00,000	24	8%	3,80,47,084	NA	3,80,47,084	NA

Source: Ambit Financial Planning Tool

2 We have assumed the loan period of twenty years and interest rate of 8 per cent per annum.

GOAL (Recurring every year)	Priority	Current Cost	Starting Year	Ending Year	Inflation
International vacation	Stability	5,00,000	2017	2050	4%

Source: Ambit Financial Planning Tool

GOAL (Recurring less frequently)	Priority	Current Cost	Starting Year	Frequency (Every how many years)	Ending Year	Inflation
Buying a car	Stability	15,00,000	2025	4	2065	4%

Source: Ambit Financial Planning Tool

Apart from the goals, the tool also has a placeholder for any future inflow or outflow. For example, it allows for future rental income from a house that Mr Kumar will buy in 2030. Thus the model shows rental income starting from 2030.

Income from Goals Achieved	Income	Starting Year	Ending Year	Growth
Rent from second house	6,00,000	2030	2050	5%

Source: Ambit Financial Planning Tool

Output:

Based on the inputs provided by Mr Kumar, the Ambit Financial Planning Tool calculates all future cash flows for him. The tool then calculates the required rate of return that his investments need to generate to ensure that he has enough capital to meet all his goals. In this case, the required rate of return for Mr Kumar to achieve all his goals is 13.3 per cent post tax. A reliable way for a man like Mr Kumar to achieve such a rate of return would be to invest 25 per cent in ETFs, 20 per cent in the Coffee Can Portfolio, 20 per cent in the Good & Clean Portfolio and 35 per cent in high-quality short-term debt mutual funds.

Exhibit 86: Mr Kumar's net worth

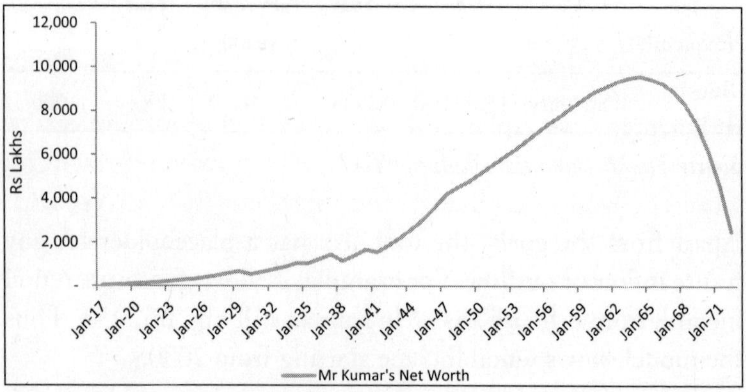

Source: Ambit Financial Planning Tool

Finally, please remember that financial planning is a dynamic exercise and needs to be carried out periodically or whenever any significant change occurs in your cash flow, assets or goals. The output from the tool will then adjust your portfolio to help you meet your goals. Whilst there are no guarantees in life, a well-planned and conservatively managed financial portfolio maximizes the chances of you and your family achieving most goals.

APPENDIX 1

Detailed Coffee Can Portfolios

In Chapter 2 we explained how Coffee Can Portfolios can be created using two simple filters: 10 per cent revenue growth for ten consecutive years alongside 15 per cent ROCE. We then highlighted the merits of investing in the Coffee Can Portfolio and leaving it untouched for ten years. Now, let's focus on an example of a real Coffee Can Portfolio.

Our first screen is for the ten-year period from FY1991 to FY2000. We take the universe of listed stocks with market capitalization of more than Rs 100 crore and look for companies that meet these parameters:

a) Revenue growth of 10 per cent and ROCE of 15 per cent every year for non-financial services companies, or

b) For financial services companies, ROE of 15 per cent and loan book growth of 15 per cent every year.

In the ten-year period between FY1991 and FY2000, we find that there are five companies that meet these requirements. These are NIIT, Cipla, Hero MotoCorp, Swaraj Engines and HDFC. This set of five companies is our 'Coffee Can Portfolio 2000' (CCP 2000), which is an equal weighted portfolio of these stocks invested on 1 July 2000. We then track the stock price performance of CCP 2000 for the next ten years (that is, from 1 July 2000 to 30 June 2010). Similarly, running the screen from FY1992 to FY2001 gives us the 'Coffee Can Portfolio 2001' (CCP 2001). We then track the stock price performance of this portfolio for the ten-year period from 1 July 2001 to 30 June 2011.

In this appendix, we have listed the details of all of the Coffee Can Portfolios from 2000 to 2017 and also provided a detailed stock-by-stock share price performance. Given that each time bucket is ten years, *we have eight fully completed Coffee Can Portfolios:* FY1991-2000 (CCP 2000), FY92-01 (CCP 2001), FY93-02 (CCP 2002), FY94-03 (CCP 2003), FY95-04 (CCP 2004), FY96-05 (CCP 2005), FY97-06 (CCP 2006) and FY98-07 (CCP 2007).

However, the Coffee Can Portfolio of companies that was constructed on the basis of financial data from FY1999 to FY2008 will complete ten years of price performance only on 30 June 2018. Similarly, Coffee Can Portfolio 2009, which uses financial data from FY2000 to FY2009, will end its ten-year stock price performance on 30 June 2019 and so on and so forth. Thus, we have nine Coffee Can Portfolios that are incomplete in the sense that they have not yet run their full duration of ten years. For these uncompleted Coffee Can Portfolios, we have used a cut-off date of 30 June 2017 to measure price performance. We have also shown the tenth incomplete Coffee Can Portfolio (CCP 2017), which commenced on 1 July 2017 and is yet to see a meaningful period of performance.

In order to measure the performance of any Coffee Can Portfolio, we have used 'total shareholder return' rather than 'share price return' of the constituent stocks. Total shareholder return assumes reinvestment of dividends received from each stock back into the same company's shares on the date of receipt of this dividend. Similarly, the benchmark return—the BSE Sensex—used to compare the outperformance of each of these portfolios is also based on the total shareholder return of the BSE Sensex rather than just the index price return.

The results can be summarized in one sentence: each of the seventeen CCPs (eight with complete price performance back-testing and nine with partially complete back-testing) have outperformed the benchmark large-cap index in India, the Sensex. In fact, as can be seen in Exhibit 87, the outperformance of the complete CCPs to the Sensex is always in excess of 5 percentage points per annum. This outperformance relative to the benchmark is called 'alpha'.

To assess the robustness of these findings, we also stress-tested the results for a subset of the CCP, i.e. its large-cap version. The large-cap version contains only those CCP stocks which were in the top 100 in India based on the market capitalization on the day the portfolio was created. Even a subset, i.e. the large-cap version of the CCP, has been successful in beating the Sensex on all seventeen occasions.

We have summarized the results of each of these seventeen iterations in exhibits 88 and 89 with a detailed description of each portfolio following it.

If you plan to use the Coffee Can method to invest money, you should read the following paragraph carefully. While each of the seventeen iterations has generated strong performance relative to the Sensex on an overall portfolio basis, not every stock in the CCPs has delivered stellar returns. To put things in perspective, over the seventeen iterations, an average Coffee Can Portfolio consists of twelve companies. Of these twelve companies, two to three companies gave stellar returns over a ten-year period (we highlight such stocks when we discuss each portfolio in detail below) and two to three companies gave low to negative returns over the same period. The rest of the portfolio has given broadly market returns. This is the nature of the construct of a Coffee Can Portfolio. However, in spite of this, every single Coffee Can Portfolio has outperformed the overall market due to the reasons listed below:

1. As the time period increases, the probability of generating positive returns increases. Using annualized Sensex returns of 16 per cent and a standard deviation of 29 per cent over the past thirty years, the probability of generating positive returns rises from around 70 per cent in a one-year horizon to almost 100 per cent if the time horizon is increased to ten years.

Exhibit 87: Probability of gains from equity investing in India increases disproportionately with increase in holding period (the chart here is for Sensex returns over the thirty-year period from March 1987 to March 2017)

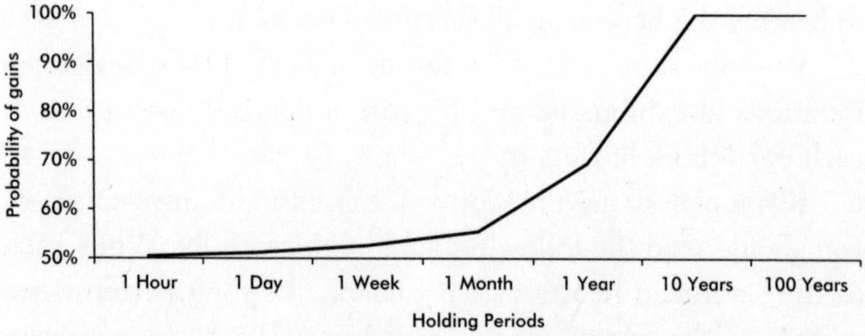

Source: Bloomberg, Ambit Capital

Note: This chart has been inspired by similar work done by Michael Mauboussin in the American context.

2. In the long run, the portfolio becomes dominated by winning stocks whilst the losing stocks keep declining to eventually become inconsequential. Thus, the positive contribution of the winners disproportionately outweighs the negative contribution of the losers to eventually help the portfolio compound handsomely.
3. Investing and holding for the long-term is the most effective way of killing 'noise' that interferes with the investment process. As soon as you try to time entry/exit, you run the risk of 'noise' rather than fundamentals driving investment decisions.
4. Lack of churn reduces transaction costs, which adds to the overall portfolio performance over the long term. A hypothetical portfolio started on 1 July, with 50 per cent churn per annum for instance, loses almost 1.2 per cent CAGR return when run for a ten-year period.

Exhibit 88: Results of back-testing of the completed eight iterations of the Coffee Can Portfolio (i.e. these portfolios have run their complete course of ten years)

Kick-off year	All-cap (start)	All-cap (end)	CAGR Return	Outperformance relative to Sensex	Large Cap (start)	Large Cap (end)	CAGR Return	Outperformance relative to Sensex
2000	500	3831	22.6%	6.6%	400	3338	23.6%	7.6%
2001	600	9802	32.2%	11.7%	300	3622	28.3%	7.8%
2002	800	7631	25.3%	5.1%	500	4176	23.6%	3.5%
2003	900	10,117	27.4%	7.2%	600	7790	29.2%	9.0%
2004	1,000	16,880	32.7%	12.9%	500	3660	22.0%	2.3%
2005	900	6659	22.2%	6.0%	500	2976	19.5%	3.4%
2006	1,000	6376	20.4%	9.0%	600	2918	17.1%	5.7%
2007	1,500	9030	19.7%	10.4%	1000	4690	16.7%	7.4%

Source: Bloomberg, Capitaline, Ambit Capital

Note: Portfolio at start denotes an equal allocation of Rs 100 for the stocks qualifying to be in the CCP for that year. Each portfolio kicks off on 1 July of the kick-off year and ends ten years later.

Exhibit 89: Results of back-testing of the incomplete nine iterations of the Coffee Can Portfolio (i.e. these iterations have not run their complete course of ten years)

Kick-off year	All-cap (start)	All-cap (end)	CAGR Return	Outperformance relative to Sensex	Large Cap (start)	Large Cap (end)	CAGR Return	Outperformance relative to Sensex
2008	1100	6471	21.8%	10.0%	800	3808	18.9%	7.1%
2009	1100	5657	22.7%	11.2%	900	3264	17.5%	6.0%
2010	700	2621	20.8%	10.7%	300	1041	19.4%	9.3%
2011	1400	3105	14.2%	3.9%	400	1037	17.2%	6.9%
2012	2200	6650	24.8%	10.9%	500	1165	18.4%	4.6%
2013	1800	5709	33.5%	19.7%	600	1438	24.4%	10.7%
2014	1700	3424	26.3%	18.1%	700	1322	23.6%	15.4%
2015	2000	2772	17.7%	11.2%	1,200	1504	11.9%	5.4%
2016	1700	2009	18.1%	2.8%	800	981	22.6%	7.3%

Source: Bloomberg, Capitaline, Ambit Capital

Note: Portfolio at start denotes an equal allocation of Rs 100 for the stocks qualifying to be in the CCP for that year. The portfolio kicks off on 1 July of the kick-off year. CAGR returns for portfolios since 2008 have been calculated till 30 June 2017.

Complete portfolio (Period 1): 2000–10 (6.6 per cent alpha relative to the Sensex; 22.6 per cent per annum absolute returns)

All-cap portfolio stocks: NIIT, Cipla, Hero MotoCorp, Swaraj Engines and HDFC

Large-cap portfolio stocks: NIIT, Cipla, Hero MotoCorp, and HDFC

In the first iteration, both versions of the CCP outperformed the benchmark. Whilst the all-cap CCP delivered a 22.6 per cent return (6.6 per cent alpha to the Sensex), the large-cap portfolio delivered a 23.6 per cent return (7.6 per cent alpha to the Sensex). The maximum drawdown, which is the largest single drop from the peak to the bottom in the value of a stock, for both the portfolios in this period was also less than the maximum drawdown for the Sensex.

Exhibit 90: Summary of the first iteration

2000–10*	All-cap CCP	Large-cap CCP	Sensex
CAGR returns	22.6%	23.6%	16.0%
Maximum drawdown**	-41.9%	-39.3%	-60.3%
Excess returns***	0.35	0.40	0.13

Source: Bloomberg, Ambit Capital

*Note: * Portfolio kicks off on 1 July 2000.*

****Excess returns have been calculated as returns in excess of risk-free rate (assumed to be 8 per cent) divided by absolute maximum drawdown. Maximum drawdown is defined as the maximum drop in cumulative returns from the highest peak to the lowest subsequent trough.*

***Maximum drawdown period was from Jan '08 to Oct '08 for the all-cap CCP, Jan '08 to Nov '08 for large-cap CCP and Jan '08 to Mar '09 for the Sensex.*

The five stocks that constituted the first iteration of the Coffee Can Portfolio consisted of one IT company, one pharma company, one non-bank lender and two companies from the automobile/auto-ancillary sector. These were NIIT, Cipla, Hero MotoCorp, HDFC Ltd and Swaraj Engines. The star performer in this portfolio was Hero MotoCorp, which proved to be a ten-bagger, i.e. its stock price rose ten times in ten years, whilst NIIT's stock price collapsed during this period. In spite of the collapse, the CCP outperformed the Sensex comfortably (see exhibit below).

Exhibit 91: Portfolio performance of CCP 2000

Stock	**Total shareholder return (TSR)* CAGR**	**PAT CAGR FY 2000–10**	**Contribution to portfolio value at start**	**Contribution to portfolio value at end**
			01/07/2000	**30/06/2010**
NIIT	-12.5%	-11.0%	20%	1%
Cipla	18.2%	23.3%	20%	14%
HDFC Ltd	29.1%	23.2%	20%	33%
Hero MotoCorp	31.1%	27.8%	20%	39%
Swaraj Engines	17.3%	7.0%	20%	13%
Total Portfolio	**22.6%**		**100%**	**100%**
Sensex TSR*	**16.0%**			

Source: Bloomberg, Ambit Capital

Note: Value at start denotes an equal allocation of Rs 100 in each stock at the start of the period. Value at end is the value of each stock at the end of the period. Thus, for this period, the value of the portfolio rose from Rs 500 at the start to Rs 3831 at the end.

**Total Shareholder Return (TSR) and Sensex TSR include dividends received and reinvested.*

Exhibit 92: Hero and HDFC rose exponentially whilst NIIT collapsed in CCP 2000

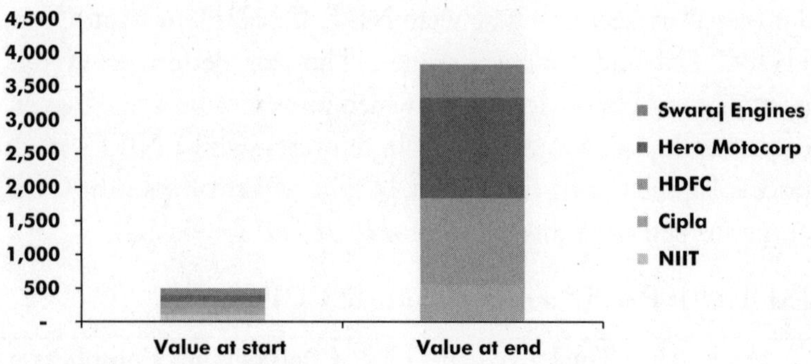

Source: Bloomberg, Ambit Capital

Note: Value at start denotes an equal allocation of Rs 100 in each stock at the start of the period. Value at end is the value of each stock at the end of the period. Thus, for this period, the value of the portfolio rose from Rs 500 at the start to Rs 3831 at the end. Total Shareholder Return (TSR) and Sensex TSR include dividends received and reinvested.

Complete portfolio (Period 2): 2001–11 (11.7 per cent alpha relative to the Sensex; 32.2 per cent per annum absolute returns)

All-cap portfolio stocks: Cipla, Hero MotoCorp, Apollo Hospitals, Roofit Inds, HDFC and LIC Housing Finance

Large-cap portfolio stocks: Cipla, Hero MotoCorp and HDFC

Both versions of the CCP performed well during the second iteration as well, beating the Sensex. The all-cap and large-cap CCP gave an impressive alpha of 11.7 per cent and 7.8 per cent respectively for this iteration. The portfolio was remarkably steady compared to the Sensex's maximum drawdown, delivering an excess return of 0.61–0.59 times (see Exhibit 93).

Exhibit 93: Summary of the second iteration

2001–11*	All-cap CCP	Large-cap CCP	Sensex
CAGR returns	32.2%	28.3%	20.5%
Maximum drawdown**	-39.8%	-34.7%	-60.3%
Excess returns* **	0.61	0.59	0.21

Source: Bloomberg, Ambit Capital

*Note: * Portfolio kicks off on 1 July 2001.*

****Excess returns have been calculated as returns in excess of risk-free rate (assumed to be 8 per cent) divided by absolute maximum drawdown. Maximum drawdown is defined as the maximum drop in cumulative returns from the highest peak to the lowest subsequent trough.*

***Maximum drawdown from Jan '08 to Nov '08 for the all-cap CCP, Apr '08 to Nov '08 for the large-cap CCP and Jan '08 to Mar '09 for the Sensex.*

During the second iteration, the Coffee Can Portfolio consisted of six stocks with three repeats (Cipla, Hero and HDFC from Period 1) and three new entries (Apollo Hospitals, Roofit Industries and LIC Housing Finance). During this period, one of the stocks in the portfolio, Roofit Industries, was delisted. Despite this, the portfolio performed admirably. The star performer was LIC Housing Finance, whose stock price rose thirty-five times, whilst Cipla was a laggard.

Exhibit 94: Portfolio performance of CCP 2001

Stock	Total Shareholder Return (TSR)* CAGR	PAT CAGR FY 2001–11	Contribution to portfolio value at start	Contribution to portfolio value at end
			01/07/2001	30/06/2011
Hero MotoCorp	34.8%	22.8%	17%	20%
Cipla	14.7%	18.6%	17%	4%
HDFC Ltd.	28.6%	24.2%	17%	13%
Apollo Hospitals	30.3%	19.6%	17%	14%
LIC Housing Finance	47.2%	22.9%	17%	49%
Roofit Industries	-26.7%	Delisted	17%	0%
Total Portfolio	**32.2%**		**100%**	**100%**
Sensex TSR*	**20.5%**			

Source: Ambit Capital research, Bloomberg

Note: Data for Roofit Ind is not available from FY03 onwards. Value at start denotes an equal allocation of Rs 100 in each stock at the start of the period. Value at end is the value of each stock at the end of the period. Thus, for this period, the value of the portfolio rose from Rs 600 at the start to Rs 9802 at the end.

**Total Shareholder Return (TSR) and Sensex TSR include dividends received and reinvested.*

Exhibit 95: LIC Housing Finance was the stellar performer of CCP 2001

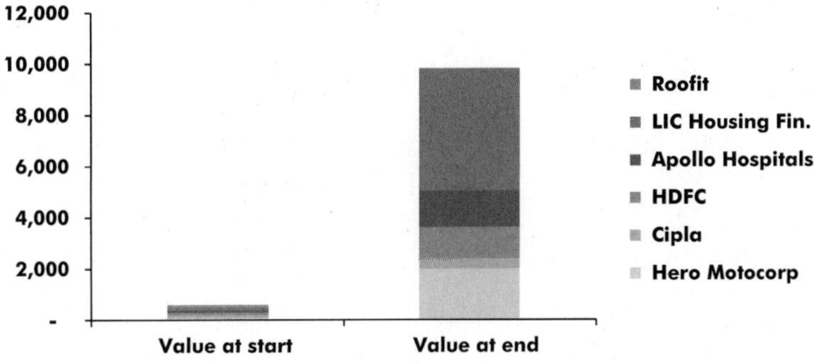

Source: Bloomberg, Ambit Capital

Note: Data for Roofit Ind is not available from FY03 onwards. Value at start denotes an equal allocation of Rs 100 in each stock at the start of the period. Value at end is the value of each stock at the end of the period. Thus, for this period, the value of the portfolio rose from Rs 600 at the start to Rs 9802 at the end. Total Shareholder Return (TSR) and Sensex TSR include dividends received and reinvested.

Complete portfolio (Period 3): 2002–12 (5.1 per cent alpha to the Sensex; 25.3 per cent per annum absolute returns)

All-cap portfolio stocks: Infosys, Hero MotoCorp, Cipla, Container Corporation of India, Gujarat Gas, Aurobindo Pharma, HDFC and LIC Housing Finance

Large-cap portfolio stocks: Infosys, Hero MotoCorp, Cipla, Container Corporation of India, HDFC Ltd

During the third iteration, the CCP delivered an alpha of 5.1 per cent whilst the large-cap CCP delivered an alpha of

3.5 per cent. Both versions of the Coffee Can performed well during maximum drawdown as well, delivering excess returns of 0.38–0.40 times.

Exhibit 96: Summary of the third iteration

2002-2012*	All-cap CCP	Large-cap CCP	Sensex
CAGR returns	25.3%	23.7%	20.2%
Maximum drawdown**	-45.9%	-39.3%	-60.3%
Excess returns * **	0.38	0.40	0.20

Source: Bloomberg, Ambit Capital

*Note: *Portfolio kicks off on 1 July 2002.*

****Excess returns have been calculated as returns in excess of risk-free rate (assumed to be 8 per cent) divided by absolute maximum drawdown. Maximum drawdown is defined as the maximum drop in cumulative returns from the highest peak to the lowest subsequent trough.*

***Maximum drawdown from Jan'08 to Nov'08 for the all-cap CCP, Jan'08 to Nov'08 for large-cap CCP and Jan'08 to Mar'09 for the Sensex.*

The Coffee Can Portfolio expanded in size during the third iteration. A total of eight stocks qualified to be part of the Coffee Can Portfolio in the third iteration. Cipla, Hero MotoCorp, HDFC and LIC Housing were repeated yet again whilst the other four stocks were Infosys, Container Corporation, Gujarat Gas and Aurobindo Pharma. LIC Housing Finance was the winner yet again, while Aurobindo Pharma lagged.

Exhibit 97: Portfolio performance of CCP 2002

Stock	Total Shareholder Return (TSR)* CAGR	PAT CAGR FY 2002–12	Contribution to portfolio value at start	Contribution to portfolio value at end
			01/07/2002	30/06/2012
Hero MotoCorp	26.2%	17.8%	13%	13%
Cipla	16.4%	18.6%	13%	6%
HDFC	28.8%	24.2%	13%	16%
Aurobindo Pharma	17.8%	11.0%	13%	7%
LIC Housing Finance	36.3%	20.1%	13%	29%
Infosys	21.5%	26.2%	13%	9%
Container Corporation	22.1%	13.2%	13%	10%
Gujarat Gas Company	22.0%	17.9%	13%	10%
Total Portfolio	**25.3%**		**100%**	**100%**
Sensex TSR*	**20.2%**			

Source: Bloomberg, Ambit Capital

Note: Value at start denotes an equal allocation of Rs 100 in each stock at the start of the period. Value at end is the value of each stock at the end of the period. Thus, for this period, the value of the portfolio rose from Rs 800 at the start to Rs 7631 at the end.

**Total Shareholder Return (TSR) and Sensex TSR include dividends received and reinvested.*

Exhibit 98: The portfolio's outperformance was led by LIC Housing Finance once again

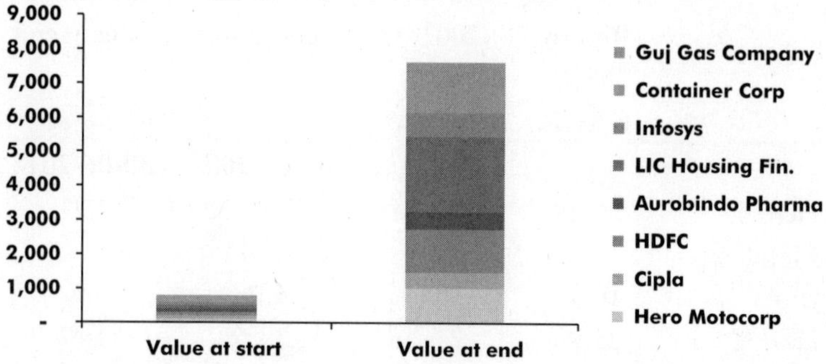

Source: Bloomberg, Ambit Capital

Note: Value at start denotes an equal allocation of Rs 100 in each stock at the start of the period. Value at end is the value of each stock at the end of the period. Thus, for this period, the value of the portfolio rose from Rs 800 at the start to Rs 7631 at the end.

**Total Shareholder Return (TSR) and Sensex TSR include dividends received and reinvested.*

Complete portfolio (Period 4): 2003–13 (7.2 per cent alpha to the Sensex; 27.4 per cent per annum absolute returns)

All-cap portfolio stocks: Infosys, Hero MotoCorp, Cipla, Sun Pharma, Container Corporation of India, Gujarat Gas, Aurobindo Pharma, HDFC and LIC Housing Finance

Large-cap portfolio stocks: Infosys, Hero MotoCorp, Cipla, Container Corporation of India, Sun Pharma and HDFC

Whilst the all-cap version of the CCP delivered a 7.2 per cent alpha, the large-cap version gave a 9 per cent alpha in the fourth iteration. In a maximum drawdown situation, both versions remained steady and beat the Sensex, delivering excess returns of 0.57–1.48 times.

Exhibit 99: Summary of the fourth iteration

2003–13*	All-cap CCP	Large-cap CCP	Sensex
CAGR returns	27.4%	29.2%	20.2%
Maximum drawdown**	-34.0%	-14.4%	-60.3%
Excess returns***	0.57	1.48	0.20

Source: Bloomberg, Ambit Capital

*Note: *Portfolio kicks off on 1 July 2003.*

****Excess returns have been calculated as returns in excess of risk-free rate (assumed to be 8 per cent) divided by absolute maximum drawdown. Maximum drawdown is defined as the maximum drop in cumulative returns from the highest peak to the lowest subsequent trough.*

***Maximum drawdown from Jan'08 to Nov'08 for the all-cap CCP, Sept'08 to Nov'08 for large-cap CCP and Jan'08 to Mar'09 for the Sensex.*

Barring one addition (Sun Pharma), the Coffee Can Portfolio in its fourth iteration was the same as that in the third iteration. Its performance was driven by Sun Pharma's stellar performance, while Gujarat Gas lagged. However, the performance of the large-cap version was better than the all-cap version of the Coffee Can Portfolio.

Exhibit 100: Portfolio performance of CCP 2003

Stock	Total Shareholder Return (TSR)* CAGR	PAT CAGR FY 2003–13	Contribution to portfolio value at start	Contribution to portfolio value at end
			01/07/2003	**30/06/2013**
Hero MotoCorp	25.5%	13.8%	11%	10%
Cipla	21.8%	20.1%	11%	7%
HDFC Ltd	29.1%	24.5%	11%	13%
Aurobindo Pharma	17.4%	13%	11%	5%
LIC Housing Finance	29.4%	19.3%	11%	13%
Infosys	21.6%	25.7%	11%	7%
Container Corporation	21.6%	13%	11%	7%
Sun Pharma	42.3%	28.2%	11%	34%
Gujarat Gas Company	17.8%	18%	11%	5%
Total Portfolio	**27.4%**		**100%**	**100%**
Sensex TSR*	**20.2%**			

Source: Bloomberg, Ambit Capital

Note: Value at start denotes an equal allocation of Rs 100 in each stock at the start of the period. Value at end is the value of each stock at the end of the period. Thus, for this period, the value of the portfolio rose from Rs 900 at the start to Rs 10,117 at the end.

**Total Shareholder Return (TSR) and Sensex TSR include dividends received and reinvested.*

Exhibit 101: Sun Pharma was the star of CCP 2003

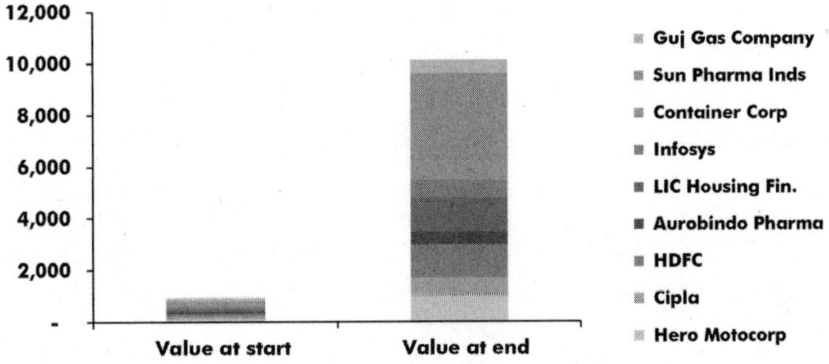

Source: Bloomberg, Ambit Capital

Note: Value at start denotes an equal allocation of Rs 100 in each stock at the start of the period. Value at end is the value of each stock at the end of the period. Thus, for this period, the value of the portfolio rose from Rs 900 at the start to Rs 10,117 at the end.

**Total Shareholder Return (TSR) and Sensex TSR include dividends received and reinvested.*

Complete portfolio (Period 5): 2004–14 (12.9 per cent alpha to the Sensex; 32.7 per cent per annum absolute returns)

All-cap portfolio stocks: Infosys, Hero MotoCorp, Cipla, Container Corporation of India, Gujarat Gas, Alok Industries, Munjal Showa, Havells India, HDFC Ltd and LIC Housing Finance

Large-cap portfolio stocks: Infosys, Hero MotoCorp, Cipla, Container Corporation of India and HDFC

The fifth iteration of our Coffee Can Portfolio yielded a whopping 12.9 per cent alpha over the Sensex. The portfolio was equally divided between large-caps and mid-caps/small-caps. The higher share of the mid-caps/small-caps vs earlier iterations was instrumental in delivering higher alpha during this period.

Exhibit 102: Summary of the fifth iteration

2004–14*	All-cap CCP	Large-cap CCP	Sensex
CAGR returns	32.7%	22.0%	19.7%
Maximum drawdown**	-64.0%	-38.3%	-60.3%
Excess returns* **	0.39	0.37	0.19

Source: Bloomberg, Ambit Capital

*Note: *Portfolio kicks off on 1 July 2004.*

****Excess returns have been calculated as returns in excess of risk-free rate (assumed to be 8 per cent) divided by absolute maximum drawdown. Maximum drawdown is defined as the maximum drop in cumulative returns from the highest peak to the lowest subsequent trough.*

***Maximum drawdown from Jan'08 to Dec'08 for the all-cap CCP, Jan'08 to Nov'08 for the large-cap CCP and Jan'08 to Mar'09 for the Sensex.*

The price performance among mid-cap/small-cap stocks was extreme: Havells' stock price rose eighty-nine times whilst Alok Industries' stock price fell significantly by the end of the iteration. As a result, the price performance of the large-cap CCP (22 per cent CAGR) lagged that of the all-cap CCP (32.7 per cent CAGR).

Exhibit 103: Portfolio performance of CCP 2004

Stock	Total Shareholder Return (TSR)* CAGR	PAT CAGR FY 2004–14	Contribution to portfolio value at start	Contribution to portfolio value at end
			01/07/2004	**30/06/2014**
Hero MotoCorp	21.7%	11.2%	10%	4%
Cipla	18.8%	16.7%	10%	3%
HDFC Ltd	27.1%	23.7%	10%	7%
Alok Industries	-8.7%	16.2%	10%	0%
Munjal Showa	20.1%	12.7%	10%	4%
Havells India	58.2%	35.8%	10%	58%
LIC Housing Finance	31.5%	22.8%	10%	9%
Infosys	18.3%	23.9%	10%	3%
Container Corporation	22.4%	9.9%	10%	4%
Gujarat Gas Company	28.4%	17.0%	10%	7%
Total Portfolio	**32.7%**		**100%**	**100%**
Sensex TSR*	**19.7%**			

Source: Bloomberg, Ambit Capital

Note: Value at start denotes an equal allocation of Rs 100 in each stock at the start of the period. Value at end is the value of each stock at the end of the period. Thus, for this period, the value of the portfolio rose from Rs 1000 at the start to Rs 16,880 at the end.

**Total Shareholder Return (TSR) and Sensex TSR include dividends received and reinvested.*

Exhibit 104: Havells was the star performer of CCP 2004

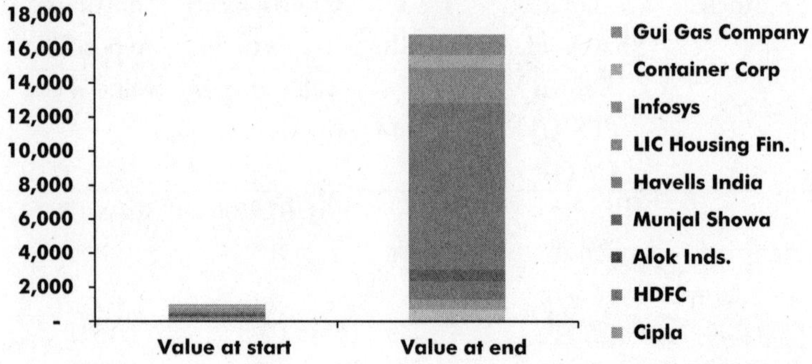

Source: Bloomberg, Ambit Capital

Note: Value at start denotes an equal allocation of Rs 100 in each stock at the start of the period. Value at end is the value of each stock at the end of the period. Thus, for this period, the value of the portfolio rose from Rs 1000 at the start to Rs 16,880 at the end. Total Shareholder Return (TSR) and Sensex TSR include dividends received and reinvested.

Complete portfolio (Period 6): 2005–15 (6.0% alpha to the Sensex; 22.2% per annum absolute returns)

All-cap portfolio stocks: Infosys, Hero MotoCorp, Cipla, Container Corporation of India, Geometric, Havells India, Ind-Swift, Munjal Showa and HDFC Ltd

Large-cap portfolio stocks: Infosys, Hero MotoCorp, Cipla, Container Corporation of India and HDFC Ltd

In the sixth iteration, our Coffee Can Portfolio again outperformed the Sensex with an alpha of 6 per cent. The large-cap version also outperformed the Sensex with an alpha of 3.4 per cent. In this period, while the all-cap version generated a higher alpha than the large-cap version on an absolute basis, on a risk-adjusted basis the large-cap version beat the all-cap version mainly on account of lower maximum drawdown (excess return of 0.32 times for large-cap versus 0.25 times for all-cap). Both versions, however, continued to perform better than Sensex on a risk-adjusted basis as well.

Exhibit 105: Summary of the sixth iteration

2005–15*	All-cap CCP	Large-cap CCP	Sensex
CAGR returns	22.2%	19.5%	16.1%
Maximum drawdown**	-56.3%	-36.2%	-60.3%
Excess returns***	0.25	0.32	0.13

Source: Bloomberg, Ambit Capital

*Note: *Portfolio kicks off on 1 July 2005.*

****Excess returns have been calculated as returns in excess of risk-free rate (assumed to be 8 per cent) divided by absolute maximum drawdown. Maximum drawdown is defined as the maximum drop in cumulative returns from the highest peak to the lowest subsequent trough.*

***Maximum drawdown from Jan'08 to Nov'08 for the all-cap CCP, Jan'08 to Nov'08 for the large-cap CCP and Jan'08 to Mar'09 for the Sensex.*

The extreme price performance among mid-cap/small-cap stocks continued during this iteration as well; Havells' stock price rose twenty-eight times whilst Ind-Swift's stock price fell almost 92 per cent by the end of the iteration.

Exhibit 106: Portfolio performance of CCP 2005

Stock	Total Shareholder Return (TSR)* CAGR	PAT CAGR FY 2005–2015	Contribution to portfolio value at start	Contribution to portfolio value at end
			01/07/2005	30/06/2015
Hero MotoCorp	19.7%	11.3%	11%	9%
Cipla	17.9%	11.2%	11%	8%
HDFC Ltd	23.8%	22.7%	11%	13%
Munjal Showa	14.5%	25.4%	11%	6%
Havells India	41.3%	28.9%	11%	48%
Geometric	1.8%	7.2%	11%	2%
Infosys	14.7%	20.6%	11%	6%
Container Corporation	19.8%	9.4%	11%	9%
Ind-Swift	-22.1%	#NUM	11%	0%
Portfolio Value	**22.2%**		**100%**	**100%**
Sensex TSR*	**16.1%**			

Source: Bloomberg, Ambit Capital

Note: Value at start denotes an equal allocation of Rs 100 in each stock at the start of the period. Value at end is the value of each stock at the end of the period. Thus, for this period, the value of the portfolio rose from Rs 900 at the start to Rs 6659 at the end.

**Total Shareholder Return (TSR) and Sensex TSR include dividends received and reinvested. #NUM = Not quantifiable since earnings became negative towards the end of the portfolio holding period.*

Exhibit 107: Havells India was the star performer of CCP 2005 too

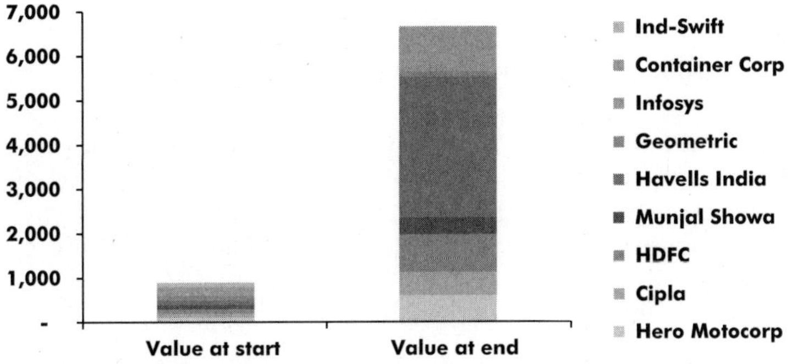

Source: Bloomberg, Ambit Capital

Note: Value at start denotes an equal allocation of Rs 100 in each stock at the start of the period. Value at end is the value of each stock at the end of the period. Thus, for this period, the value of the portfolio rose from Rs 900 at the start to Rs 6659 at the end. Total Shareholder Return (TSR) and Sensex TSR include dividends received and reinvested.

Complete portfolio (Period 7): 2006–16 (9.0 per cent alpha to the Sensex; 20.4 per cent per annum absolute returns)

All-cap portfolio stocks: Infosys, Cipla, Hero MotoCorp, Container Corporation of India, Geometric, Havells India, Suprajit Engineering, Munjal Showa, HDFC Ltd and HDFC Bank

Large-cap portfolio stocks: Infosys, Hero MotoCorp, Cipla, Container Corporation of India, HDFC Ltd and HDFC Bank

In the seventh iteration our Coffee Can Portfolio again outperformed the Sensex with an alpha of 9 per cent. The large-cap version also outperformed the Sensex with an alpha of 5.7 per cent. On a risk-adjusted basis too, both versions beat the Sensex with excess return of 0.23–0.24 times as against 0.06 times for the Sensex.

Exhibit 108: Summary of the seventh iteration

2006–16*	**All-cap CCP**	**Large-cap CCP**	**Sensex**
CAGR returns	20.4%	17.1%	11.4%
Maximum drawdown**	-52.3%	-40.5%	-60.3%
Excess returns* **	0.24	0.23	0.06

Source: Bloomberg, Ambit Capital

*Note: *Portfolio kicks off on 1 July 2006.*

****Excess returns have been calculated as returns in excess of risk-free rate (assumed to be 8 per cent) divided by absolute maximum drawdown. Maximum drawdown is defined as the maximum drop in cumulative returns from the highest peak to the lowest subsequent trough.*

***Maximum drawdown from Jan'08 to Nov'09 for the all-cap CCP, Jan'08 to Nov'08 for the large-cap CCP and Jan'08 to Mar'09 for the Sensex.*

Mid-cap/small-cap stocks again outperformed in this period with Havells and Suprajit Engineering's stock prices rising by eleven and seven times respectively.

Exhibit 109: Portfolio performance of CCP 2006

Stock	Total Shareholder Return (TSR)* CAGR	PAT CAGR FY 2006–16	Contribution to portfolio value at start	Contribution to portfolio value at end
			01/07/2006	**30/06/2016**
Hero MotoCorp	18.6%	12.4%	10%	9%
Cipla	9.5%	8.4%	10%	4%
HDFC Ltd	20.0%	22.4%	10%	10%
Munjal Showa	15.7%	11.7%	10%	7%
Havells India	30.6%	35.3%	10%	23%
Geometric	11.4%	15.1%	10%	5%
Infosys	13.7%	18.5%	10%	6%
Container Corporation	13.1%	6.3%	10%	5%
Suprajit Engineering	29.1%	30.1%	10%	20%
HDFC Bank	23.0%	30.7%	10%	12%
Total Portfolio	**20.4%**		**100%**	**100%**
Sensex TSR	**11.4%**			

Source: Bloomberg, Ambit Capital

Note: Value at start denotes an equal allocation of Rs 100 in each stock at the start of the period. Value at end is the value of each stock at the end of the period. Thus, for this period, the value of the portfolio rose from Rs 1000 at the start to Rs 6376 at the end.

**Total Shareholder Return (TSR) and Sensex TSR include dividends received and reinvested.*

Exhibit 110: Mid-caps continued their outperformance in CCP 2006

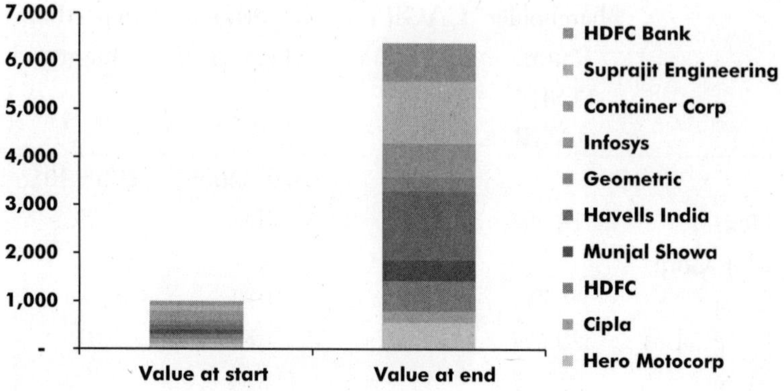

Source: Bloomberg, Ambit Capital research

Note: Value at start denotes an equal allocation of Rs 100 in each stock at the start of the period. Value at end is the value of each stock at the end of the period. Thus, for this period, the value of the portfolio rose from Rs 1000 at the start to Rs 6376 at the end. Total Shareholder Return (TSR) and Sensex TSR include dividends received and reinvested.

Complete portfolio (Period 8): 2007–17 (10.4 per cent alpha to the Sensex; 19.7 per cent per annum absolute returns)

All-cap portfolio stocks: Infosys, Wipro, Cipla, Tech Mahindra, Hindalco, Hero MotoCorp, Container Corporation of India, Asian Paints, Havells India, Geometric, Aftek, Munjal Showa, Suprajit Engineering, HDFC Ltd and HDFC Bank

Large-cap portfolio stocks: Infosys, Wipro, Cipla, Tech Mahindra, Hindalco, Hero MotoCorp, Container Corporation of India, Asian Paints, HDFC Ltd and HDFC Bank

In the eighth iteration, our Coffee Can Portfolio continued its outperformance versus the Sensex on both absolute as well as risk-adjusted basis. The large-cap CCP matched the all-cap CCP on a risk-adjusted basis (0.21 times for both portfolios).

Exhibit 111: Summary of the eighth iteration

2007–17*	All-cap CCP	Large-cap CCP	Sensex
CAGR returns	19.7%	16.7%	9.3%
Maximum drawdown**	-54.3%	-42.1%	-60.3%
Excess returns* **	0.21	0.21	0.02

Source: Bloomberg, Ambit Capital

*Note: *Portfolio kicks off on 1 July 2007.*

****Excess returns have been calculated as returns in excess of risk-free rate (assumed to be 8 per cent) divided by absolute maximum drawdown. Maximum drawdown is defined as the maximum drop in cumulative returns from the highest peak to the lowest subsequent trough.*

***Maximum drawdown from Jan'08 to Mar'09 for the all-cap CCP, Jan'08 to Mar'09 for the large-cap CCP and Jan'08 to Mar'09 for the Sensex.*

In this iteration, large-caps led the charge with Asian Paints being the star performer with a jump in stock price of almost fifteen times. Extreme movements were seen in mid-cap stocks again with stocks like Suprajit Engineering rising almost twenty-five times whereas Aftek lost 97 per cent of its value before suspension in May 2015.

Exhibit 112: Portfolio performance of CCP 2007

Stock	Total Shareholder Return (TSR)* CAGR	PAT CAGR FY 2007–17	Contribution to portfolio value at start	Contribution to portfolio value at end
			01/07/2007	30/06/2017
Hero MotoCorp	22.1%	15.4%	7%	8%
Cipla	11.0%	4.2%	7%	3%

(*Cont.*)

Stock	Total Shareholder Return (TSR)* CAGR	PAT CAGR FY 2007–17	Contribution to portfolio value at start	Contribution to portfolio value at end
HDFC Ltd	16.2%	20.3%	7%	5%
Munjal Showa	18.9%	8.1%	7%	6%
Havells India	26.6%	17.1%	7%	12%
Geometric	9.4%	DNA	7%	3%
Infosys	8.9%	14.0%	7%	3%
Container Corporation	7.8%	2.0%	7%	2%
Suprajit Engineering	37.8%	26.7%	7%	27%
HDFC Bank	22.7%	29.5%	7%	9%
Wipro	7.8%	11.2%	7%	2%
Tech Mahindra	1.8%	36.9%	7%	1%
Hindalco	3.8%	-3.1%	7%	2%
Asian Paints	31.3%	21.3%	7%	17%
Aftek	-29.7%	DNA	7%	0%
Total Portfolio	**19.7%**		**100%**	**100%**
Sensex TSR*	**9.3%**			

Source: Bloomberg, Ambit Capital

Note: Value at start denotes an equal allocation of Rs 100 in each stock at the start of the period. Value at end is the value of each stock at the end of the period. Thus, for this period, the value of the portfolio rose from Rs 1500 at the start to Rs 9030 at the end.

**Total Shareholder Return (TSR) and Sensex TSR include dividends received and reinvested. DNA = Data not available.*

Exhibit 113: Suprajit Engineering and Asian Paints were the star performers of CCP 2007

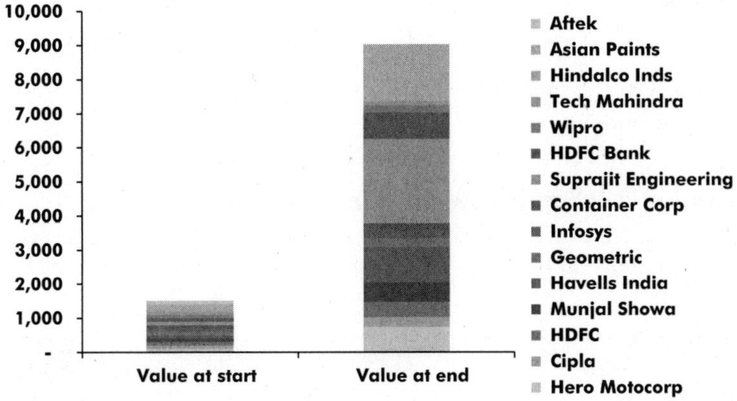

Source: Bloomberg, Ambit Capital

Note: Value at start denotes an equal allocation of Rs 100 in each stock at the start of the period. Value at end is the value of each stock at the end of the period. Thus, for this period, the value of the portfolio rose from Rs 1500 at the start to Rs 9030 at the end. Total Shareholder Return (TSR) and Sensex TSR include dividends received and reinvested.

Incomplete portfolio (Period 9): 2008–Present (10 per cent alpha to the Sensex; 21.8 per cent per annum absolute returns)

All-cap portfolio stocks: Infosys, Wipro, Cipla, Asian Paints, Tech Mahindra, Havells India, Automotive Axles, Geometric, HDFC Ltd, HDFC Bank and Punjab National Bank

Large-cap portfolio stocks: Infosys, Wipro, Cipla, Asian Paints, Tech Mahindra, HDFC Ltd, HDFC Bank and Punjab National Bank

The ninth iteration of the CCP that began life in July 2008 has so far 'outperformed' the Sensex with an alpha of 10 per cent. The large-cap version also beat the Sensex with an alpha of 7.1 per cent. The large-cap version, on account of lower drawdown, saw a risk-adjusted return of 0.25 times as compared to 0.26 times for the all-cap version and 0.01 times for the Sensex.

Exhibit 114: Summary of the ninth iteration

2008–17*	All-cap CCP	Large-cap CCP	Sensex
CAGR returns	21.8%	18.9%	11.8%
Maximum drawdown**	-52.6%	-43.4%	-47.1%
Excess returns* **	0.26	0.25	0.08

Source: Bloomberg, Ambit Capital

*Note: *Portfolio kicks off on 1 July 2008.*

****Excess returns have been calculated as returns in excess of risk-free rate (assumed to be 8 per cent) divided by absolute maximum drawdown. Maximum drawdown is defined as the maximum drop in cumulative returns from the highest peak to the lowest subsequent trough.*

***Maximum drawdown from August'08 to Mar'09 for the all-cap CCP, August'08 to Mar'09 for the large-cap CCP and August'08 to Mar'09 for the Sensex.*

Both large-caps and mid-caps shared the outperformance during this iteration with Asian Paints and HDFC Bank's stock prices rising 31 per cent and 28 per cent respectively on an annualized basis whilst Havells India continued its strong run with a 36 per cent annualized return.

Exhibit 115: Portfolio performance of CCP 2008

Stock	Total Shareholder Return (TSR)* CAGR	PAT CAGR FY 2008–17	Contribution to portfolio value at start	Contribution to portfolio value at end
			01/07/2008	**30/06/2017**
Cipla	12.3%	4.1%	9%	4%
HDFC Ltd	19.3%	16.9%	9%	8%
Havells India	35.7%	13.2%	9%	24%
Geometric	24.2%	DNA	9%	11%
Infosys	11.2%	13.3%	9%	4%
Punjab National Bank	9.9%	-13.2%	9%	4%
Automotive Axles	16.5%	-1.5%	9%	6%
HDFC Bank	27.9%	28.5%	9%	14%
Wipro	11.3%	11.1%	9%	4%
Tech Mahindra	10.2%	26.9%	9%	4%
Asian Paints	30.8%	18.9%	9%	17%
Portfolio Value	**21.8%**		**100%**	**100%**
Sensex TSR*	**11.8%**			

Source: Bloomberg, Ambit Capital

Note: Value at start denotes an equal allocation of Rs 100 in each stock at the start of the period. Value at end is the value of each stock at the end of the period. Thus, for this period, the value of the portfolio rose from Rs 1100 to Rs 6471.

**Total Shareholder Return (TSR) and Sensex TSR include dividends received and reinvested. DNA = Data not available.*

Exhibit 116: Large-caps and mid-caps both outperformed in CCP 2008

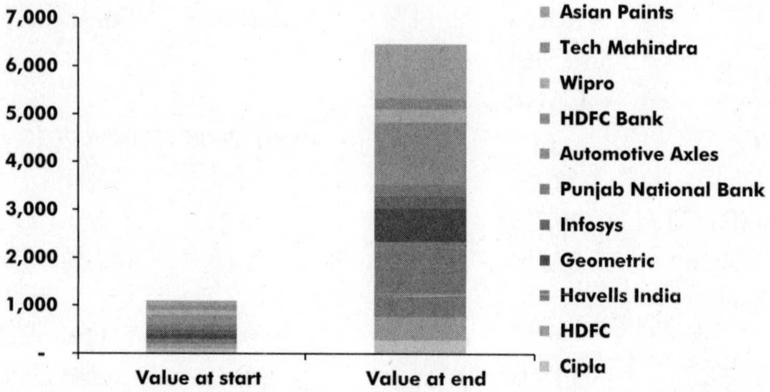

Source: Bloomberg, Ambit Capital

Note: Value at start denotes an equal allocation of Rs 100 in each stock at the start of the period. Value at end is the value of each stock at the end of the period. Thus, for this period, the value of the portfolio rose from Rs 1100 at the start to Rs 6471 at the end. Total Shareholder Return (TSR) and Sensex TSR include dividends received and reinvested.

Incomplete portfolio (Period 10): 2009–Present (11.2 per cent alpha to the Sensex; 22.7 per cent per annum absolute returns)

All-cap portfolio stocks: Infosys, Wipro, Jindal Steel, Cipla, Asian Paints, Oracle Financial Services, Tech Mahindra, Motherson Sumi, HDFC Ltd, HDFC Bank and Punjab National Bank

Large-cap portfolio stocks: Infosys, Wipro, Jindal Steel, Cipla, Asian Paints, Oracle Financial Services, HDFC Ltd, HDFC Bank and Punjab National Bank

In the iteration beginning 2009, the all-cap and large-cap CCP again beat the Sensex comprehensively with alphas of

11.2 per cent and 6 per cent respectively. On a risk-adjusted basis too, they gave a stable performance with excess returns of 0.49–0.55 times.

Exhibit 117: Summary of the tenth iteration

2009–17*	All-cap CCP	Large-cap CCP	Sensex
CAGR returns	22.7%	17.5%	11.5%
Maximum drawdown**	-26.5%	-19.4%	-26.7%
Excess returns* **	0.55	0.49	0.13

Source: Bloomberg, Ambit Capital

*Note: *Portfolio kicks off on 1 July 2009.*

****Excess returns have been calculated as returns in excess of risk-free rate (assumed to be 8 per cent) divided by absolute maximum drawdown. Maximum drawdown is defined as the maximum drop in cumulative returns from the highest peak to the lowest subsequent trough.*

***Maximum drawdown from August'15 to Feb'16 for the all-cap CCP, Jan'11 to Oct'11 large-cap CCP and Nov'10 to Dec'11 for the Sensex.*

Motherson Sumi was the star performer in this iteration with its stock price rising twenty-two times.

Exhibit 118: Portfolio performance of CCP 2009

Stock	Total Shareholder Return (TSR)* CAGR	PAT CAGR FY 2009–17	Contribution to portfolio value at start	Contribution to portfolio value at end
			01/07/2009	30/06/2017
Cipla	11.4%	3.4%	9%	4%
HDFC Ltd	18.3%	21.6%	9%	7%

(*Cont.*)

Stock	Total Shareholder Return (TSR)* CAGR	PAT CAGR FY 2009–17	Contribution to portfolio value at start	Contribution to portfolio value at end
Jindal Steel	-13.9%	#NUM	9%	1%
Motherson Sumi	47%	31.3%	9%	38%
Oracle Financial Services	18%	6.1%	9%	7%
Infosys	11.8%	11.5%	9%	4%
Punjab National Bank	1.9%	-18.6%	9%	2%
HDFC Bank	24.7%	27.0%	9%	10%
Wipro	13.9%	10.2%	9%	5%
Tech Mahindra	10.2%	13.6%	9%	4%
Asian Paints	33.5%	21.9%	9%	18%
Portfolio Value	**22.7%**		**100%**	**100%**
Sensex TSR*	**11.5%**			

Source: Bloomberg, Ambit Capital

Note: Value at start denotes an equal allocation of Rs 100 in each stock at the start of the period. Value at end is the value of each stock at the end of the period. Thus, for this period, the value of the portfolio rose from Rs 1100 at the start to Rs 5657 at the end.

**Total Shareholder Return (TSR) and Sensex TSR include dividends received and reinvested. #NUM = Not quantifiable as earnings became negative towards the end of the portfolio holding period.*

Exhibit 119: Motherson Sumi was the star performer of CCP 2009

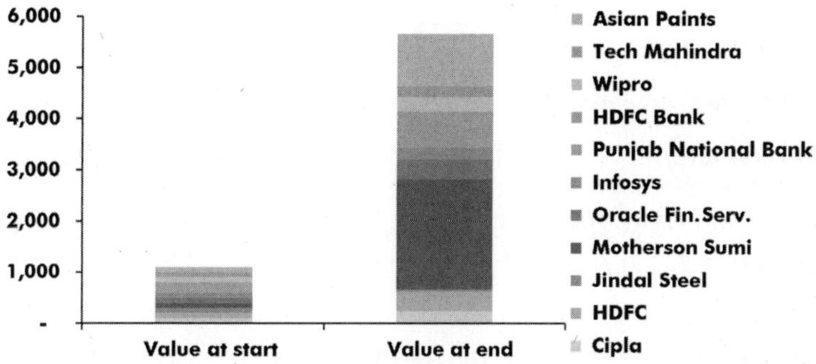

Source: Bloomberg, Ambit Capital

Note: Value at start denotes an equal allocation of Rs 100 in each stock at the start of the period. Value at end is the value of each stock at the end of the period. Thus, for this period, the value of the portfolio rose from Rs 1100 at the start to Rs 5657 at the end. Total Shareholder Return (TSR) and Sensex TSR include dividends received and reinvested.

Incomplete portfolio (Period 11): 2010–Present (10.7 per cent alpha to the Sensex; 20.8 per cent per annum absolute returns)

All-cap portfolio stocks: Asian Paints, Amar Remedies, Motherson Sumi, Tulip Telecom, HDFC Bank, Punjab National Bank and Dewan Housing Finance

Large-cap portfolio stocks: Asian Paints, HDFC Bank and Punjab National Bank

In this iteration, our Coffee Can Portfolio outperformed the Sensex with an alpha of 10.7 per cent. The large-cap version beat the Sensex in this iteration with an outperformance of 9.3 per cent.

Exhibit 120: Summary of the eleventh iteration

2010–17*	All-cap CCP	Large-cap CCP	Sensex
CAGR returns	20.8%	19.5%	10.1%
Maximum drawdown**	-33.0%	-24.3%	-26.7%
Excess returns***	0.39	0.47	0.08

Source: Bloomberg, Ambit Capital

*Note: *Portfolio kicks off on 1 July 2010.*

****Excess returns have been calculated as returns in excess of risk-free rate (assumed to be 8 per cent) divided by absolute maximum drawdown. Maximum drawdown is defined as the maximum drop in cumulative returns from the highest peak to the lowest subsequent trough.*

***Maximum drawdown from August'15 to Feb'16 for the all-cap CCP, May'13 to Sept'13 for the large-cap CCP and Nov'10 to Dec'11 for the Sensex.*

The performance of the portfolio in this iteration was led by Motherson Sumi and Asian Paints in this iteration. In spite of suspension of trading in two of the constituent stocks through the period (Amar Remedies and Tulip Telecom), the portfolio gave a stellar performance with a 20.8 per cent CAGR.

Exhibit 121: Portfolio performance of CCP 2009

Stock	Total Shareholder Return (TSR)* CAGR	PAT CAGR FY 2010–17	Contribution to portfolio value at start	Contribution to portfolio value at end
			01/07/2010	30/06/2017
Dewan Housing Finance	23.8%	50.7%	14%	17%

(*Cont.*)

Stock	Total Shareholder Return (TSR)* CAGR	PAT CAGR FY 2010–17	Contribution to portfolio value at start	Contribution to portfolio value at end
Motherson Sumi	41.5%	30.4%	14%	43%
Punjab National Bank	-3.6%	-23.4%	14%	3%
HDFC Bank	24.2%	26.1%	14%	17%
Asian Paints	26.1%	12.8%	14%	19%
Amar Remedies	-29.9%	DNA	14%	0%
Tulip Telecom	-48.9%	DNA	14%	0%
Portfolio Value	**20.8%**		**100%**	**100%**
Sensex TSR*	**10.1%**			

Source: Bloomberg, Ambit Capital

Note: Value at start denotes an equal allocation of Rs 100 in each stock at the start of the period. Value at end is the value of each stock at the end of the period. Thus, for this period, the value of the portfolio rose from Rs 700 at the start to Rs 2630 at the end.

**Total Shareholder Return (TSR) and Sensex TSR include dividends received and reinvested. DNA = Data not available.*

Exhibit 122: Motherson Sumi was the star performer of CCP 2010 as well

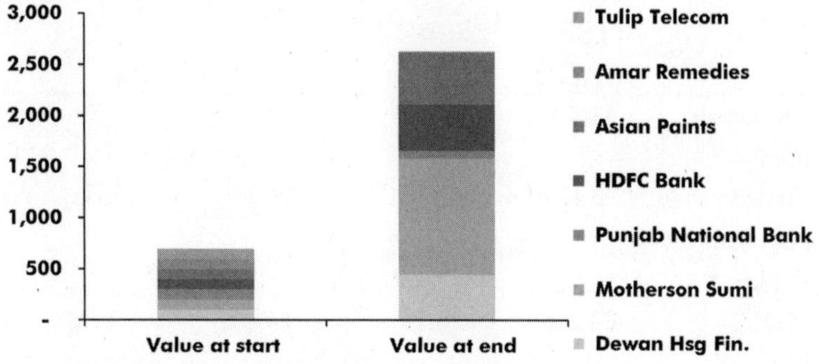

Source: Bloomberg, Ambit Capital

Note: Value at start denotes an equal allocation of Rs 100 in each stock at the start of the period. Value at end is the value of each stock at the end of the period. Thus, for this period, the value of the portfolio rose from Rs 700 at the start to Rs 2630 at the end. Total Shareholder Return (TSR) and Sensex TSR include dividends received and reinvested.

Incomplete portfolio (Period 12): 2011–Present (3.9 per cent alpha to the Sensex; 14.2 per cent per annum absolute returns)

All-cap portfolio stocks: ITC, Asian Paints, Motherson Sumi, Ipca, Tulip Telecom, Zylog Systems, Pratibha industries, Unity Infra, Amar Remedies, Setco Automotive, HDFC Bank, Punjab National Bank, Dewan Housing and City Union Bank

Large-cap portfolio stocks: ITC, Asian Paints, HDFC Bank and Punjab National Bank

Amongst all the Coffee Can Portfolios, this iteration gave the weakest result in terms of absolute performance. The large-cap version outperformed in this iteration by beating both the all-cap version and the Sensex on absolute as well as risk-adjusted basis.

Exhibit 123: Summary of the twelfth iteration

2011–17*	All-cap CCP	Large-cap CCP	Sensex
CAGR returns	14.2%	17.2%	10.3%
Maximum drawdown**	-30.2%	-21.8%	-21.6%
Excess returns***	0.21	0.42	0.11

Source: Bloomberg, Ambit Capital

*Note: *Portfolio kicks off on 1 July 2011.*

****Excess returns have been calculated as returns in excess of risk-free rate (assumed to be 8 per cent) divided by absolute maximum drawdown. Maximum drawdown is defined as the maximum drop in cumulative returns from the highest peak to the lowest subsequent trough.*

***Maximum drawdown from August'15 to Feb'16 for the all-cap CCP, May'13 to Aug'13 for the large-cap CCP and Jan'15 to Feb'16 for the Sensex.*

Extreme price performance among mid-cap/small-cap stocks was seen during this iteration. Motherson Sumi's stock price rose seven times during this period whilst Zylog Systems lost 98 per cent of its value.

Exhibit 124: Portfolio performance of CCP 2011

Stock	Total Shareholder Return (TSR)* CAGR	PAT CAGR FY 2011–17	Contribution to portfolio value at start	Contribution to portfolio value at end
			01/07/2011	30/06/2017
Dewan Housing Finance	28.8%	42.9%	7%	15%
Motherson Sumi	39.7%	25.9%	7%	24%
City Union Bank	30.7%	25.9%	7%	16%

(*Cont.*)

Stock	Total Shareholder Return (TSR)* CAGR	PAT CAGR FY 2011–17	Contribution to portfolio value at start	Contribution to portfolio value at end
Pratibha Industries	-25.7%	#NUM	7%	1%
ITC	17.9%	12.7%	7%	9%
Ipca Laboratories	6.9%	-4.9%	7%	5%
Punjab National Bank	-5.8%	-28.4%	7%	2%
Setco Automotive	11.5%	#NUM	7%	6%
Unity Infrastructure	-30.7%	#NUM	7%	0%
Zylog Systems	-47.7%	-52.5%	7%	0%
HDFC Bank	23.0%	25.0%	7%	11%
Asian Paints	23.3%	14.9%	7%	11%
Amar Remedies	-36.9%	DNA	7%	0%
Tulip Telecom	-53.5%	DNA	7%	0%
Portfolio Value	**14.2%**		**100%**	**100%**
Sensex TSR*	**10.3%**			

Source: Bloomberg, Ambit Capital

Note: Value at start denotes an equal allocation of Rs 100 in each stock at the start of the period. Value at end is the value of each stock at the end of the period. Thus, for this period, the value of the portfolio rose from Rs 1400 to Rs 3112.

**Total Shareholder Return (TSR) and Sensex TSR include dividends received and reinvested. #NUM = Not quantifiable since earnings became negative towards the end of the portfolio holding period. DNA =Data not available.*

Exhibit 125: Extreme price performance was seen in mid/small caps in CCP 2011

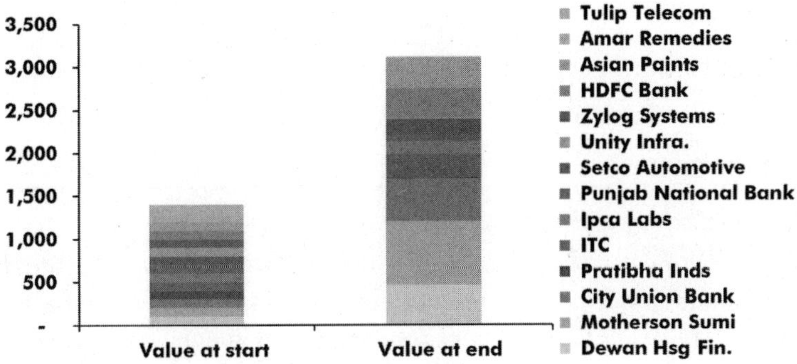

Source: Bloomberg, Ambit Capital research

Note: Value at start denotes an equal allocation of Rs 100 in each stock at the start of the period. Value at end is the value of each stock at the end of the period. Thus, for this period, the value of the portfolio rose from Rs 1400 at the start to Rs 3112 at the end. Total Shareholder Return (TSR) and Sensex TSR include dividends received and reinvested.

Incomplete portfolio (Period 13): 2012–Present (10.9 per cent alpha to the Sensex; 24.8 per cent per annum absolute returns)

All-cap portfolio stocks: ITC, Asian Paints, Marico, Opto Circuits, Ipca Labs, Berger paints, Page Industries, Balkrishna Industries, Grindwell Norton, Zylog Systems, Tecpro Systems, Pratibha Industries, Astral Poly Technik, Amar Remedies, Unity Infra, Setco Automotive, HDFC Bank, Axis Bank, Punjab National Bank, Allahabad Bank, Dewan Housing and City Union Bank

Large-cap portfolio stocks: ITC, Asian Paints, HDFC Bank, Axis Bank and Punjab National Bank

The all-cap version again came to the fore, beating the Sensex by 4.6 per cent.

Exhibit 126: Summary of the thirteenth iteration

2012–17*	All-cap CCP	Large-cap CCP	Sensex
CAGR returns	24.8%	18.4%	13.9%
Maximum drawdown**	-23.3%	-28.8%	-21.6%
Excess returns	0.72	0.36	0.27

Source: Bloomberg, Ambit Capital
*Note: *Portfolio kicks off on 1 July 2012. Excess returns have been calculated as returns in excess of risk-free rate (assumed to be 8 per cent) divided by absolute maximum drawdown. Maximum drawdown is defined as the maximum drop in cumulative returns from the highest peak to the lowest subsequent trough.*
***Maximum drawdown from April'15 to Feb'16 for the all-cap CCP, May'13 to Sept'13 for the large-cap CCP and Jan'15 to Feb'16 for the Sensex.*

With twenty-two companies making the cut in this iteration, this was the biggest Coffee Can Portfolio in terms of number of constituent companies. Astral Poly Technik was the star performer in this iteration with an almost sixteen-time increase in the stock price. Zylog Systems and Tecpro Systems, on the other hand, lost almost their entire value with declines of 99 per cent and 98 per cent respectively.

Exhibit 127: Portfolio performance of CCP 2012

Stock	Total Shareholder Return (TSR)* CAGR	PAT CAGR FY 2012–17	Contribution to portfolio value at start	Contribution to portfolio value at end
			01/07/2012	30/06/2017
Dewan Housing Finance	43.3%	54.0%	5%	9%

(*Cont.*)

Stock	Total Shareholder Return (TSR)* CAGR	PAT CAGR FY 2012–17	Contribution to portfolio value at start	Contribution to portfolio value at end
Allahabad Bank	-13.0%	#NUM	5%	1%
Astral Poly	73.0%	29.6%	5%	23%
Balkrishna Inds	46.7%	21.7%	5%	10%
Berger Paints	39.2%	21.3%	5%	8%
Marico	30.0%	20.9%	5%	6%
Opto Circuits	-43.3%	#NUM	5%	0%
Page Industries	43.5%	24.2%	5%	9%
Grindwell Norton	28.4%	3.0%	5%	5%
Tecpro Systems	-54.6%	DNA	5%	0%
Axis Bank	21.6%	-1.3%	5%	4%
City Union Bank	33.4%	43.0%	5%	6%
Pratibha Industries	-28.0%	#NUM	5%	0%
ITC	15.5%	10.5%	5%	3%
Ipca Laboratories	6.9%	-6.8%	5%	2%
Punjab National Bank	-1.7%	-34.3%	5%	1%
Setco Automotive	7.3%	#NUM	5%	2%
Unity Infra.	-31.3%	#NUM	5%	0%

(*Cont.*)

Stock	Total Shareholder Return (TSR)* CAGR	PAT CAGR FY 2012–17	Contribution to portfolio value at start	Contribution to portfolio value at end
Zylog Systems	-58.1%	-61.8%	5%	0%
HDFC Bank	25.0%	23.8%	5%	5%
Asian Paints	24.3%	14.4%	5%	4%
Amar Remedies	-46.0%	DNA	5%	0%
Total Portfolio	**24.8%**		**100%**	**100%**
Sensex TSR*	**13.8%**			

Source: Bloomberg, Ambit Capital

Note: Value at start denotes an equal allocation of Rs 100 in each stock at the start of the period. Value at end is the value of each stock at the end of the period. Thus, for this period, the value of the portfolio rose from Rs 2200 at the start to Rs 6650 at the end.

**Total Shareholder Return (TSR) and Sensex TSR include dividends received and reinvested. #NUM = Not quantifiable since earnings became negative towards the end of the portfolio holding period. DNA = Data not available.*

Exhibit 128: Astral Poly Technik outperformed other stocks in CCP 2012

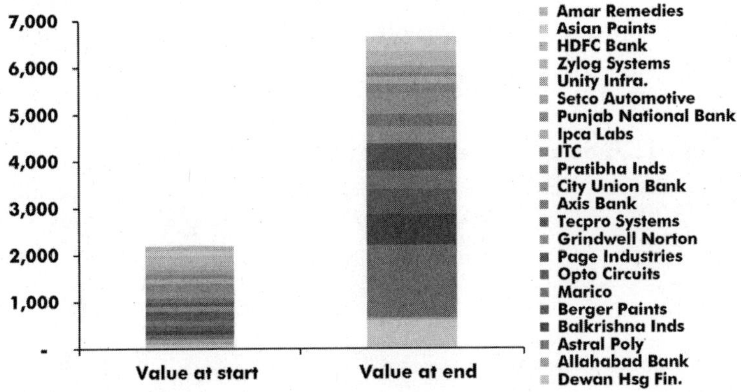

Source: Bloomberg, Ambit Capital research

Note: Value at start denotes an equal allocation of Rs 100 in each stock at the start of the period. Value at end is the value of each stock at the end of the period. Thus, for this period, the value of the portfolio rose from Rs 2200 at the start to Rs 6650 at the end. Total Shareholder Return (TSR) and Sensex TSR include dividends received and reinvested.

Incomplete portfolio (Period 14): 2013–Present (19.7 per cent alpha to the Sensex; 33.5 per cent per annum absolute returns)

All-cap portfolio stocks: ITC, HCL Technologies, Asian Paints, Marico, Berger Paints, Ipca, Page Industries, Balkrishna Industries, Solar Industries, Astral Poly Technik, Pratibha Industries, Unity Infra, Sarla Performance Fibers, HDFC Bank, Axis Bank, Indian Bank, City Union Bank and Dewan Housing

Large-cap portfolio stocks: ITC, HCL Tech, Asian Paints, Marico, HDFC Bank, Axis Bank

This iteration has given the best results thus far with a whopping return of 33.5 per cent on a compounded annualized basis. The Sensex generated a CAGR return of 13.7 per cent over the same period whereas the large-cap portfolio generated a CAGR return of 24.4 per cent.

Exhibit 129: Summary of the fourteenth iteration

2013–17*	All-cap CCP	Large-cap CCP	Sensex
CAGR returns	33.5%	24.4%	13.8%
Maximum drawdown**	-21.4%	-18%	-21.6%
Excess returns	1.19	0.91	0.27

Source: Bloomberg, Ambit Capital

*Note: *Portfolio kicks off on 1 July 2013. Excess returns have been calculated as returns in excess of risk-free rate (assumed to be 8 per cent) divided by absolute maximum drawdown. Maximum drawdown is defined as the maximum drop in cumulative returns from the highest peak to the lowest subsequent trough.*

***Maximum drawdown from August'15 to Feb'16 for the all-cap CCP, Sept'16 to Dec'16 for the large-cap CCP and Jan'15 to Feb'16 for the Sensex.*

Mid-cap stocks led the performance of the profile in this iteration with some of the stock prices rising almost four to eight times since the beginning of this portfolio in June 2013. These stocks included names like Astral Poly Technik, Solar Industries, Balkrishna Industries and Page Industries.

Exhibit 130: Portfolio performance of CCP 2013

Stock	Total Shareholder Return (TSR)* CAGR	PAT CAGR FY 2013–17	Contribution to portfolio value at start	Contribution to portfolio value at end
			01/07/2013	30/06/2017
Dewan Housing Finance	56.4%	57.8%	6%	10%
HCL Technologies	25.1%	20.8%	6%	4%
Astral Poly	57%	24.3%	6%	11%
Balkrishna Industries	69%	19.6%	6%	14%
Berger Paints	32.4%	21.3%	6%	5%
Marico	35.3%	19.2%	6%	6%
Indian Bank	27.2%	-2.5%	6%	5%
Page Industries	43.3%	24%	6%	7%
Axis Bank	18.9%	-6.8%	6%	4%
City Union Bank	35.3%	36.7%	6%	6%
Pratibha Industries	-24.9%	#NUM	6%	1%
ITC	12.6%	7.8%	6%	3%
Ipca Laboratories	-6.8%	-11.9%	6%	1%
Sarla Performance	36.1%	10.2%	6%	6%
Solar Industries	45.6%	12.4%	6%	8%
Unity Infra.	-28.9%	#NUM	6%	0%
HDFC Bank	26.3%	22.1%	6%	4%
Asian Paints	24.8%	14.9%	6%	4%

(*Cont.*)

Stock	Total Shareholder Return (TSR)* CAGR	PAT CAGR FY 2013–17	Contribution to portfolio value at start	Contribution to portfolio value at end
Total Portfolio	33.5%		100%	100%
Sensex TSR*	13.7%			

Source: Bloomberg, Ambit Capital

Note: Value at start denotes an equal allocation of Rs 100 in each stock at the start of the period. Value at end is the value of each stock at the end of the period. Thus, for this period, the value of the portfolio rose from Rs 1800 at the start to Rs 5709 at the end.

**Total Shareholder Return (TSR) and Sensex TSR include dividends received and reinvested. NUM = Not quantifiable since earnings became negative towards the end of the portfolio holding period.*

Exhibit 131: Mid-caps led the charge in CCP 2013 and generated most of the portfolio's value

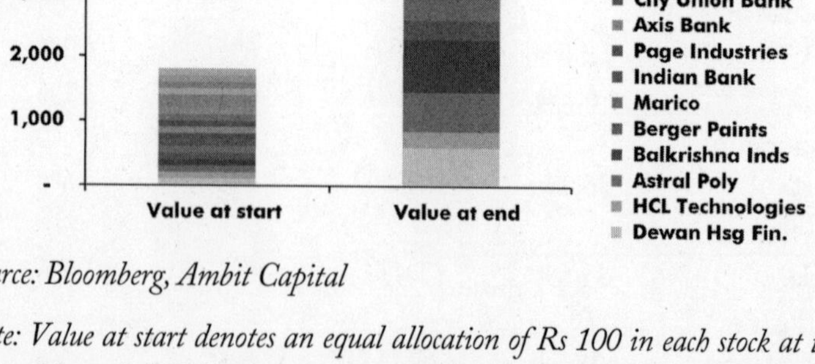

Source: Bloomberg, Ambit Capital

Note: Value at start denotes an equal allocation of Rs 100 in each stock at the start of the period. Value at end is the value of each stock at the end of the period. Thus, for this period, the value of the portfolio rose from Rs 1800 to Rs 5709. Total Shareholder Return (TSR) and Sensex TSR include dividends received and reinvested.

Incomplete portfolio (Period 15): 2014–Present (18.3 per cent alpha to the Sensex; 26.4 per cent absolute returns till date)

All-cap portfolio stocks: ITC, Asian Paints, Godrej Consumer, Marico, Ipca, Berger Paints, Page Industries, Balkrishna Industries, eClerx Services, Mayur Uniquoters, V-Guard Industries, HCL Tech, HDFC Bank, Axis Bank, City Union Bank and Gruh Finance

Large-cap portfolio stocks: ITC, Asian Paints, Godrej Consumer, Marico, HCL Tech, HDFC Bank and Axis Bank

The returns shown in the tables below denote the performance of the portfolio since 1 July 2014. This Coffee Can Portfolio outperformed the Sensex by a handsome margin of 18.3 per cent over this period.

Exhibit 132: Summary of the fifteenth iteration

2014–17*	All-cap CCP	Large-cap CCP	Sensex
CAGR returns	26.29%	23.6%	8.16%
Maximum drawdown**	-15.95%	-17.69%	-21.56%
Excess returns	1.15	0.88	0.01

Source: Bloomberg, Ambit Capital

*Note: *Portfolio kicks off on 1 July 2014. Excess returns have been calculated as returns in excess of risk-free rate (assumed to be 8 per cent) divided by absolute maximum drawdown. Maximum drawdown is defined as the maximum drop in cumulative returns from the highest peak to the lowest subsequent trough.*

***Maximum drawdown from Oct'16 to Dec'16 for the all-cap CCP, Sept'16 to Dec'16 for the large-cap CCP and Jan'15 to Feb'16 for the Sensex.*

The strong performance was led by V-Guard, which generated a CAGR return of 61 per cent during this period.

Exhibit 133: Portfolio performance of CCP 2014

Stock	Total Shareholder Return (TSR)* CAGR	PAT CAGR FY 2014–17	Contribution to portfolio value at start	Contribution to portfolio value at end
			01/07/2014	30/06/2017
Astral Poly	24.1%	22.4%	6%	6%
eClerx Services	16.7%	11.5%	6%	5%
Godrej Consumer	34.5%	19.7%	6%	7%
GRUH Finance	32%	18.8%	6%	7%
V-Guard Industries	61.3%	29.3%	6%	12%
Mayur Uniquoters	-1.1%	11.6%	6%	3%
HCL Technologies	7%	10.6%	6%	4%
Balkrishna Industries	32%	14.7%	6%	7%
Berger Paints	33.6%	23.8%	6%	7%
Marico	37.7%	18%	6%	8%
Page Industries	33.7%	20.1%	6%	7%
Axis Bank	11.1%	-14.4%	6%	4%
City Union Bank	34.2%	26.6%	6%	7%
ITC	16.5%	5%	6%	5%
Ipca Laboratories	-17.1%	-25.9%	6%	2%
HDFC Bank	27.1%	20.4%	6%	6%

(*Cont.*)

Stock	Total Shareholder Return (TSR)* CAGR	PAT CAGR FY 2014–17	Contribution to portfolio value at start	Contribution to portfolio value at end
Asian Paints	24.7%	16.7%	6%	6%
Portfolio Value	**26.3%**		**100%**	**100%**
Sensex TSR*	8.2%			

Source: Bloomberg, Ambit Capital research

Note: Value at start denotes an equal allocation of Rs 100 in each stock at the start of the period. Value at end is the value of each stock at the end of the period. Thus, for this period, the value of the portfolio rose from Rs 1600 to Rs 3233.

**Total Shareholder Return (TSR) and Sensex TSR include dividends received and reinvested.*

Exhibit 134: V-Guard Industries was the best performer of CCP 2014

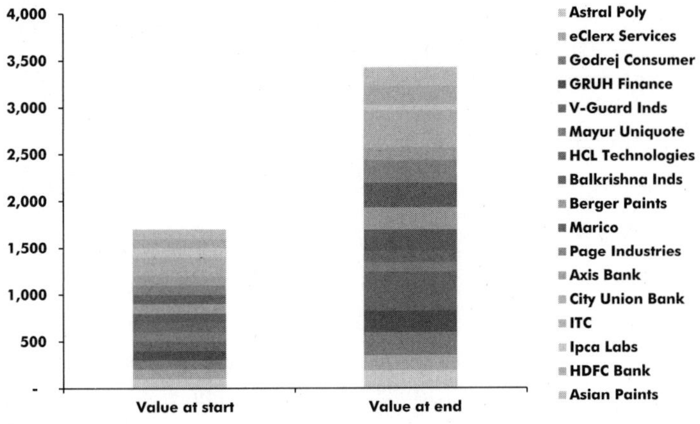

Source: Bloomberg, Ambit Capital

Note: Value at start denotes an equal allocation of Rs 100 in each stock at the start of the period. Value at end is the value of each stock at the end of the period. Thus, for this period, the value of the portfolio rose from Rs 1600 at the start to Rs 3233 at the end. Total Shareholder Return (TSR) and Sensex TSR include dividends received and reinvested.

Incomplete portfolio (Period 16): 2015–Present (11.2 per cent alpha to the Sensex; 17.7 per cent absolute returns to date)

All-cap portfolio stocks: ITC, HCL Tech, Lupin, Asian Paints, Cadila, Britannia, Marico, GSK Consumer, Colgate, Amara Raja, Page Industries, Berger Paints, eClerx Services, Astral, V-Guard, Cera Sanitaryware, HDFC Bank, Axis Bank, LIC HF, Gruh Finance

Large-cap portfolio stocks: ITC, HCL Tech, Lupin, Asian Paints, Cadila, Britannia, Marico, GSK Consumer, Colgate, HDFC Bank, Axis Bank, LIC HF

This Coffee Can portfolio outperformed the Sensex by a handsome margin of 11.2 per cent over this period.

Exhibit 135: Summary of the sixteenth iteration

2015–17*	All-cap CCP	Large-cap CCP	Sensex
CAGR returns	17.7%	11.9%	6.5%
Maximum drawdown**	-16.5%	-15.9%	-11.1%
Excess returns***	0.59	0.25	(0.13)

Source: Bloomberg, Ambit Capital

*Note: *Portfolio kicks off on 1 July 2015.*

****Excess returns have been calculated as returns in excess of risk-free rate (assumed to be 8 per cent) divided by absolute maximum drawdown. Maximum drawdown is defined as the maximum drop in cumulative returns from the highest peak to the lowest subsequent trough.*

***Maximum drawdown from Sept'16 to Dec'16 for the all-cap CCP, Sept'16 to Dec'08 for the large-cap CCP and Sept'16 to Nov'16 for the Sensex.*

The all-cap portfolio was able to outperform the Sensex and the large-cap portfolio on the back of strong performance of V-guard and Astral Poly, which generated CAGR of 65 per cent and 33 per cent respectively.

Exhibit 136: Portfolio performance of CCP 2015

Stock	Total Shareholder Return (TSR)* CAGR	PAT CAGR FY 2015–17	Contribution to portfolio value at start	Contribution to portfolio value at end
			01/07/2015	30/06/2017
eClerx Services	8.7%	24.1%	5%	4%
Astral Poly	32.9%	38.0%	5%	6%
GRUH Finance	31.6%	20.6%	5%	6%
V-Guard Industries	64.8%	46.4%	5%	10%
LIC Housing Finance	29.4%	17.9%	5%	6%
HCL Technologies	-2.4%	8.6%	5%	3%
Berger Paints	32.3%	33.7%	5%	6%
Marico	20.2%	18.0%	5%	5%
Page Industries	6.1%	16.5%	5%	4%
Axis Bank	-4.6%	-27.1%	5%	3%
Amara Raja Batteries	-2.0%	7.9%	5%	3%
Britannia Industries	16.9%	13.3%	5%	5%
Cadila Healthcare	21.3%	13.8%	5%	5%

(*Cont.*)

Stock	Total Shareholder Return (TSR)* CAGR	PAT CAGR FY 2015–17	Contribution to portfolio value at start	Contribution to portfolio value at end
GlaxoSmith Consumer Healthcare	-6.1%	6.1%	5%	3%
Colgate-Palmolive	5.1%	1.6%	5%	4%
Lupin	-24.5%	3.2%	5%	2%
Cera Sanitaryware	20.5%	19.9%	5%	5%
ITC	26.8%	3.2%	5%	6%
HDFC Bank	25.5%	19.4%	5%	6%
Asian Paints	21.4%	17.9%	5%	5%
Total Portfolio	**17.7%**		**100%**	**100%**
Sensex TSR*	**6.5%**			

Source: Bloomberg, Ambit Capital

Note: Value at start denotes an equal allocation of Rs 100 in each stock at the start of the period. Value at end is the value of each stock at the end of the period. Thus, for this period, the value of the portfolio rose from Rs 2000 at the start to Rs 2772 at the end.

**Total Shareholder Return (TSR) and Sensex TSR include dividend received and reinvested.*

Exhibit 137: V-Guard was the best performer of CCP 2015

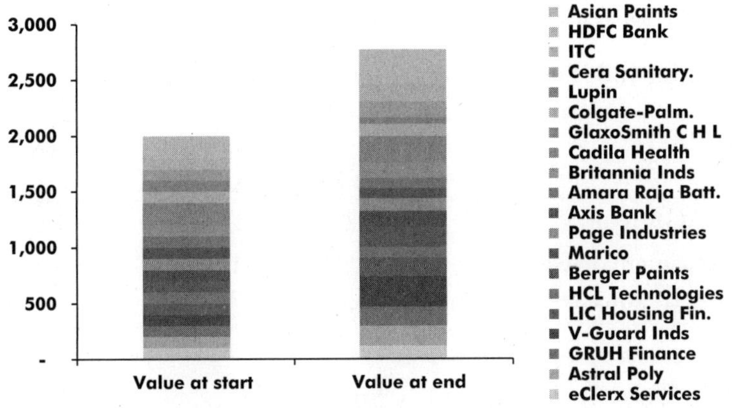

Source: Bloomberg, Ambit Capital

Note: Value at start denotes an equal allocation of Rs 100 in each stock at the start of the period. Value at end is the value of each stock at the end of the period. Thus, for this period, the value of the portfolio rose from Rs 2000 at the start to Rs 2772 at the end. Total Shareholder Return (TSR) and Sensex TSR include dividends received and reinvested.

Incomplete portfolio (Period 17): 2016–Present (2.8 per cent alpha to the Sensex; 18.1 per cent absolute returns till date)

All-cap portfolio stocks: HCL Tech, Lupin, Asian Paints, Cadila, Britannia, Amara Raja, Page Industries, eClerx Services, Astral, Cera Sanitaryware, HDFC Bank, Axis Bank, LIC HF, Gruh Finance, Relaxo Footwear, Repco Home Fin, Dr Lal PathLabs

Large-cap portfolio stocks: HCL Tech, Lupin, Asian Paints, Cadila, Britannia, HDFC Bank, Axis Bank, LIC HF

The CCP beginning 2016 has just completed a year, with both all-cap and large-cap CCPs beating the Sensex with alpha of 2.8 per cent and 7.3 per cent respectively.

Exhibit 138: Summary of the seventeenth iteration

2016–17*	All-cap CCP	Large-cap CCP	Sensex
CAGR returns	18.2%	22.6%	15.3%
Maximum drawdown**	-15.8%	-15.0%	-11.1%
Excess returns* **	0.64	0.98	0.66

Source: Bloomberg, Ambit Capital

*Note: *Portfolio kicks off on 1 July 2016.*

****Excess returns have been calculated as returns in excess of risk-free rate (assumed to be 8 per cent) divided by absolute maximum drawdown. Maximum drawdown is defined as the maximum drop in cumulative returns from the highest peak to the lowest subsequent trough.*

***Maximum drawdown from Sept'16 to Dec'16 for the all-cap CCP, Sept'16 to Dec'16 for large-cap CCP and Sept'16 to Nov'16 for the Sensex.*

HDFC Bank, Gruh Finance, LIC Housing Finance, Astral Poly and Cadila Healthcare were the top performers in the period by giving one-year returns of 42 per cent, 59 per cent, 50 per cent, 42 per cent and 61 per cent respectively, while Lupin's value dropped by 32 per cent.

Exhibit 139: Portfolio performance of CCP 2016

Stock	Total Shareholder Return (TSR)* CAGR	PAT CAGR FY 2016–17	Contribution to portfolio value at start	Contribution to portfolio value at end
			01/07/2016	30/06/2017
eClerx Services	-7.8%	-2.5%	6%	5%
Astral Poly	41.8%	43.3%	6%	7%

(*Cont.*)

Stock	Total Shareholder Return (TSR)* CAGR	PAT CAGR FY 2016–17	Contribution to portfolio value at start	Contribution to portfolio value at end
GRUH Finance	58.6%	21.8%	6%	8%
LIC Housing Finance	50.4%	16.5%	6%	7%
HCL Technologies	19.8%	17.6%	6%	6%
Relaxo Footwear	-3.0%	2.2%	6%	5%
Repco Home Finance	7.3%	21.8%	6%	5%
Page Industries	19.9%	15.0%	6%	6%
Axis Bank	-3.8%	-52.7%	6%	5%
Amara Raja Batteries	-2.5%	-2.7%	6%	5%
Britannia Industries	32.3%	7.3%	6%	7%
Cadila Healthcare	61.1%	-23.1%	6%	8%
Lupin	-31.5%	13.1%	6%	3%
Cera Sanitaryware	20.6%	16.6%	6%	6%
HDFC Bank	41.6%	19.2%	6%	7%
Asian Paints	11.0%	11.1%	6%	6%
Dr Lal PathLabs	-7.3%	16.5%	6%	5%
Total Portfolio	**18.1%**		**100%**	**100%**
Sensex TSR*	**15.3%**			

Source: Bloomberg, Ambit Capital

Note: Value at start denotes an equal allocation of Rs 100 in each stock at the start of the period. Value at end is the value of each stock at the end of the period. Thus, for this period, the value of the portfolio rose from Rs 1700 to Rs 2009.

**Total Shareholder Return (TSR) and Sensex TSR include dividends received and reinvested.*

Exhibit 140: Gruh Finance, LIC Housing Finance, Astral Poly, Cadila Healthcare and HDFC Bank were the best performers of CCP 2016

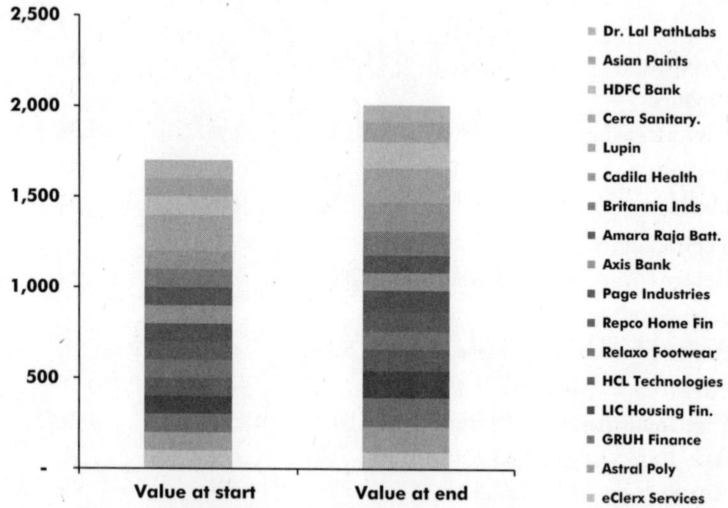

Source: Bloomberg, Ambit Capital research

Note: Value at start denotes an equal allocation of Rs 100 in each stock at the start of the period. Value at end is the value of each stock at the end of the period. Thus, for this period, the value of the portfolio rose from Rs 1700 at the start to Rs 2009 at the end. Total Shareholder Return (TSR) and Sensex TSR include dividends received and reinvested.

Incomplete portfolio (Period 18): 2017–Present

All-cap stocks: HDFC Bank, HCL Technologies, Lupin, LIC HF, Page Industries, Gruh Fin, Amara Raja Batteries, Abbott India, Astral Poly, Dr Lal PathLabs, Repco Home Finance, Muthoot Capital Services

Large-cap stocks: HDFC Bank, HCL Technologies, Lupin and LIC Housing Finance

A total of twelve companies made it to the eighteenth Coffee Can Portfolio. Of these, one was a bank (HDFC Bank) and four were NBFCs. The exhibit below shows the complete list of the companies for the 2017 iteration of the CCP.

Exhibit 141: Portfolio composition of CCP 2017

Company Name	Amount Invested (Rs)	Market Cap (Rs Cr)	Market Cap ($ Mn)
HDFC Bank	100	4,55,427	71,160
HCL Technologies	100	1,21,180	18,934
Lupin	100	44,633	6974
LIC Housing Finance	100	33,505	5235
Page Industries	100	19,581	3059
GRUH Finance	100	18,486	2888
Amara Raja Batteries	100	13,355	2087
Abbott India	100	9054	1415
Astral Poly	100	8204	1282
Dr Lal PathLabs	100	6682	1044
Repco Home Finance	100	4064	635
Muthoot Capital Services	100	729	114

Source: Ambit Capital, Bloomberg. Market capitalization data is as on 30 August 2017.

APPENDIX 2

How Punchy Can the P/E Multiple of a Great Company Be?

A large proportion of investors and financial analysts use shortcuts to value companies. Some of these include using three/five/ten-year historical average P/E[1] or P/B[2] multiples to arrive at the absolute valuation, or using PEG (i.e. the ratio P/E divided by expected earnings growth of a stock) ratios to identify overvaluation or undervaluation relative to peers. All these methods anchor themselves either to history or to peers' performance no matter how unjustified these comparisons might be in the future.

We present a simple example of how ratios like P/E and PEG can skew the actual picture of shareholder value creation

[1] The P/E ratio measures the market price of a company's stock relative to its corporate earnings, which can then be compared with other companies.

[2] The price-to-book ratio (P/B Ratio) is a ratio used to compare a stock's market value to its book value. It is calculated by dividing the current closing price of the stock by the latest quarter›s book value per share.

and make it look rosier than it actually is. Take two hypothetical companies X and Y which make revenues of Rs 1 million in Year 1 and have the same projected revenue growth of 5 per cent and profit margin of 10 per cent until Year 5. However, as shown in the table below, Company X needs to reinvest 50 per cent of its earnings each year to maintain 5 per cent growth in revenues and earnings, while Company Y needs to reinvest 25 per cent of its earnings. Thus, in Year 1, Company X generates Rs 50,000 in free cash flow while Company Y generates Rs 75,000 in free cash flow. In both cases, those free cash flow figures grow at 5 per cent per year, just like the earnings and revenue figures do. To value each company then, would you look at free cash flows or earnings?

Exhibit 142: Comparison of two firms with similar earnings but different cash flows

Company X (in ₹)	Year 1	Year 2	Year 3	Year 4	Year 5
Revenue	10,00,000	10,50,000	11,02,500	11,57,625	12,15,506
Earnings	1,00,000	1,05,000	1,10,250	1,15,763	1,21,551
Investment	-50,000	-52,500	-55,125	-57,881	-60,775
Free cash flow*	50,000	52,500	55,125	57,881	60,775
Company Y (in ₹)					
Revenue	10,00,000	10,50,000	11,02,500	11,57,625	12,15,506
Earnings	1,00,000	1,05,000	1,10,250	1,15,763	1,21,551
Investment	-25,000	-26,250	-27,563	-28,941	-30,388
Free cash flow*	75,000	78,750	82,688	86,822	91,163

Source: Adapted by Ambit Capital from Value: the Four Cornerstones of Corporate Finance *(2010) by Tim Koller, Richard Dobbs and Bill Huyett, McKinsey & Company.*

* *Free cash flow is calculated as 'Earnings minus investment'.*

The interesting thing about earnings is that not only can they be manipulated according to the whims of the management team, but they only provide information about how much profit a business can generate every year and NOT about the re-investments of those earnings necessary to keep the business running. The cash flow figures, on the other hand, describe clearly how much of the profit is actually left for shareholders.

Using these free cash flow figures and plugging them in a simple DCF model with an assumption of 5 per cent growth rate (forever) discounted at cost of capital of 15 per cent results in Company X being valued at Rs 500k versus Company Y at Rs 750k, an obvious answer given that Company Y requires less reinvestment (for the same earnings) and so generates more free cash flow. Now let's look at what the conventional methods of ascertaining value would project in this case.

Assuming both companies were trading at a fair price, Company X would have a P/E of 5 versus Company Y which has a P/E of 7.5.[3] The PEG ratio for Company X would be 1 while for Company Y it would be 1.5.[4] Most investors would look at these two companies and conclude that Company X is a better value than Company Y because you are paying a lower P/E and a lower PEG ratio for the same earnings and the same growth in earnings.

While this assessment is not harmful as both companies are fairly valued at this price, issues arise when we change the prices. For instance, if Company X was trading at Rs 600k while Company Y was trading at Rs 650k, Company X would

---

3 P/E ratio is computed as DCF based fair value divided by Year 1 earnings, i.e. PE ratio of Company X = Rs 5,00,000/Rs 1,00,000 = 5 and PE ratio of Company Y = Rs 7,50,000/Rs 1,00,000 = 7.5.

4 PEG ratio is computed as PE divided by earnings growth rate, i.e. PEG ratio of Company X = 5/5 = 1.0; and PEG ratio of Company Y = 7.5/5 = 1.5.

have a P/E of 6 versus 6.5 for Company Y. The PEG ratios of these two companies would be 1.2 and 1.3 respectively. In this scenario, concluding on the basis of the P/E and PEG ratios that Company X was a better value than Company Y would be wrong. It's actually the contrary.

Company Y was able to justify higher valuations for the same levels of growth and earnings because of its higher 'marginal return on capital'. As the example above clearly highlights, Company Y was able to generate incremental earnings of Rs 5000 in Year 2 by investing Rs 25,000 into the business as compared to Company X which had to invest Rs 50,000 to achieve the same growth. This means that the marginal return on capital for Company Y was 20 per cent versus 10 per cent for Company X. Once this finding comes through, one realizes the flaw in traditional metrics of plainly using earnings as a determinant of 'value'.

Besides the need to factor in the cash generative nature of a business in the valuation methodology, the added flaw in using a PEG ratio or P/E multiple is that these methodologies do NOT adequately capture the longevity of a franchise. For instance, let us assume that the two companies cited in the example above had the same investment requirements and cash generation for the next five years. However, there is a difference in the sustainability of the two firms' competitive strengths. While X can sustain its competitive advantages for ten years, Y can sustain its competitive advantages for twenty years. In this case, Company Y deserves a significantly higher P/E multiple than Company X despite delivering the same set of financials over the next five years.

So how punchy can the fair value of a 'great' company be? Let us assume that the Coffee Can philosophy has identified a company, ABC, which will deliver the following financial performance:

- Sustain an ROCE of 35 per cent for the next twenty years (from 2017 to 2037),
- Maintain a dividend payout ratio of 30 per cent, i.e. it reinvests the balance 70 per cent earnings in the business and generates 35 per cent ROCE on this incremental capital employed.

Let us also assume that the popular theory of 'mean reversion' applies to its P/E multiple after another twenty years and, hence, in 2037, Company ABC will trade at the market average P/E multiple of twenty times. This is possible if in 2037 there is no visibility of another twenty-year runway for growth.

Now the big question is: At what P/E multiple in 2016 will this company deliver market average returns over the next twenty years? The following points answer this question:

- The BSE Sensex has delivered 11.1 per cent CAGR over the past twenty-five years. So let's assume 11 per cent CAGR to be the likely market return over the next twenty years.
- If the said company's P/E multiple in 2017 is 210 times (yes, you read that right, 210!) then this company will deliver 11 per cent compounded annualized returns over the twenty years assuming a steady decline in its P/E to twenty times by 2037.
- If, more realistically, ABC is available for investment at fifty times the P/E in 2017, then it will deliver 19.5 per cent share price CAGR over the next twenty years even as the company's P/E declines from fifty times in 2017 to twenty times in 2037.

The exhibit below shows the result of this exercise for a company which is expected to generate 35 per cent ROCE consistently over the next twenty years while reinvesting 70 per cent of its operating cash flows back into the business. Even if the P/E multiple of such a company is fifty times today and de-rates gradually to twenty times, i.e. close to the market average P/E, over the next twenty years, investors buying the company's shares today will realize a healthy 19.5 per cent CAGR in Total Shareholder Returns over the next twenty years.

Exhibit 143: Conviction on fundamentals will give healthy returns even with high entry P/E

Year	Earnings	EPS growth	Capital employed	ROCE	Reinvestment of Earnings	P/E	Twenty-year investment CAGR
0	100		286	35%	70%	50	
1	125	24.5%	356	35%	70%	49	
2	155	24.5%	443	35%	70%	47	
3	193	24.5%	551	35%	70%	46	
4	240	24.5%	686	35%	70%	44	
17	4,148	24.5%	11,853	35%	70%	25	
18	5,165	24.5%	14,756	35%	70%	23	
19	6,430	24.5%	18,372	35%	70%	22	
20	8,005	24.5%	22,873	35%	70%	20	19.5%

Source: Bloomberg, Ambit Capital Research

Note: Exhibit reproduced without any changes.

APPENDIX 3

Should Investors Sell Coffee Can Stocks When Markets Are Richly Valued?

We consider five scenarios to analyse whether buying and holding the Coffee Can Portfolio makes sense in India. The description and results for each scenario are given below.

Scenario 1: We sell when the Nifty's trailing P/E multiple goes above twenty times and invest in government bonds. We wait for a year before making the reinvestment decision and such a decision is taken only if the multiple has dropped below twenty times (at that juncture we reinvest in the fresh ongoing CCP as at that time). So, for example, when the Nifty exceeds twenty times the trailing earnings in October 2007, we SELL the entire portfolio. We then wait until October 2008 and BUY the CCP FY08 at that point.

As can be seen below, barring a couple of portfolios with minor outperformance, none of the CCP portfolios following the Scenario 1 strategy were able to beat their 'buy and hold' counterparts.

Exhibit 144: Selling the Coffee Can Portfolio when the Nifty P/E is above 20 does not outperform 'Buy and Hold'

Total returns (CAGR)**							
	Absolute returns from CCP			Alpha from CCP		Sell when Nifty P/E>20x	
Year	CCP	Sensex	BSE 200	vs Sensex	vs BSE 200	Scenario 1	Difference
2000	22.6%	16.0%	17.5%	6.6%	5.1%	23.5%	0.9%
2001	32.2%	20.5%	22.4%	11.7%	9.8%	28.3%	-3.9%
2002	25.4%	20.3%	20.5%	5.1%	4.9%	25.4%	-0.1%
2003	27.4%	20.2%	19.8%	7.2%	7.7%	23.0%	-4.5%
2004	32.6%	19.9%	19.3%	12.7%	13.4%	30.8%	-1.8%
2005	22.1%	16.1%	15.9%	6.0%	6.2%	23.3%	1.2%
2006	20.4%	11.4%	12.3%	9.0%	8.1%	18.8%	-1.5%
2007	19.2%	9.4%	10.3%	9.8%	9.0%	16.5%	-2.7%
2008	21.3%	11.5%	12.6%	9.9%	8.8%	13.4%	-8.0%
2009	23.0%	11.8%	13.0%	11.3%	10.0%	14.1%	-9.0%
2010	20.8%	10.1%	10.9%	10.7%	10.0%	13.2%	-7.7%
2011	14.1%	10.5%	12.0%	3.7%	2.1%	11.5%	-2.6%
2012	23.4%	14.2%	16.1%	9.3%	7.3%	18.9%	-4.5%
2013	33.3%	14.4%	17.6%	18.9%	15.7%	26.0%	-7.3%
2014	21.1%	5.5%	9.1%	15.6%	12.1%	9.9%	-11.3%
2015	18.9%	11.6%	14.8%	7.2%	4.1%	5.5%	-13.3%
2016	17.3%	18.8%	19.9%	-1.5%	-2.6%	3.8%	-13.5%

Source: Bloomberg, Ambit Capital

Note: We apply a brokerage cost of 50 Bps on buying or selling. Prices updated until 30 May 2017.

***Total returns include dividends received and reinvested, both for CCPs as well as for the indices.*

Scenario 2: We sell when the Nifty trailing P/E multiple goes above twenty times and invest in government bonds. We wait for the multiple to drop below fourteen times to reinvest in a fresh CCP at that time (equal allocation of all new stocks). So, for example, when the Nifty exceeded twenty times the trailing earnings in July 2009, we sell the entire portfolio and buy government bonds. We then wait until December 2011 and BUY the CCP FY11 at that point.

In this scenario, while the completed CCP portfolios (until the ones initiated in 2006) show marginal outperformance, the incomplete ones underperform the 'buy & hold' CCP strategy significantly.

Exhibit 145: Selling at high multiples and buying at low multiples underperform 'buy & hold' in most cases

	Total returns (CAGR)						
	Absolute returns from CCP			Alpha from CCP		BUY when Nifty P/E<14x	
Year	CCP	Sensex	BSE 200	vs Sensex	vs BSE 200	Scenario 2	Difference
2000	22.6%	16.0%	17.5%	6.6%	5.1%	23.5%	0.9%
2001	32.2%	20.5%	22.4%	11.7%	9.8%	29.2%	-3.1%
2002	25.4%	20.3%	20.5%	5.1%	4.9%	30.2%	4.8%
2003	27.4%	20.2%	19.8%	7.2%	7.7%	27.5%	0.0%
2004	32.6%	19.9%	19.3%	12.7%	13.4%	34.4%	1.7%
2005	22.1%	16.1%	15.9%	6.0%	6.2%	25.0%	2.9%
2006	20.4%	11.4%	12.3%	9.0%	8.1%	20.8%	0.4%
2007	19.2%	9.4%	10.3%	9.8%	9.0%	18.4%	-0.8%
2008	21.3%	11.5%	12.6%	9.9%	8.8%	15.5%	-5.9%
2009	23.0%	11.8%	13.0%	11.3%	10.0%	16.4%	-6.6%
2010	20.8%	10.1%	10.9%	10.7%	10.0%	15.9%	-5.0%
2011	14.1%	10.5%	12.0%	3.7%	2.1%	11.9%	-2.2%

(*Cont.*)

Total returns (CAGR)							
	Absolute returns from CCP			Alpha from CCP		BUY when Nifty P/E<14x	
Year	CCP	Sensex	BSE 200	vs Sensex	vs BSE 200	Scenario 2	Difference
2012	23.4%	14.2%	16.1%	9.3%	7.3%	19.5%	-3.9%
2013	33.3%	14.4%	17.6%	18.9%	15.7%	26.8%	-6.5%
2014*	21.1%	5.5%	9.1%	15.6%	12.1%	10.9%	-10.2%
2015*	18.9%	11.6%	14.8%	7.2%	4.1%	7.1%	-11.7%
2016*	17.3%	18.8%	19.9%	-1.5%	-2.6%	3.8%	-13.5%

Source: Bloomberg, Ambit Capital

Note: We apply a brokerage cost of 50 Bps on buying or selling.

*The live portfolios are used for the analysis. Prices updated till 30 May 2017.

**Total Returns include dividends received and reinvested, both for CCPs as well as for the indices.

We ran three more scenarios to test the robustness of the 'buy and hold' strategy.

1. **Scenario 3A**: In this scenario, rather than selling when valuations are rich, we stay put and when the Nifty trailing P/E drops below fourteen times, we exit the old CCP and enter into the fresh CCP as at that moment. The money is allocated equally to all the new CCP stocks.
2. **Scenario 3B**: In this scenario, rather than selling when valuations are rich, we buy more when the Nifty trailing P/E drops below fourteen times. We double the investment amount whenever this happens and the money is allocated equally to all the existing CCP stocks.
3. **Scenario 3C**: As in the previous scenario, rather than selling when valuations are rich, we buy more when the

Nifty trailing P/E drops below fourteen times. However, we remain cognizant of the compounding benefits enjoyed by outperforming stocks in a CCP. So as to not penalize them by equally allocating new money, in this scenario, we double the total investment amount but allocate this amount as per the stocks' existing weights.

Interestingly, we find that even in these scenarios, there is no outperformance as compared to the 'buy and hold' strategy.

The findings above make sense when one realizes that the firms that do make it to the CCPs enjoy sustainable competitive advantages over their competitors, which reflects in their share price performance. Thus, trying to time the market and using market-level valuations as a guide to especially make 'sell' decisions prove to be counter-productive as companies with sound fundamentals and excellent return ratios will continue to look expensive.

APPENDIX 4

How Coffee Can Portfolios Outperform during Market Stress

Only when the tide goes out do you discover who's been swimming naked. This insight from Warren Buffett has repeatedly proved correct when it comes to investing in stocks. When the broader market is undergoing a euphoric or bullish phase, most stocks do well regardless of the quality of their underlying fundamentals. However, when the euphoria ends, stocks with poor underlying fundamentals are decimated, leading to significant capital erosion for investors who did not adequately understand the weak fundamentals of their portfolio companies.

As shown in the exhibit below, during periods of market stress (encircled in the exhibit below), the performance trajectory of the Coffee Can Portfolios (CCPs) consistently generate the following outcomes:

- The CCPs tend to fall less than the overall stock market,
- The recovery following the crash is faster and stronger for CCPs compared to that of the broader market.

Exhibit 146: Coffee Can Portfolio (CCP) vs Sensex (one-year holding period using Total Shareholder Returns)

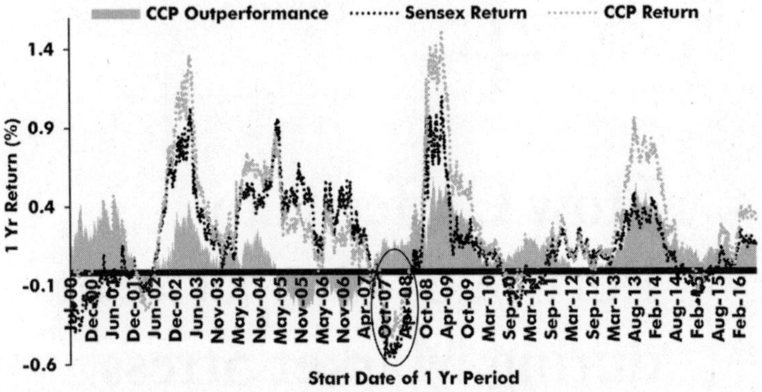

Source: Bloomberg, Ambit Capital. The CCP return is taken as average of all live Coffee Can portfolios for the period.

The only period when Coffee Can Portfolios underperformed compared to the broader market for more than a year was from May 2005 to August 2007. This was a period of irrational exuberance in cyclical sectors like infrastructure, real estate and utilities. However, it is worth noting that despite this relative underperformance during the broader market's euphoric phase, the CCPs continued to generate healthy absolute returns of 20 per cent to 25 per cent.

Understanding CCPs' resilience via histograms of annual share price returns

Let us begin by putting the Sensex's annual returns for the last twenty-five financial years on a histogram (see Exhibit 147). As the histogram shows, ten of the last twenty-five years, i.e. 40 per cent of the instances, have seen a negative return from the Sensex with the remaining fifteen years, i.e. 60 per cent of the instances, having delivered a positive return.

Exhibit 147: Sensex's histogram of annual return—positive returns in 60 per cent of the instances

NEGATIVE RETURNS				POSITIVE RETURNS			
					FY98		
					FY05		
					FY07		FY94
			FY97		FY08		FY00
		FY95	FY99		FY11		FY04
FY93		FY03	FY02	FY96	FY14		FY06
FY09	FY01	FY12	FY16	FY13	FY17	FY15	FY10
Less than -30%	**-20% to -30%**	**-10% to -20%**	**0% to -10%**	**0% to +10%**	**+10% to +20%**	**+20% to +30%**	**More than +30%**

Source: Bloomberg, Ambit Capital. The period under consideration is FY1993 to FY2017.

Next, we replicate these twenty-five-year histograms for some of the stocks that have frequently formed part of our Coffee Can Portfolios. In these stock-specific histograms, we have shaded the years in which the direction of the stock price movement was reverse of the direction of Sensex, i.e. years when the Sensex delivered negative return and the stock still delivered a positive return and vice versa.

There are two key conclusions from these stock-specific histograms (exhibits 148 to 155):

- **Conclusion No. 1**: Most of the stock-specific histograms of CCP companies are skewed to the right, i.e. while 60 per cent of the instances show a positive return for Sensex, the corresponding number for CCP companies is more like 80 per cent to 90 per cent.

- **Conclusion No. 2:** There have been several years in which the stock gave a positive return, whilst in ten out of the last twenty-five years the Sensex gave a negative return. The number of such instances is anywhere between three and six (out of ten years of Sensex's negative returns) in each of the histograms shown below.

Exhibit 148: Marico's histogram of annual share price returns

NEGATIVE RETURNS				POSITIVE RETURNS			
							FY99
						FY11	FY04
					FY02	FY12	FY05
					FY03	FY13	FY06
				FY98	FY07	FY16	FY10
FY00		FY09	FY01	FY14	FY08	FY17	FY15
Less than -30%	**-20% to -30%**	**-10% to -20%**	**0% to -10%**	**0% to +10%**	**+10% to +20%**	**+20% to +30%**	**More than +30%**

Source: Bloomberg, Ambit Capital. The period under consideration is FY1993 to FY2017.

***Shaded** cell: Stock delivering **positive** return when Sensex gave **negative** return*

***Bordered** cell: Stock delivering **negative** return when Sensex gave **positive** return*

Exhibit 149: Berger Paints' histogram of annual share price returns

NEGATIVE RETURNS				POSITIVE RETURNS			
							FY94
							FY95
							FY98
							FY99
							FY00
							FY04
							FY05
							FY06
							FY10
							FY11
FY93			FY03		FY12		FY13
FY96		FY01	FY08		FY14		FY15
FY07		FY02	FY09	FY97	FY16		FY17
Less than -30%	-20% to -30%	-10% to -20%	0% to -10%	0% to +10%	+10% to +20%	+20% to +30%	More than +30%

Source: Bloomberg, Ambit Capital. The period under consideration is FY1993 to FY2017.

***Shaded** cell: Stock delivering **positive** return when Sensex gave **negative** return*

***Bordered** cell: Stock delivering **negative** return when Sensex gave **positive** return*

Exhibit 150: Asian Paints' histogram of annual share price returns

NEGATIVE RETURNS				POSITIVE RETURNS			
							FY94
							FY00
							FY02
							FY04
					FY95		FY06
					FY96	FY05	FY08
				FY93	FY98	FY11	FY10
		FY97		FY03	FY07	FY12	FY13
FY09		FY99	FY01	FY16	FY14	FY17	FY15
Less than -30%	-20% to -30%	-10% to -20%	0% to -10%	0% to +10%	+10% to +20%	+20% to +30%	More than +30%

Source: Bloomberg, Ambit Capital. The period under consideration is FY1993 to FY2017.

***Shaded** cell: Stock delivering **positive** return when Sensex gave **negative** return*

***Bordered** cell: Stock delivering **negative** return when Sensex gave **positive** return*

Exhibit 151: Britannia's histogram of annual share price returns

NEGATIVE RETURNS				POSITIVE RETURNS			
							FY94
							FY98
							FY99
							FY05
	FY95				FY97		FY06
	FY96				FY01	FY04	FY12
FY93	FY02			FY08	FY10	FY16	FY14
FY00	FY07	FY13	FY03	FY09	FY11	FY17	FY15
Less than -30%	-20% to -30%	-10% to -20%	0% to -10%	0% to +10%	+10% to +20%	+20% to +30%	More than +30%

Source: Bloomberg, Ambit Capital. The period under consideration is FY1993 to FY2017.

***Shaded** cell: Stock delivering **positive** return when Sensex gave **negative** return*

***Bordered** cell: Stock delivering **negative** return when Sensex gave **positive** return*

Exhibit 152: Amara Raja's histogram of annual share price returns

NEGATIVE RETURNS				POSITIVE RETURNS			
							FY95
							FY98
							FY99
							FY05
							FY06
							FY07
							FY08
FY93							FY10
FY00							FY12
FY01				FY02	FY94		FY13
FY03				FY16	FY04		FY14
FY09	FY96		FY97	FY17	FY11		FY15
Less than -30%	-20% to -30%	-10% to -20%	0% to -10%	0% to +10%	+10% to +20%	+20% to +30%	More than +30%

Source: Bloomberg, Ambit Capital. The period under consideration is FY1993 to FY2017.

***Shaded** cell: Stock delivering **positive** return when Sensex gave **negative** return*

***Bordered** cell: Stock delivering **negative** return when Sensex gave **positive** return*

Exhibit 153: Relaxo's histogram of annual share price returns

NEGATIVE RETURNS				POSITIVE RETURNS			
							FY04
							FY10
						FY05	FY13
						FY06	FY14
FY02				FY03		FY08	FY15
FY09			FY07	FY12	FY16	FY11	FY17
Less than -30%	-20% to -30%	-10% to -20%	0% to -10%	0% to +10%	+10% to +20%	+20% to +30%	More than +30%

Source: Bloomberg, Ambit Capital. The period under consideration is FY1993 to FY2017.

***Shaded** cell: Stock delivering **positive** return when Sensex gave **negative** return*

***Bordered** cell: Stock delivering **negative** return when Sensex gave **positive** return*

Exhibit 154: HDFC Bank's histogram of annual share price returns

NEGATIVE RETURNS				POSITIVE RETURNS			
							FY97
							FY98
							FY00
							FY04
							FY05
							FY06
							FY08
						FY07	FY10
			FY99	FY02	FY12	FY11	FY15
	FY09	FY01	FY03	FY16	FY14	FY13	FY17
Less than -30%	-20% to -30%	-10% to -20%	0% to -10%	0% to +10%	+10% to +20%	+20% to +30%	More than +30%

Source: Bloomberg, Ambit Capital. The period under consideration is FY1993 to FY2017.

***Shaded** cell: Stock delivering **positive** return when Sensex gave **negative** return*

***Bordered** cell: Stock delivering **negative** return when Sensex gave **positive** return*

Exhibit 155: Gruh Finance's histogram of annual share price returns

NEGATIVE RETURNS				POSITIVE RETURNS			
							FY02
							FY04
							FY05
							FY06
							FY07
							FY10
							FY11
							FY12
		FY94					FY13
		FY97	FY95				FY14
FY96		FY99	FY03		FY01		FY15
FY09	FY98	FY00	FY16		FY08		FY17
Less than -30%	-20% to -30%	-10% to -20%	0% to -10%	0% to +10%	+10% to +20%	+20% to +30%	More than +30%

Source: Bloomberg, Ambit Capital. The period under consideration is FY1993 to FY2017.

***Shaded** cell: Stock delivering **positive** return when Sensex gave **negative** return*

***Bordered** cell: Stock delivering **negative** return when Sensex gave **positive** return*

So why does the Coffee Can philosophy outperform the broader market even during periods of market stress?

As highlighted in Chapter 2, the Coffee Can philosophy seeks firms which can deliver healthy and consistent revenue growth and ROCE over long periods of time. This implies that even when the broader macroeconomic environment or the competitive landscape becomes difficult for a CCP company, the firm is able to deliver healthy revenue growth and ROCE. These characteristics ensure that during prolonged periods of stock-market stress, CCP companies would, more often than not, deliver positive returns due to one of the following two factors:

- **Earnings growth more than offsets the P/E de-rating during periods of stock market stress:** Stressed periods of the stock market usually occur due to deterioration in earnings growth prospects of the constituent stocks compared to what are already factored into the share prices. Since the CCP companies can maintain healthy growth even in a disruptive external environment, the ripple effect of a stressed stock market's P/E multiple de-rating tends to be more than offset by a CCP company's earnings growth delivered during the same period. As a result, the share price of such a company could end up giving positive returns even during periods of stress in the broader stock market. The table below highlights some of these instances for firms like Asian Paints, Amara Raja and ITC.

Exhibit 156: Examples of CCP stocks' earnings offsetting P/E de-rating during periods of stress in broader stock market (using trailing 12-month EPS and P/E multiples)

	Asian Paints (FY03)	ITC (FY12)	Asian Paints (FY16)	Amara Raja (FY16)
EPS at the start of the period	1.1	4.1	14.8	24.1
EPS at the end of the period	1.4	5.2	18.5	28.7
Share price at start	21.9	121.4	811.3	833.1

(*Cont.*)

	Asian Paints (FY03)	ITC (FY12)	Asian Paints (FY16)	Amara Raja (FY16)
Share price at end	22.0	151.3	868.4	877.6
P/E at start	19.9	29.6	54.9	34.6
P/E at end	15.7	29.1	46.8	30.6
EPS growth	27%	27%	25%	19%
P/E rerating*	-21%	-2%	-15%	-12%
Share price growth	1%	25%	7%	5%
Sensex EPS growth	13%	6%	-10%	-10%
Sensex P/E re-rating	-22%	-16%	1%	1%
Sensex price growth	-12%	-10%	-9%	-9%

Source: Ambit Capital research, Bloomberg, Ace Equity

**A negative sign in front of the number indicates P/E de-rating, i.e. a drop in P/E.*

- **P/E does not derate because the market incrementally factors in longevity of earnings:** As CCP stocks tend to deliver consistent revenue and earnings growth during periods of weakness in fundamentals for the broader market, it is likely that P/E multiples of CCP companies start factoring in a greater degree of sustainability of earnings growth over the longer term in future. For example, in FY12, Asian Paints delivered 28 per cent share price growth whilst the Sensex declined by 10 per cent. During this period, Sensex earnings grew by 6 per cent and its trailing P/E multiple declined by 16 per cent. However, despite this market-wide derating in the P/E multiple, Asian Paints' P/E multiple increased by 10 per cent and its EPS grew by 17 per cent in FY12.

APPENDIX 5

The Role of Starting Period Valuations in Determining Investment Returns

Our analysis shows that contrary to popular expectations, starting period valuations do not play a role in determining returns over a medium-to-long term horizon. As shown in the exhibits that follow, the BSE 200 universe of stocks has had no significant correlation between starting period valuations (as at the beginning of the concerned period) and subsequent long-term returns no matter which phase of the stock market one looks at.

Scenario 1 (defensive phase of the stock market): The first scenario considers the five-year period of FY2012–17 and the three-year period of FY2014–17 during which high-quality stocks were in vogue. As can be seen clearly, there is no significant correlation between the returns profile and the starting price multiples of the index constituents.

Exhibit 157: No correlation of three-year returns with starting P/E multiple

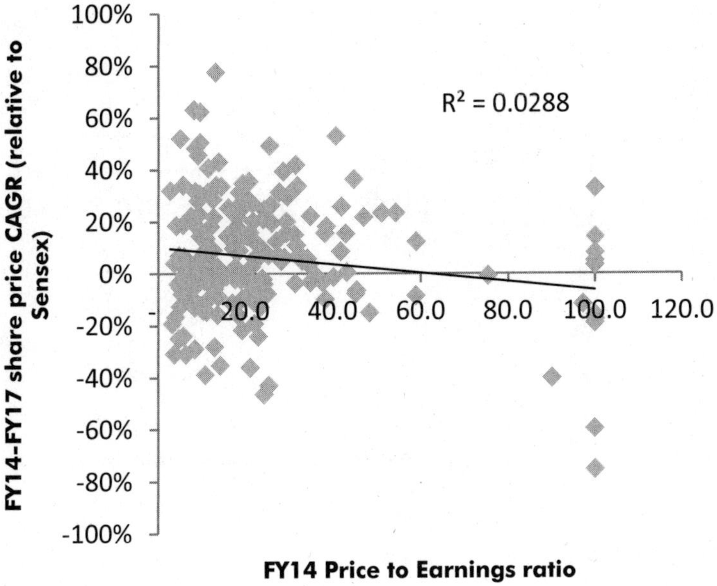

Source: Ambit Capital

Note: Returns here are stock returns relative to the Sensex. Trailing P/E has been restricted to 100.

Exhibit 158: No correlation of three-year returns with starting P/B multiple

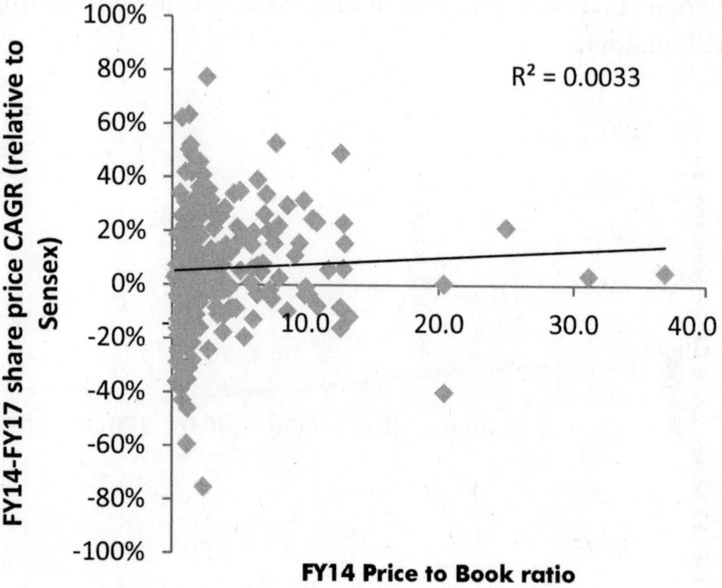

Source: Ambit Capital

Note: Returns here are stock returns relative to the Sensex.

Exhibit 159: No correlation of five-year returns with starting P/E multiple

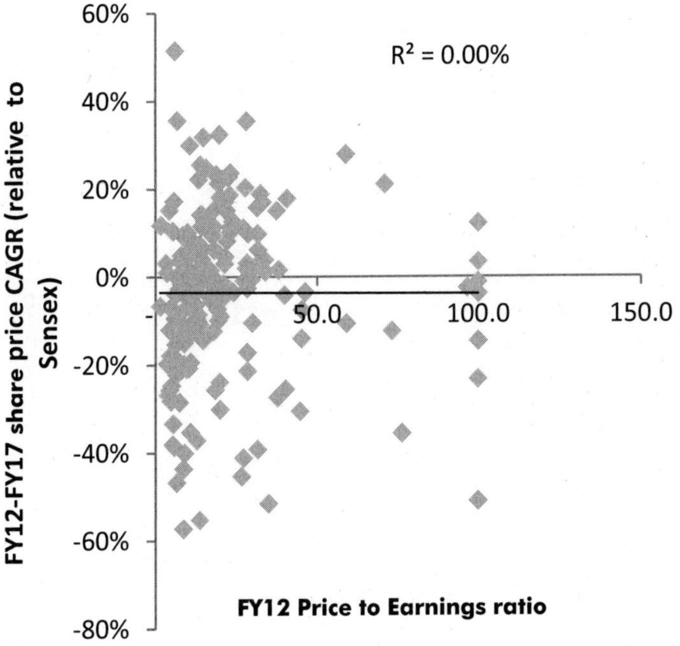

Source: Ambit Capital

Note: Returns here are stock returns relative to the Sensex. Trailing P/E has been restricted to 100.

Exhibit 160: No correlation of five-year returns with starting P/B multiple

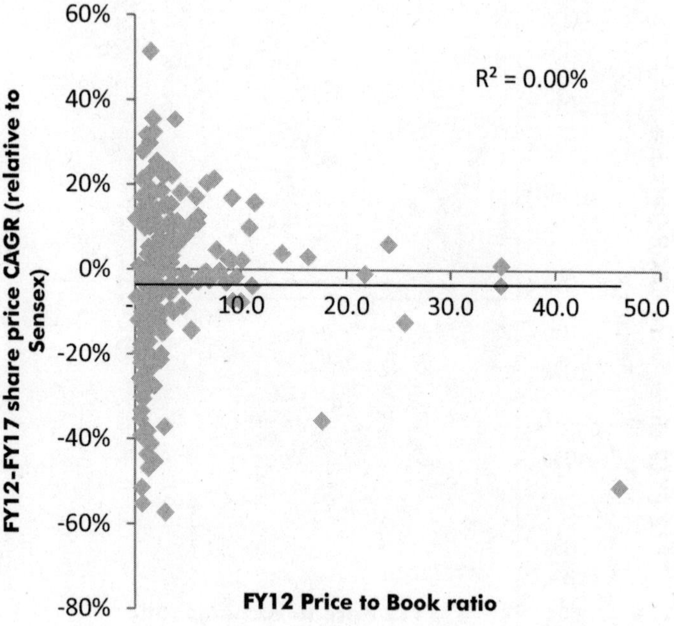

Source: Ambit Capital
Note: Returns here are stock returns relative to the Sensex.

Scenario 2 (bullish phase of the stock market): To ensure that the returns profile is not influenced by the underlying period, in the second scenario we consider the bull periods of FY2003–06 and FY2003–08. Unlike the previous scenario, this was a period of strong macroeconomic activity, and yet even in this scenario there is no clear correlation between starting period multiples and the subsequent returns.

Exhibit 161: No correlation of three-year returns with starting P/E multiple

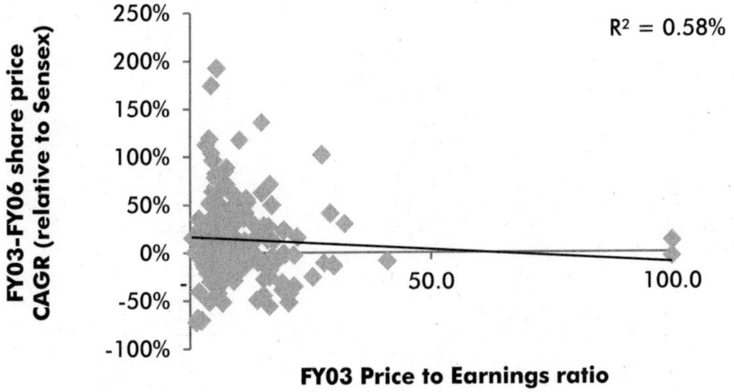

Source: Ambit Capital

Note: Returns here are stock returns relative to the Sensex. Trailing P/E has been restricted to 100.

Exhibit 162: No correlation of three-year returns with starting P/B multiple

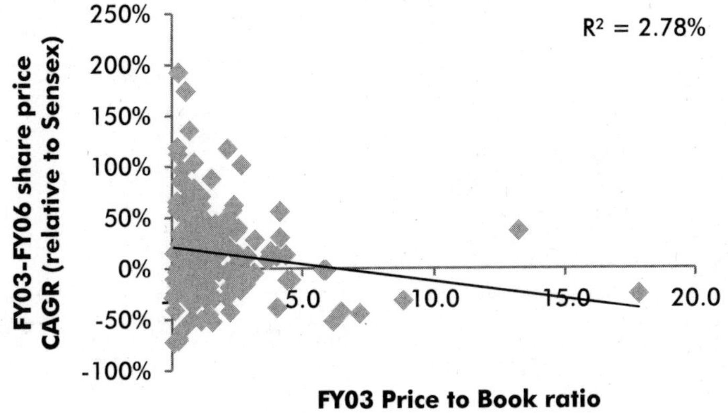

Source: Ambit Capital

Note: Returns here are stock returns relative to the Sensex.

Exhibit 163: No correlation of five-year returns with starting P/E multiple

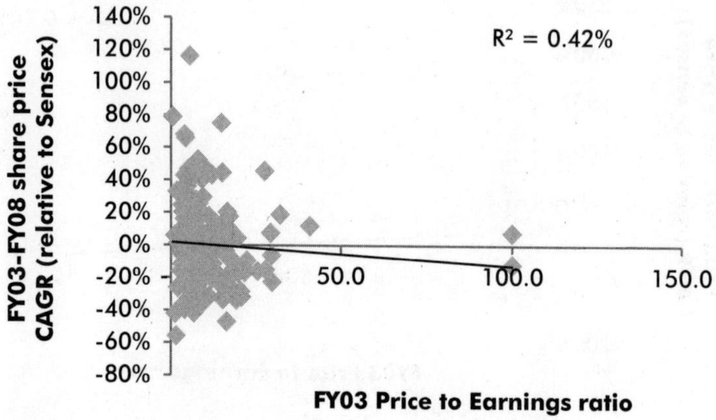

Source: Ambit Capital

Note: Returns here are stock returns relative to the Sensex. Trailing P/E has been restricted to 100.

Exhibit 164: No correlation of five-year returns with starting P/B multiple

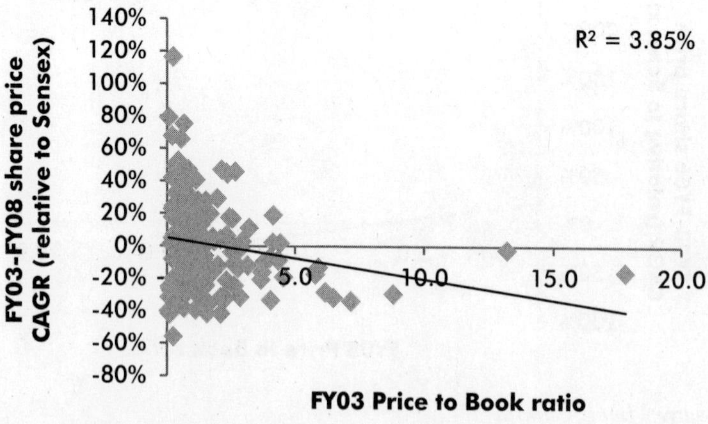

Source: Ambit Capital

Note: Returns here are stock returns relative to the Sensex.

Scenario 3 (cross-cyclical phase): Lastly, we examine returns over an extended period of ten years (FY07–17). The results obtained are largely similar to those over shorter time frames, i.e. there is no evidence to suggest that buying stocks which look cheap on P/E or P/B leads to superior investment returns in the long run.

Exhibit 165: Insignificant correlation of ten-year returns with starting P/E multiple

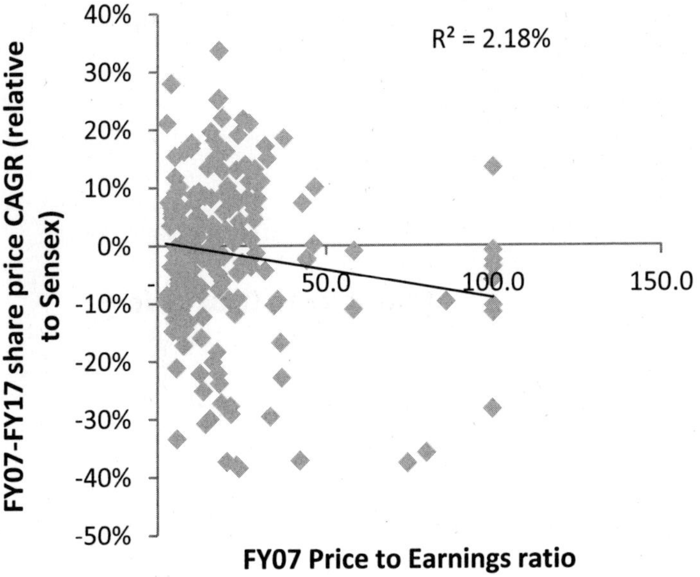

Source: Ambit Capital

Note: Returns here are stock returns relative to the Sensex. Trailing P/E has been restricted to 100.

Exhibit 166: Insignificant correlation of ten-year returns with starting P/B multiple

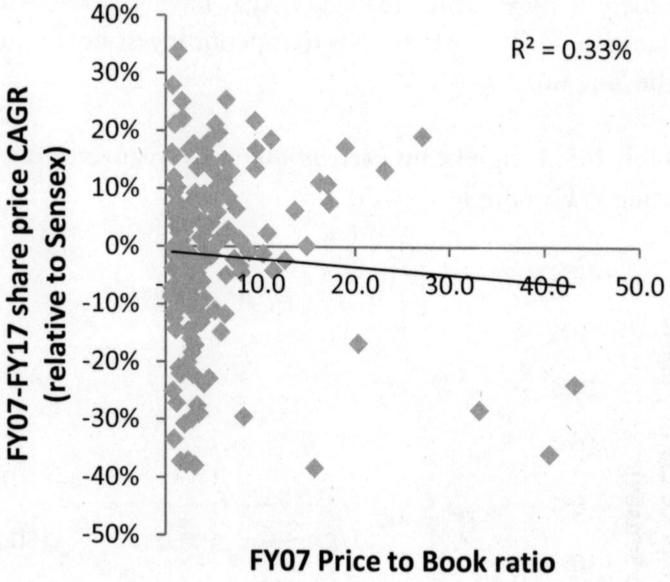

Source: Ambit Capital

Note: Returns here are stock returns relative to the Sensex.